LAWN & GARDEN

TIME
LIFE
BOOKS ®

Other Publications:

MYSTERIES OF THE UNKNOWN

TIME FRAME

FIX IT YOURSELF

FITNESS, HEALTH & NUTRITION

SUCCESSFUL PARENTING

HEALTHY HOME COOKING

UNDERSTANDING COMPUTERS

LIBRARY OF NATIONS

THE ENCHANTED WORLD

THE KODAK LIBRARY OF CREATIVE PHOTOGRAPHY

GREAT MEALS IN MINUTES

THE CIVIL WAR

PLANET EARTH

COLLECTOR'S LIBRARY OF THE CIVIL WAR

THE EPIC OF FLIGHT

THE GOOD COOK

WORLD WAR II

HOME REPAIR AND IMPROVEMENT

THE OLD WEST

LAWN & GARDEN

TIME-LIFE BOOKS
ALEXANDRIA, VIRGINIA

Fix It Yourself was produced by
ST. REMY PRESS

MANAGING EDITOR	Kenneth Winchester
MANAGING ART DIRECTOR	Pierre Léveillé

Staff for *Lawn & Garden*

Series Editor	Kathleen M. Kiely
Editor	Elizabeth W. Lewis
Series Art Director	Diane Denoncourt
Art Director	Philippe Arnoldi
Research Editor	Katherine Zmetana
Designer	Solange Pelland
Editorial Assistants	Fiona Gilsenan, Michael Kleiza
Contributing Writers	Kent J. Farrell, Elyse Greenberg, Grant Loewen, Brian Parsons, Wayne Voce, Rachel Wareham, Carolyn A. Warren
Contributing Illustrators	Gérard Mariscalchi, Jacques Proulx, Elayne Sears
Cover	Robert Monté
Index	Christine M. Jacobs
Administrator	Denise Rainville
Coordinator	Michelle Turbide
Systems Manager	Shirley Grynspan
Systems Analyst	Simon Lapierre
Studio Director	Daniel Bazinet
Photographer	Maryo Proulx

Time-Life Books Inc. is a wholly owned subsidiary of
TIME INCORPORATED

FOUNDER	Henry R. Luce 1898-1967
Editor-in-Chief	Jason McManus
Chairman and Chief Executive Officer	J. Richard Munro
President and Chief Operating Officer	N. J. Nicholas Jr.
Editorial Director	Ray Cave
Executive Vice President, Books	Kelso F. Sutton
Vice President, Books	George Artandi

TIME-LIFE BOOKS INC.

EDITOR	George Constable
Executive Editor	Ellen Phillips
Director of Design	Louis Klein
Director of Editorial Resources	Phyllis K. Wise
Editorial Board	Russell B. Adams Jr., Dale M. Brown, Roberta Conlan, Thomas H. Flaherty, Lee Hassig, Donia Ann Steele, Rosalind Stubenberg, Kit van Tulleken, Henry Woodhead
Director of Photography and Research	John Conrad Weiser
PRESIDENT	Christopher T. Linen
Chief Operating Officer	John M. Fahey Jr.
Senior Vice President	James L. Mercer
Vice Presidents	Stephen L. Bair, Ralph J. Cuomo, Neal Goff, Stephen L. Goldstein, Juanita T. James, Hallett Johnson III, Carol Kaplan, Susan J. Maruyama, Robert H. Smith, Paul R. Stewart, Joseph J. Ward
Director of Production Services	Robert J. Passantino

Editorial Operations

Copy Chief	Diane Ullius
Production	Celia Beattie
Library	Louise D. Forstall
Correspondents	Elizabeth Kraemer-Singh (Bonn); Maria Vincenza Aloisi (Paris); Ann Natanson (Rome).

THE CONSULTANTS

The Montreal Botanical Garden provided special assistance for this book. Third largest of its kind in the world, it is internationally recognized for its educational programs and scientific research. Director **Pierre Bourque** is also Chief Horticulturist of the City of Montreal. Agronomist **Nicole Ouimet** has taught gardening and landscaping techniques.

Consulting Editor **David L. Harrison** served as an editor of several Time-Life Books do-it-yourself series, including *Home Repair and Improvement*, *The Encyclopedia of Gardening* and *The Art of Sewing*.

Stuart Robertson, horticultural consultant and lecturer for 12 years, is the gardening columnist for *The Gazette* and a regular contributor to radio and television shows in Montreal, Canada.

A. Cort Sinnes of Kansas City, Missouri is associate editor of *Flower & Garden* magazine, as well as the author and editor of numerous books on gardening.

Barbara Peck, senior editor of *Travel & Leisure* magazine, is an avid gardener in New York City.

Library of Congress Cataloging-in-Publication Data
Lawn & garden
p. cm. – (Fix it yourself)
Includes index.
ISBN 0-8094-6228-1
ISBN 0-8094-6229-X (lib. bdg.)
1. Gardening. 2. Lawns. I. Time-Life Books.
II. Title: Lawn and garden. III. Series.
SB453.L355   1988
635.9 – dc 19   88-2373
                                                    CIP

For information about any Time-Life book, please write:
Reader Information
Time-Life Customer Service
P.O. Box C-32068
Richmond, Virginia
23261-2068

CONTENTS

HOW TO USE THIS BOOK

Lawn & Garden is divided into three sections. The Emergency Guide on pages 8 through 13 provides information that can be indispensable in the event of an emergency affecting you or your plants. Take the time to study this section *before* you need the important advice it contains.

The Repairs section—the heart of the book—is a system for troubleshooting and fixing problems that may arise with your lawn or garden. Pictured below are four sample pages from the chapter on kitchen gardens, with captions describing the various features of the book and how they work. If your seeds don't germinate, for example, the Troubleshooting Guide will offer a number of possible causes. If the problem is that the seeds were sown at the wrong depth, you will be directed to page 39 for detailed, step-by-step instructions for reseeding.

Each job has been rated by degree of difficulty and by the average time it will take for a do-it-yourselfer to complete. Keep in mind that this rating is only a suggestion. Before deciding whether you should attempt a repair, first read all the instructions carefully. Then be guided by your own confidence, and the tools and time available to you. For more complex or time-consuming repairs, such as installing a drainage system or pruning a large tree, you may wish to call for professional

---

Introductory text
Describes the lawn, garden or group of plants, their most common problems and basic repair procedures.

Troubleshooting Guide
To use this chart, locate the symptom that most closely resembles your problem, review the possible causes in column 2, then follow the recommended procedure in column 3. Simple fixes may be explained on the chart; in most cases you will be directed to an illustrated, step-by-step repair sequence.

KITCHEN GARDENS

KITCHEN GARDENS

A kitchen garden burgeoning with ripe, succulent vegetables, fruits and herbs is for many homeowners the ultimate expression of satisfying domesticity. The work of planning and caring for such a garden is more than compensated for by the luxury of fresh produce a stone's throw from the back door.

In the winter, design your garden based on a realistic assessment of the time and energy you are able to spend gardening. Expect to spend at least half an hour every couple of days during late spring and summer tending a typical vegetable garden like the one illustrated below. Before planting, consult a reputable gardening guide and talk with neighboring gardeners and nursery professionals. To learn how to cope with particular problems confronting local gardens, contact your cooperative extension service.

When you are ready to plant, read the Soil Management chapter *(page 16)* and prepare the soil carefully. A loamy soil, rich in organic matter and free from rocks and debris, is ideal for vegetables. Most crops flourish in a soil within a pH range of 5.5 to 7.0. Buy only certified disease-free seeds. Examine nursery transplants carefully for evidence of insects and disease before buying them; select stocky, robust plants with rich green foliage and without flowers or fruit.

Once the seeds and plants are in the ground, your job of policing the garden begins, mostly in the form of defending it against the environment and arresting the spread of pests and diseases. Don't wait until harvest for bitter leafy or root vegetables to tell you that your garden wasn't irrigated enough or adequately protected against the burning sun. Learn what your plants need and act on it. For instance, most vegetables require about 1 to 2 inches of water a week. Splashing the leaves with the spray from a hose or sprinkler system can encourage the spread of disease; consider saving watering time by laying down a soaker hose, digging water furrows *(page 35)* or installing a drip irrigation system *(page 36)*, all of which will ensure that water reaches the critical root zone. Then, to regulate soil moisture and temperature while cutting down on weed growth and discouraging insects, maintain an adequate mulch *(page 38)*. Finally, protect plants, particularly younger ones, from harsh wind, sun, rain and frost: Choose from among an array of covering materials and erect a tunnel *(page 43)* over vulnerable garden rows.

Even a well-maintained garden can fall victim to an unhospitable environment—the Troubleshooting Guide below details likely symptoms and lists their possible causes. The Pests and Diseases chapter *(page 112)* will help you diagnose and treat specific ills. Read Tools & Techniques *(page 129)* for advice on pesticidal control procedures and good horticultural practices.

Vine vegetables
Support climbing vegetable plants (pole beans, peas) on a fence (p. 44) to keep their fruit off the ground.

Heavy feeders
Some vegetables such as corn and tomatoes need plenty of water and should be side dressed with nitrogen fertilizer (p. 38) during growing season.

Fruit canes
To produce well, should be severely pruned annually and trained on a trellis (p. 47).

Tomatoes
Should be caged or staked (p. 45) to save space and produce a healthier crop.

Cucurbits
Members of the cucumber family (cucumbers, melons, squash) can be hand-pollinated (p. 38); should be mulched with plastic to speed ripening and prevent contact with soil fungi.

Root vegetables
Include carrots, radishes, onions; usually grown from seed and need to be thinned (p. 40) early for healthy growth.

Companion plants
Benefit from growing close together. Lettuce and strawberries do well together; cabbage and strawberries don't. Consult an organic gardening guide or your cooperative extension service.

Drip irrigation system
Can be assembled from a kit (p. 36); provides regular, deep moisture for vegetables and reduces watering by hand.

32

TROUBLESHOOTING GUIDE

continued ▶

SYMPTOM	POSSIBLE CAUSE	PROCEDURE
Garden doesn't thrive due to environmental stress: Seeds don't germinate, foliage dull, plants wilt and die, fruit poor	Soil too moist due to excessive watering or rainfall	Check soil moisture (p. 18) □○ and decrease watering
	Soil structure poor	Evaluate soil texture (p. 20) □○ and amend (p. 21) ●○; reseed (p. 39) ●●
	Soil draining poorly	Evaluate drainage (p. 27) ●○, raise soil bed (p. 28) ●●, change soil bed structure (p. 28) ●● or install a drainage system (p. 30) ■●; reseed (p. 39) ●●
	Soil too dry	Check soil moisture (p. 18) □○ and increase watering; mulch (p. 38) □○; consider furrow watering (p. 35) □○ or installing a drip irrigation system (p. 36) ●●
Seeds don't germinate	Seeds old or require longer germination time	Check seed packets for issue date and germination time; if seeds older than 2 years, reseed (p. 39) ●● with new seed
	Seeds sown too early; low soil temperature slowing germination	Ask cooperative extension service when to sow; reseed (p. 39) ●● in warmer weather
	Heavy rains or excessive watering have washed seed away; birds are eating seeds	Reseed and add a row cover (p. 39) ●●
	Crusted soil inhibiting sprouting	If soil dry, keep moistened with mist spray from hose or sprinkler and wait for germination. If soil moist, cultivate (p. 19) □○ and reseed (p. 39) ●● with soilless mix
	Seed-rotting fungi flourishing in wet soil	Check soil moisture (p. 18) □○ and decrease watering. If wet soil persists, evaluate soil drainage (p. 27) ●○, raise soil bed (p. 28) ●●, change soil bed structure (p. 28) ●● or install drainage system (p. 30) ■●; reseed (p. 39) ●● with fungicide-treated seeds
	Seeds sown at wrong depth	Reseed (p. 39) ●● at depth recommended on seed packets
Spindly growth; flowers sparse and may drop	Sun blocked by tree or shrub	Prune tree or shrub (p. 94) ■○; in future, choose planting site with a minimum of six hours sun a day
	Seedlings overcrowded	Thin to proper spacing (step 5, p. 40) □○, and weed (p. 35) □○
	Vegetables overcrowded or unsupported	Erect a support fence (p. 44) ●○ for climbing peas, beans and cucumbers. Cage (p. 45) ●○ or stake (p. 45) □○ tomatoes. Weed (p. 35) □○ and mulch (p. 38) □○
	Temperature too high or too low	When below 55°F, install a protective tunnel (p. 43) ●● over shorter vegetables (tomatoes, peppers, eggplant); when above 85-90°F, mulch (p. 38) □○
Pale green or yellow leaves	Soil pH unsuitable; nitrogen deficiency	See Pests and Diseases (p. 119); test soil pH (p. 23) ●○ and amend if necessary
	Vegetable planted too deeply	Replant at correct depth (step 5, p. 42) ●○

DEGREE OF DIFFICULTY: □ Easy ● Moderate ■ Complex
ESTIMATED TIME: ○ Less than 1 hour ● 1 to 3 hours ● Over 3 hours

33

Anatomy diagrams
Locate and describe the components of the garden or the special characteristics of the group of plants.

Degree of difficulty and time
Rate the complexity of each repair and how much time the job should take for a homeowner with average do-it-yourself skills.

Cross-references
Direct you to important information elsewhere in the book, including diagnosing pests and diseases and amending soil.

service. However, you will still have saved time and money by diagnosing the problem yourself.

Most of the repairs in Lawn & Garden can be made with a garden fork, a garden trowel, a hoe, a spade and pruning shears. For pruning trees and shrubs you will need lopping shears, a pruning knife, a pruning saw and a step ladder. You may also need power tools for some of the heavier repairs, particularly when working on a lawn.

Basic gardening tools—and the proper way to use them—are presented in the Tools & Techniques section starting on page 129. If you are a novice when it comes to the application of pesticides or the use of a power tiller, for example, read this section in preparation for a major job.

Gardening can lead to injury unless you take certain basic precautions. Wear safety goggles when spraying pesticides overhead, and work gloves to prevent blisters when using tools for a long period of time. If you are applying herbicides, protect your hands with heavy neoprene gloves and mix the chemicals outdoors. When dusting with a pesticide, wear a respirator. Be kind to your back—work with a helper when lifting heavy shrubs or bags of mulch. Most important, follow all safety tips in the Emergency Guide and throughout the book.

Name of repair
You will be referred by the Troubleshooting Guide to the first page of a specific repair job.

Insets
Illustrate close-up views of specific steps.

Step-by-step procedures
Follow the numbered repair sequence carefully. Depending on the result of each step, you may be directed to a later step, or to another part of the book, to complete the repair.

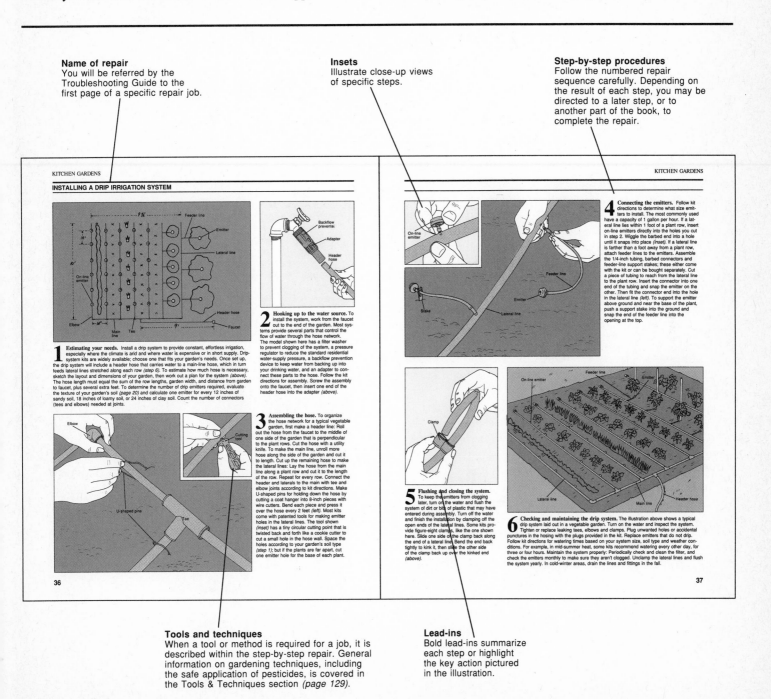

Tools and techniques
When a tool or method is required for a job, it is described within the step-by-step repair. General information on gardening techniques, including the safe application of pesticides, is covered in the Tools & Techniques section (page 129).

Lead-ins
Bold lead-ins summarize each step or highlight the key action pictured in the illustration.

EMERGENCY GUIDE

Preventing problems in the garden. Garden emergencies fall into two categories: situations that threaten your family's health and safety, such as accidents with pesticides or tools, and situations that threaten the garden itself, such as heavy storms or early frosts that hit with little, if any, warning.

The Troubleshooting Guide on page 9 puts emergency procedures at your fingertips. It provides you with suggestions for quick action to take, and refers you to the procedures on pages 10 through 13 for more detailed information. Read these emergency instructions thoroughly before you need them.

Accidents can befall even the most careful gardener. Sharp tools can slip. Machinery can malfunction. Pesticides contain ingredients that can burn skin and eyes, and cause illness if ingested by a child or pet. Bee stings can induce painful and sometimes serious allergic reactions.

Most garden accidents can be prevented if you follow the Safety Tips presented at right and familiarize yourself with the Tools & Techniques *(page 129)* and Lawns *(page 70)* chapters of this book, both of which describe the safe use of garden tools, machinery and pesticides.

Pesticides include insecticides, herbicides, miticides and other pest killers. Minimize the risk of pesticide poisoning by carefully reading product labels; they provide information for your protection. Study the sample pesticide label on page 10 to learn what to look for. Read the label before you buy a product to make sure it's what you need. Observe specific directions for safely mixing and using the product. Study the first aid instructions on the label so you'll know what to do before an accident occurs and, finally, follow directions for safe storage and disposal.

Poison oak and poison ivy can be troublesome if they are growing in the garden where they can easily come into contact with skin. The rash they induce spreads quickly, is very uncomfortable and may require medical attention. Methods for identifying and safely removing these poisonous plants are covered on page 12.

Keep a well-equipped first-aid kit within easy access of the garden. Stock it with a mild antiseptic, sterile gauze dressings, a roll of gauze bandage, adhesive tape, adhesive bandages, scissors, tweezers, a packet of needles, and a bottle of calamine lotion for sunburn, insect bites or rashes.

Keep a supply of old sheets or burlap on hand for weather emergencies. They can quickly be laid over beds of valuable plants, such as ripening vegetables, and anchored with rocks to afford some protection against sudden heavy rain, hail or an unexpected light frost.

If you doubt your ability to handle an emergency properly, call for help. Post numbers for your local hospital and poison control center near the telephone. Your County Cooperative Extension Service of the Department of Agriculture can answer many questions about gardening-related emergencies. Your local environmental protection agency can answer questions about toxic pesticide use and disposal.

SAFETY TIPS

1. Before beginning any repair in this book, read the entire procedure. Familiarize yourself with the specific safety information presented in each chapter.

2. Never leave garden tools—especially sharp rakes—lying on the ground where they can be tripped over or stepped on.

3. Wear gloves when working in the garden to guard against cuts, insect bites and contact with pesticides.

4. Before using a pesticide, carefully read the label, and follow the instructions concerning use and storage.

5. Do not eat, drink or smoke while working with pesticides; the combination can cause illness.

6. When mixing pesticides, wear rubber gloves and long sleeves. Never use kitchen utensils to mix pesticides. Do not mix together different pesticides except as the label directs.

7. Do not use a pesticide on fruits or vegetables unless the label says it is safe, and then only as close to harvest time as the label indicates. Wash fruits and vegetables before eating them.

8. When applying a pesticide, wear rubber gloves, boots and long sleeves, and safety goggles if spraying overhead. If there is a breeze, spray with it at your back. Don't spray if it's windy.

9. Keep children and pets away from the area while you're spraying pesticides, and do not let them play on a sprayed lawn until the product label indicates it is safe.

10. Store pesticides in a cool, dry, locked cupboard, tightly capped, and in their original labeled containers. If you put pesticides in other containers, label them accurately. Never use old food or drink containers; the chemical could be consumed by mistake.

11. Never pour unused pesticides down a drain, since they may harm septic tanks, sewage systems and water supplies. Do not re-use empty containers. Call your environmental protection agency to learn how to safely dispose of chemicals and containers.

12. Clean pesticide equipment thoroughly when you have finished and store it in a locked cupboard. Then wash your face and hands and launder contaminated clothes separately.

13. Before mowing a lawn, remove all rocks, sticks and children's toys. Mow only when grass is dry. Wear boots or heavy shoes and long pants. Keep children and pets away. If you are mowing a slope with a push mower, mow side to side, not up and down.

14. Before using a power tiller, carefully read the operating instructions and know how to turn it off. When starting the machine, put it in neutral and stand clear of wheels and blades. If you lose control of the tiller during operation, slip it into neutral.

15. Before cleaning or repairing a power tool such as a lawn mower or tiller, make sure that an electric model is unplugged and that a gas-powered model has been emptied of gas and the spark plug lead disconnected from the spark plug.

16. Empty gas out of gas-powered garden equipment for storage during winter or other long periods. Store gasoline in a tightly closed gas can away from heat or open flame.

17. Keep a fire extinguisher rated ABC or BC in the garden shed, basement or garage where you store pesticides and gasoline, and know how to use it *(p. 11)*.

18. Post the numbers of your local hospital, poison control center and county cooperative extension service near the phone.

TROUBLESHOOTING GUIDE

PROBLEM	PROCEDURE
Pesticide, fertilizer or other garden chemical in eye	Flush eye with water for 10 minutes *(p. 11)*
	Consult a physician immediately and bring product container with you
Pesticide, fertilizer or other garden chemical on skin	Wash thoroughly with soap and water, and refer to product label for additional directions
	If skin irritation develops, consult a physician and bring the product container with you
Pesticide, fertilizer or other garden chemical on clothes	Prerinse and launder clothes separately in hot water with plenty of detergent; rinse twice
	Dry clothes on a clothesline to prevent contamination of dryer
Pesticide, fertilizer or other garden chemical swallowed	Read and follow emergency instructions on the product label; call the poison control center
	Go to the emergency room or physician immediately and bring the container with you
Faintness or dizziness when mixing or using pesticide or other garden chemical	Stop working immediately and rest away from the chemical; refer to product label for instructions
	If symptoms persist or worsen, consult a physician and bring the product container with you
Pesticide or other garden chemical spilled	Keep people away from the spill area and clean area thoroughly *(p. 10)*
	Consult your local environmental protection agency for directions for disposing of toxic materials
Fire in pesticide, gasoline or other garden chemical	Have someone call the fire department immediately
	If there is heavy smoke or the fire is spreading quickly, wait outside for the fire department
	If the fire is small and well contained, use an ABC or BC fire extinguisher *(p. 11)* to extinguish it
Illness after eating fruits or vegetables that have been sprayed with pesticides	Identify the pesticides that have been sprayed on the plant
	Seek medical attention immediately and bring the pesticide container with you
Illness after child eats berries, leaves or other plant material	Determine which plant and plant parts have been ingested
	Seek medical attention immediately and bring a sample of the plant with you
Cut or minor wound	Wrap with a clean cloth, elevate affected limb and apply pressure to stop bleeding *(p. 11)*
	If bleeding doesn't stop or the wound is deep or gaping, seek medical attention
	Wash the area with soap and water and bandage it
	If a puncture, or caused by a rusty or dirty tool, consult a physician about a tetanus shot
Bee sting	Remove stinger and poison sac with a sterilized needle *(p. 11)*, not tweezers
	Wash the area with soap and water; apply calamine lotion or a cold compress to relieve pain
	Consult a physician immediately if a victim has multiple stings or becomes weak, swollen or has difficulty breathing
Insect bite	Wash the area with soap and water, and apply calamine lotion to reduce pain or itching
	Consult a physician if symptoms worsen
Itchy rash after working or playing in garden	Wash affected skin area thoroughly with soap and water, and avoid scratching
	Apply calamine lotion to reduce itching; consult a physician if symptoms persist or worsen
	Check garden for poison ivy or poison oak *(p. 12)*
Faintness or dizziness when working in hot sun	Lay the victim down with feet slightly elevated in a cool, shaded place
	Sponge the victim with cool water; if symptoms persist, seek medical attention immediately
Electric lawn mower or other electric power tool gives off sparks or shocks user	Unplug power cord without touching the machine
	Have machine serviced before using it again
Unseasonable frost is forecast	Harvest as many near-ripe fruits and vegetables as can be used
	Cover the garden for quick protection *(p. 13)*, or mist-water the garden continuously through the night that a frost is expected, until temperatures the next morning rise above freezing
Heavy rain, hail or wind is forecast	Harvest as many near-ripe fruits and vegetables as can be used
	Cover the garden for quick protection *(p. 13)*
Heavy rain, hail or wind has badly damaged the garden	Immediately replant uprooted plants *(p. 13)*; wait for garden to dry before clearing debris *(p. 13)*
	Call a professional arborist if large trees have fallen or split

READING A PESTICIDE LABEL

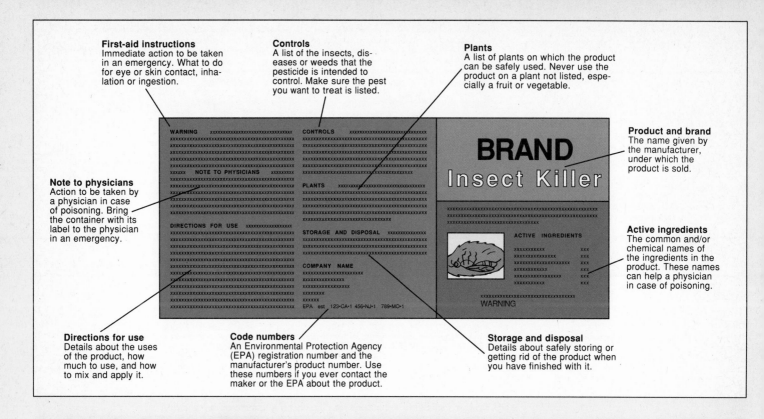

First-aid instructions
Immediate action to be taken in an emergency. What to do for eye or skin contact, inhalation or ingestion.

Controls
A list of the insects, diseases or weeds that the pesticide is intended to control. Make sure the pest you want to treat is listed.

Plants
A list of plants on which the product can be safely used. Never use the product on a plant not listed, especially a fruit or vegetable.

Product and brand
The name given by the manufacturer, under which the product is sold.

Note to physicians
Action to be taken by a physician in case of poisoning. Bring the container with its label to the physician in an emergency.

Active ingredients
The common and/or chemical names of the ingredients in the product. These names can help a physician in case of poisoning.

Directions for use
Details about the uses of the product, how much to use, and how to mix and apply it.

Code numbers
An Environmental Protection Agency (EPA) registration number and the manufacturer's product number. Use these numbers if you ever contact the maker or the EPA about the product.

Storage and disposal
Details about safely storing or getting rid of the product when you have finished with it.

CLEANING UP A PESTICIDE SPILL

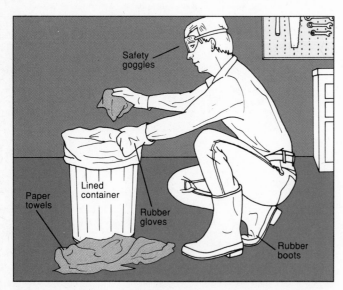

Safety goggles

Paper towels

Lined container

Rubber gloves

Rubber boots

Detergent-and-water solution

1 Sponging up spilled pesticides. Keep people and pets away. Ventilate the area and extinguish any flame. Put on rubber gloves, boots, long sleeves, goggles and, in the case of spilled powder, a dust mask. Sweep up spilled powder with a broom and dustpan and empty it into a container double-lined with heavy-duty plastic garbage bags. Spread absorbent cloths or paper towels over a liquid spill, then sweep the material into a pile and carefully place it in the container *(above)*.

2 Washing the spill site. Use the same broom to scrub the area with a detergent-and-water solution *(above)*. Scrub all corners and crevices well. Pick up the soap solution and dispose of it as in step 1, and repeat. Seal in plastic bags all residue, broken containers and the broom and dustpan. Contact your local environmental protection agency for directions for safe disposal. Wash gloves and boots with a strong detergent-and-water solution, change, and launder clothing separately.

EXTINGUISHING A FIRE

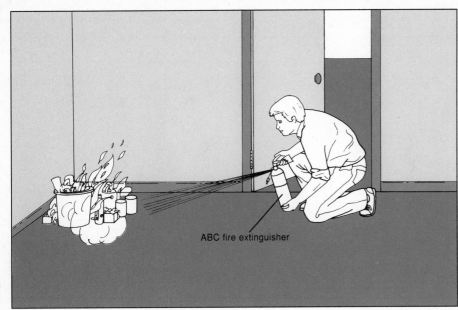

ABC fire extinguisher

Fighting a chemical fire. If an enclosed area is completely filled with smoke, leave and call for help. Otherwise, to snuff a small fire involving pesticides or gasoline, have someone call the fire department, and use a carbon-dioxide fire extinguisher, rated BC, or a dry-chemical fire extinguisher, rated ABC. Note the nearest exit and position yourself 6 to 10 feet from the fire. Hold the extinguisher upright, pull the lock pin out of the handle and aim the nozzle at the base of the flames. Squeeze the handle and spray in a quick side-to-side motion until the fire is completely out. Watch for "flashback," or rekindling, and be prepared to spray again. If the fire spreads, leave the area. Dispose of burned waste or contaminated runoff following the advice of your fire department. Have a fire extinguisher recharged professionally after any use.

FIRST AID TREATMENTS

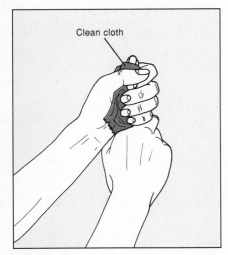

Clean cloth

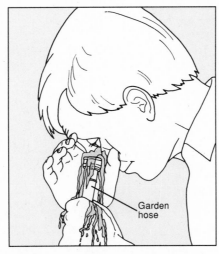

Garden hose

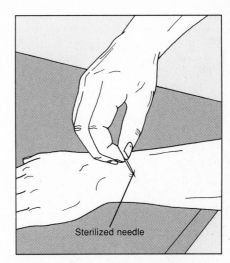

Sterilized needle

Treating cuts and scratches. To stop a wound from bleeding, wrap it with a clean cloth and apply direct pressure, elevating the affected limb *(above)*. If the cloth becomes blood-soaked, wrap another around it. Continue applying pressure, with the limb elevated, until the bleeding stops. Wash a minor wound with soap and water, then bandage it. Seek medical attention if bleeding persists or if the wound is deep or gaping.

Flushing chemicals from the eyes. Liquid or powdered chemicals that accidentally enter the eye must be washed out quickly. Hold the eyelids apart with your fingers and use a steady, gentle flow of cool water from a garden hose to flush the eye *(above)* for 10 minutes. Then cover the eye with a sterile gauze dressing and seek medical attention immediately.

Extracting a bee stinger. Remove the stinger and poison sac from a bee sting immediately. Sterilize a needle with a match flame or rubbing alcohol, then scrape the stinger out from under the skin with the tip of the needle *(above)*. Do not use tweezers, which can squeeze out more venom. Wash the area with soap and water and apply a cold compress to relieve pain. Seek immediate medical attention if the victim becomes weak, swollen or has difficulty breathing.

ERADICATING POISON IVY AND POISON OAK

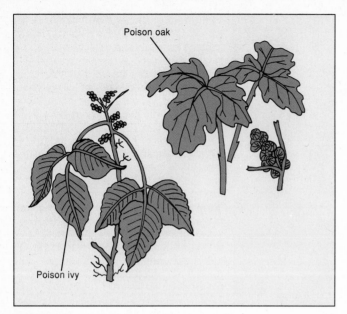

Identifying poison ivy and poison oak. These perennial plants grow as either upright bushes or climbing vines. They are identified by their leaf distribution: Only one leaf, composed of three leaflets, grows from each stem node. The center leaflet has a longer stem than the other two. Poison ivy leaflets are oval, tapered to a pointed tip *(above, left)*, and red in spring. Poison oak leaflets are rounder, and lobed like oak leaves *(above, right)*, hairy on top and velvety underneath. The plants may have greenish flowers in late spring and berries later; poison ivy berries remain all winter.

Uprooting poisonous bushes. Have a lawn care professional remove poison ivy or poison oak if you are allergic. Grub out small patches of plants in early spring or late fall. Wear heavy-duty vinyl or plastic gloves, boots and a rain suit. Do not wear rubber, which may absorb plant oils. Wet the soil thoroughly, and dig down 10 inches around plants with a spade to loosen them. Grab plants at the base and pull out their roots and runners. Seal the plants in double-lined garbage bags for trash disposal; do not burn them. Watch the area carefully for regrowth for one year.

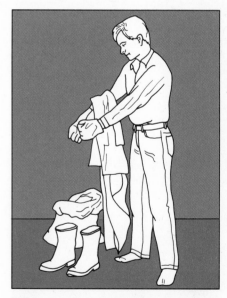

Removing poisonous vines. Remove poison ivy or poison oak vines as soon as you spot them. Wear heavy-duty gloves, boots and a rain suit of vinyl or plastic, not rubber. Cut the vine at ground level, and wait a few days until it wilts. Remove a vine growing in a hedge or shrub by pulling it out with a rake *(above, left)*. To remove a vine from a fence or tree, pull it down by hand *(above, right)*. Seal cut vines in double-lined garbage bags for trash disposal. Don't burn them; the smoke is poisonous. In the future, carefully watch the stems that remain in the ground and spray *(page 77)* regrowth with ammonium sulphamate, triclopyr or glyphosate to kill the roots. Repeat if necessary.

Safely cleaning contaminated clothing. Before removing your gloves, wash all tools with a detergent-and-water solution, and remove and wash your boots. Remove the rain suit, then the gloves *(above)*. Put them in the washing machine, with the other clothing you wore, and launder them thoroughly.

QUICK PROTECTION AGAINST FROST AND HAIL

Covering the garden. Listen for forecasts of bad weather, and learn the warning signs of damaging conditions. A fast-moving, turbulent, green-gray cloud front preceded by a sudden temperature drop in summer may mean hail and heavy rain. If the temperature at bedtime in late spring or late summer is 40°F to 45°F on a still, clear, dry night, there may be light frost. If your fruits or vegetables are almost ripe, harvest those you can conveniently use, to keep them from being damaged. Protect vegetable and flower beds by covering them with sheets of burlap or old bedsheets *(left)*, anchored along the edges with rocks. Cover larger, free-standing plants with inverted cardboard boxes. Stake *(page 45)* freestanding tall plants to help protect them against strong storm winds. Install a protective tunnel *(page 43)* over vegetables when there is risk of frost.

CLEANING UP AFTER A STORM

Replanting uprooted plants. If a storm has left plants covered with mud, mist-water the garden to clean them off. Replant uprooted plants immediately. Lay a wide board in the garden to walk on so you don't compact wet soil. Lift a fallen plant gently, scoop out a hole and put it back in the ground, mounding extra soil around the stem *(above)*. Support plants by tying them to small stakes, driven no closer than 4 to 6 inches away. Remove broken flowers, fruits or leaves before new growth starts.

Removing debris. Let the garden dry before grooming it so you don't compact the soil or spread disease. Harvest vegetables mature enough to eat. Collect debris from the ground *(above)*, and torn leaves, broken tips and damaged fruits and flowers from plants. Dig up badly damaged plants. Prune trees *(page 94)* to remove small, damaged branches. Call a professional arborist to assess damage to large trees. Don't fertilize plants until new growth shows, and watch for rots, molds, or leaf spots *(page 112)*.

YOUR LAWN AND GARDEN

The picture-perfect yard has a harmonious quality that suggests tranquility and order: the lawn unrolling in a welcoming green carpet; trees and shrubs offering shade and privacy; the kitchen garden heavy with ripening vegetables; flowers blooming in controlled profusion. Your house, too, is part of this ecosystem: It forms a pleasing backdrop for climbing plants and flowering bushes, shelters shade-loving ground cover, and by its underground drainage system, determines the types of trees that will grow nearby.

A healthy garden includes plants suitable not only to the region of the country in which you live, but also to the particular microclimate of your lot. There may even be variations from one part of your yard to another. In one corner the soil may be loamy—rich in nutrients and useful microorganisms—and plants will flourish with minimal care. Elsewhere, the soil may be sandy and require frequent watering and amending for plants to survive. Yet another area may be exposed to wind and frost, or it may be so sheltered that plants from a more temperate region can thrive there.

Identify the character of the soil around your home by evaluating its texture and by testing its pH and nutrient levels. Make a sketch of your yard and note soil types, drainage, amount of sunlight received and other factors for future reference. Then choose carefully what will grow best in each area. Botanical gardens, reputable garden centers and your local Cooperative Extension Service are useful places to gather information before you start to plant. Be patient; it may take time and experimentation before you reach a compromise between your fantasies and the dictates of the environment.

Since plants are not assembly-line products, learning to recognize their symptoms of ill-health—and knowing when to intervene—are as important as the repairs themselves. This is where the Troubleshooting Guides in this book, and your detective skills, come into play. Sometimes this diagnosis will be obvious. It isn't difficult to understand that a wilting tomato plant growing in dry soil needs watering, or that an anemic-looking petunia planted in the sun needs more shade. At other times, the symptoms may be subtler: a maple tree that turns color earlier than its neighbor, or a rosebush whose blooms are not as profuse as last year. Even more difficult to diagnose and treat are problems caused by multiple factors, each of which must be identified and corrected for the plant to return to health. When such signs are ignored, the plant's ability to resist infection declines dramatically. Even in the healthiest of gardens, expect to see some evidence of pests and disease; keep their damage under control by treating problems as soon as possible and practicing careful husbandry. To ensure plants receive an inch of water a week, supplement rainfall as required and water to the full depth of their roots. Remove weeds whenever you see them; consider mulching to lessen the amount of watering and weeding you will otherwise have to do. Keep a gardening journal to monitor what is happening to your plants; much can be learned by comparing their health to that of your neighbor's plants and to their condition in previous years.

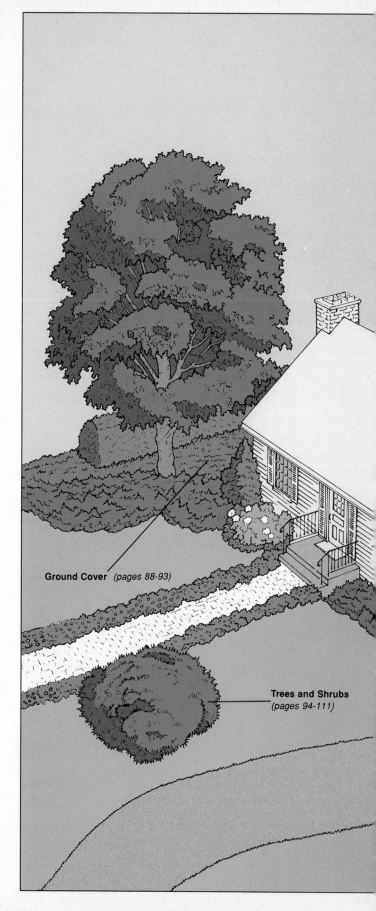

Ground Cover *(pages 88-93)*

Trees and Shrubs *(pages 94-111)*

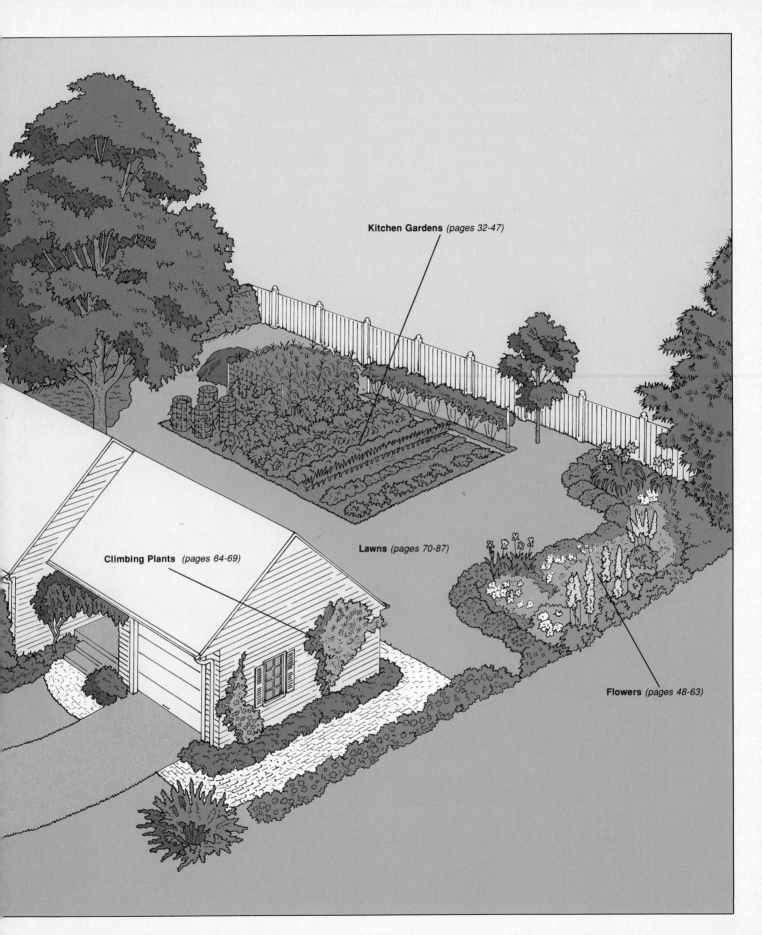

Kitchen Gardens *(pages 32-47)*

Lawns *(pages 70-87)*

Climbing Plants *(pages 64-69)*

Flowers *(pages 48-63)*

SOIL MANAGEMENT

Soil may be simply dirt to some people; to the gardener, it is precious black gold. Rarely is soil naturally barren; although it may involve tedious work, even a poor soil can be managed so that in time it produces healthy plants.

Symptoms of soil problems are presented in the Trouble-shooting Guide *(page 17)* and may be detected either in the soil itself or in the plants. For more detailed plant symptoms and their repairs, consult the appropriate chapter.

Soil sustains plants by supplying their roots with a steady diet of air, water and essential nutrients. Before planting, focus your attention on the condition of the soil; look at it, touch it, even smell it. Soil type is commonly defined by texture *(page 20)*, which reflects the relative proportions of sand, silt and clay particles present. Sand particles are the largest and clay

the smallest, with silt particles falling in between. The ideal garden soil is loam, a friable, or crumbly, mixture of sand, clay, silt and organic matter in various stages of decay. Its acidity, known as the pH level, is between 5.5 and 7.0. At this slightly acidic level the major nutrients, nitrogen, phosphorus and potassium, and the micronutrients, or trace elements, are absorbed by plants most efficiently. When soil is too sandy, it needs regular fertilizing to compensate for the loss of nutrients, which tend to be flushed rapidly through its looser texture by water. When organic materials such as peat moss are used as fertilizer, they can also modify soil texture and pH level. At the other extreme, a soil that has a high clay content will retain water longer, allowing soil nutrients to be absorbed by plant roots. A too-clayey soil may hold water so well that

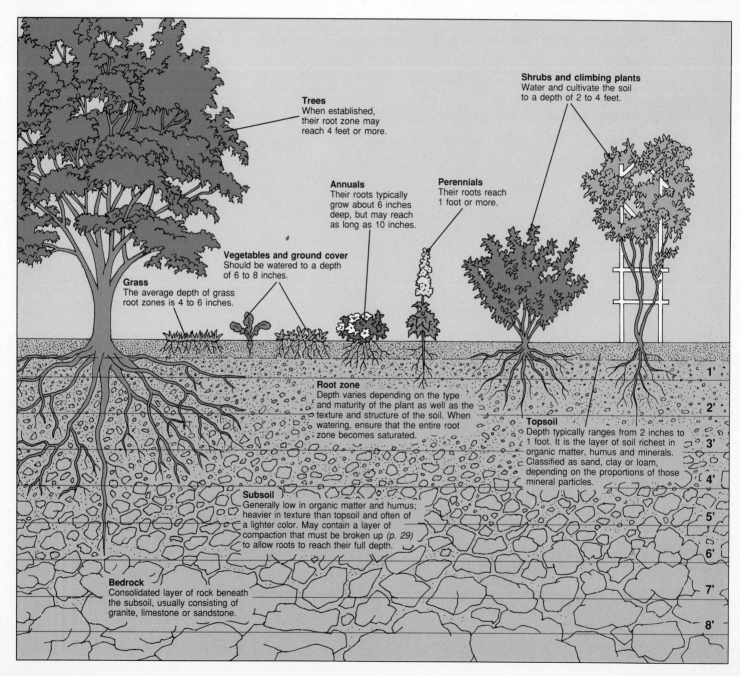

Trees
When established, their root zone may reach 4 feet or more.

Shrubs and climbing plants
Water and cultivate the soil to a depth of 2 to 4 feet.

Annuals
Their roots typically grow about 6 inches deep, but may reach as long as 10 inches.

Perennials
Their roots reach 1 foot or more.

Vegetables and ground cover
Should be watered to a depth of 6 to 8 inches.

Grass
The average depth of grass root zones is 4 to 6 inches.

Root zone
Depth varies depending on the type and maturity of the plant as well as the texture and structure of the soil. When watering, ensure that the entire root zone becomes saturated.

Topsoil
Depth typically ranges from 2 inches to 1 foot. It is the layer of soil richest in organic matter, humus and minerals. Classified as sand, clay or loam, depending on the proportions of those mineral particles.

Subsoil
Generally low in organic matter and humus; heavier in texture than topsoil and often of a lighter color. May contain a layer of compaction that must be broken up *(p. 29)* to allow roots to reach their full depth.

Bedrock
Consolidated layer of rock beneath the subsoil, usually consisting of granite, limestone or sandstone.

1'
2'
3'
4'
5'
6'
7'
8'

the roots become waterlogged. If cultivated, or walked or driven over, clayey soil will become compacted and airless. Amending the soil *(page 21)* and allowing it to dry out between waterings will alleviate this condition.

Regular testing of soil pH *(page 23)* and fertility *(page 25)* can be performed at home, but have the tests done professionally when major adjustments need to be made. Your Cooperative Extension Service can refer you to a reputable laboratory. Also test whether your soil needs watering *(page 18)*. If the soil appears hard or cracked, assist water penetration by cultivating first *(page 19)*. Water using the best method for the plant type; see the appropriate chapter. Study the cross-section at left for the range of plant root-zone depths, and water to the full depth of the plant roots.

As with plant-related problems, repairing soil problems demands a commitment in both time and effort. While you can perform some soil repairs, such as installing a drainage system *(page 30)*, immediately, repairs such as changing soil pH *(page 24)* may take a season to show their full effect. Others, such as changing the structure of the soil bed *(page 28)* may require that you wait until the following spring.

If you choose to perform major repairs when there are plants in the ground, turn to the relevant chapter for information on how to dig up and store the plants and replant them once the repair is completed. Keep in mind, however, that a plant that is already showing the ill effects of a soil problem will suffer even more being removed from the ground, and may need to be replaced.

TROUBLESHOOTING GUIDE
continued ▶

SYMPTOM	POSSIBLE CAUSE	PROCEDURE
Soil is heavy and wet, sticks to tools; water puddles on soil. On plants, lower leaves turn yellow, plant growth slow, roots shallow and rotting	Too much rain; overwatering	Evaluate soil moisture *(p. 18)* □○ and water less frequently
	Soil too clayey (high clay content)	Evaluate soil texture *(p. 20)* ◪○; amend *(p. 21)* ◪○ and cultivate soil *(p. 19)* □○ or change soil bed structure with amendments, such as a 50/50 mixture of sand and peat moss *(p. 28)* ◪◕
	Poor drainage due to subsurface soil compaction	Evaluate soil drainage *(p. 27)* ◪○; water and mulch *(p. 21)* around plants; install drainage system *(p. 30)* ■●. Before planting, raise soil bed *(p. 28)* ◪◕ or change soil bed structure *(p. 28)* ◪◕
	Poor drainage due to underlying bedrock	Raise soil bed *(p. 28)* ◪◕; plant only shallow-rooted plants such as grass or annuals, or move garden site
	High water table	Evaluate soil drainage *(p. 27)* ◪○; install drainage system *(p. 30)* ■●, or before planting next season, raise soil bed *(p. 28)* ◪◕
Soil slides off tools or is too fine to lift with garden fork; dries out quickly. On plants, foliage is brown, plants wilt and die	Insufficient rain or water; plants dehydrated by sun, heat or wind	Evaluate soil moisture *(p. 18)* □○ and water deeply and more frequently; cultivate soil *(p. 19)* □○ and mulch around plants
	Soil too sandy	Evaluate soil moisture *(p. 18)* □○ and soil texture *(p. 20)* ◪○; water deeply and more frequently, cultivate soil *(p. 19)* □○ and mulch around plants with organic matter such as peat moss or manure. Before planting next season, amend *(p. 21)* ◪○ and cultivate *(p. 19)* □○, or change soil bed structure *(p. 28)* ◪◕ with amendments such as peat moss
	Shallow layer of topsoil overlying subsurface soil compaction	Evaluate soil drainage *(p. 27)* ◪○; water and mulch *(p. 21)* ◪○ around plants. Before planting next season, raise soil bed *(p. 28)* ◪◕ or change soil bed structure *(p. 28)* ◪◕
	Shallow layer of topsoil overlying bedrock	Raise soil bed *(p. 28)* ◪◕; plant only shallow-rooted plants such as grass or annuals, or move garden site
Soil is encrusted with white or dark powdery material	Soil watered too lightly	Evaluate soil moisture *(p. 18)* □○; leach soil *(p. 19)* □○; water deeply. Cultivate *(p. 19)* □○; mulch around plants *(p. 21)* ◪○
	Soil too alkaline	Gather soil sample *(p. 23)* □○; test soil pH *(p. 23)* ◪○▲; lower soil pH *(p. 24)* ◪○
	Excessive fertilizing	Leach soil *(p. 19)* □○; in the future, test soil fertility *(p. 25)* ◪○▲ before fertilizing and fertilize *(p. 26)* ◪○ correctly
	Soil salty due to poor drainage	Evaluate soil drainage *(p. 27)* ◪○; install drainage system *(p. 30)* ■●, or before planting next season, raise soil bed *(p. 28)* ◪◕ or change soil bed structure *(p. 28)* ◪◕
Soil is eroded	Excessive water or wind, particularly on a slope	Evaluate soil moisture *(p. 18)* □○ and water correctly in the future. Amend soil and mulch around plants *(p. 21)* ◪○; on a slope, consider mulching with plastic *(p. 41)* ◪○ and replanting with dense, low-lying ground cover

DEGREE OF DIFFICULTY: □ Easy ◪ Moderate ■ Complex
ESTIMATED TIME: ○ Less than 1 hour ◕ 1 to 3 hours ● Over 3 hours

▲ Special tool required

TROUBLESHOOTING GUIDE (continued)

SYMPTOM	POSSIBLE CAUSE	PROCEDURE
Bare spots in soil amid plants	Soil compaction due to excessive foot or machine traffic	Reroute traffic; water, cultivate *(p. 19)* □○ and mulch *(p. 21)* ◨○ around plants
	Soil structure poor	Evaluate soil texture *(p. 20)* ◨○; cultivate soil *(p. 19)* □○ and mulch *(p. 21)* ◨○ around plants with organic matter such as peat moss or manure. Before planting, amend *(p. 21)* ◨○ and cultivate *(p. 19)* □○, or change soil bed structure *(p. 28)* ◨●
Plants spindly and weak; foliage pale green or yellow	Soil pH unsuitable; nitrogen deficiency	Test soil pH *(p. 23)* ◨○▲ and adjust *(p. 24)* ◨○; test soil nitrogen *(p. 25)* ◨○▲ and fertilize *(p. 26)* ◨○
Leaves curl and dry; may turn brown along edges	If soil encrusted white or black, road salt or fertilizer salt accumulated in soil	Leach and cultivate soil *(p. 19)* □○
	Soil pH unsuitable; potassium deficiency	Test soil pH *(p. 23)* ◨○▲ and adjust *(p. 24)* ◨○; test soil fertility *(p. 25)* ◨○▲ and fertilize correctly in the future *(p. 26)* ◨○
	Foliage damaged by fertilizer or pesticide	Apply fertilizer *(p. 27)* □○ or pesticide *(p. 139)* ◨● correctly
Leaves purplish-red; plant growth stunted	Soil pH unsuitable; phosphorus deficiency	Test soil pH *(p. 23)* ◨○▲ and adjust *(p. 24)* □○; test soil fertility *(p. 25)* ◨○▲ and fertilize correctly in the future *(p. 26)* ◨○
Soil smells unpleasant	Compost material not decomposed before application	Return undecomposed material to compost heap. Ensure that only appropriate materials are composted, aerate compost and cover with polyethylene sheet *(p. 22)* ◨○
	Lack of oxygen in soil due to heavy soil compaction	Add amendments *(p. 21)* ◨○ and cultivate soil *(p. 19)* □○, or change soil bed structure *(p. 28)* ◨●
	If sour smelling, soil too acidic	Test soil pH *(p. 23)* ◨○▲ and raise pH *(p. 24)* ◨○ as necessary
Soil is rocky; root vegetables deformed	Soil inadequately cultivated before planting	Remove rocks larger than 1 1/2 inches in diameter. Before planting next season, amend *(p. 21)* ◨○ and cultivate soil *(p. 19)* □○, or change soil bed structure *(p. 28)* ◨●

DEGREE OF DIFFICULTY: □ **Easy** ◨ **Moderate** ■ **Complex**
ESTIMATED TIME: ○ **Less than 1 hour** ◨ **1 to 3 hours** ● **Over 3 hours**　　　　　▲ **Special tool required**

EVALUATING SOIL MOISTURE

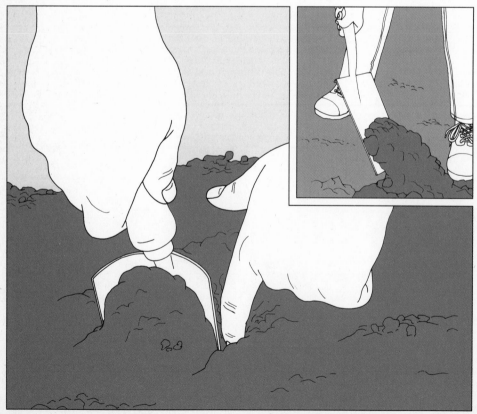

Assessing moisture. Evaluate soil moisture, and supplement rainfall by watering, if necessary, so that plants receive an inch or so of water a week. Recognize when to water by feeling the soil: Use a trowel to make a hole about 2 inches deep, and wide enough to insert your finger *(left)*. When the soil feels cool and barely moist, water deeply and thoroughly. If the soil feels damp or wet to the touch, use a spade to dig down about 6 to 8 inches deeper *(inset)* and assess the soil. If it is barely moist at this depth, wait a day, then water thoroughly. If it is wet, let it dry out. If it doesn't dry out after three rain-free days, check the soil drainage *(page 27)*.

Don't ever let the soil get hard and dry; this damages the plants. Immediately soak dry soil thoroughly with a hose or sprinkler for at least 15 minutes. The following day, evaluate soil moisture again and water if necessary. If the soil dries out very fast after watering, or it continues to feel wet even when it hasn't been recently watered, evaluate its texture *(page 20)* and amend it if necessary *(page 21)*. Sandy soil requires more frequent watering with less water; in clay soil, the water penetrates more slowly and is retained for a longer period.

LEACHING THE SOIL

Leaching salts from the soil. To leach plant-damaging salts from the topsoil, water deeply enough so that the salts are washed into the subsoil below the plants' root zones. First loosen hard, compacted soil with a cultivator *(below)* to assist water penetration. Use a hose with an adjustable nozzle or spray gun, or a sprinkler, to water until puddles start to form on the soil surface *(left)*. Then allow 3 to 4 hours for the soil to absorb the water before assessing the depth to which the soil is saturated. Use a spade to dig a hole in the soil about 1 foot deep and push the handle away from you, using the blade to keep the hole open. Feel the soil; if it is dry, water again until it feels cold and sticky.

CULTIVATING THE SOIL

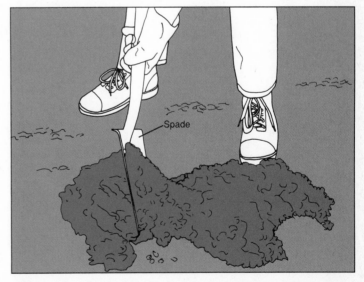

Spade

1 **Cultivating during the growing season.** Many garden beds require weekly cultivation to aerate the soil and encourage water penetration. Evaluate soil moisture *(page 18)* and cultivate when it feels cool and barely moist. Let wet soil dry out first; water over-dry soil two days before cultivating. Loosen crusted or compacted soil with the tines of a cultivator; dig no closer than 3 inches from the base of the plants *(above)*, and no deeper than 4 inches to prevent damaging the plant roots. In the spring, use this method to work decomposed winter mulch into the ground around perennial plants.

2 **Cultivating during the dormant season.** For shallow cultivation—a depth of 6 to 8 inches—use a spade. On a large area, consider using a power tiller *(page 132)*. If amendments *(page 21)* or pH adjustors *(page 24)* are required, spread them over the ground to the recommended depth, but not more than 4 inches. Dig deeply into the ground, pressing down on the blade with one foot. Lift up a bladeful of soil and turn the spade sideways *(above)*, allowing the soil to fall off the spade rather than turning it over completely. Repeat throughout the area to be cultivated. Then smooth down the cultivated soil with a garden rake. If, when digging down with the spade, you hit a hard surface, go to page 28, step 1.

EVALUATING SOIL TEXTURE

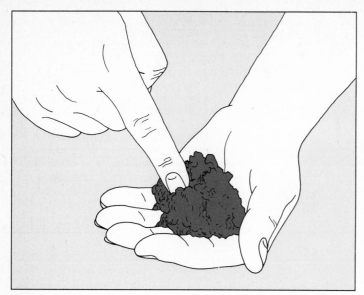

1 **Performing a touch test.** To evaluate the texture of the soil, pick up a handful, lightly moisten it and squeeze it into a ball in the palm of your hand. Release the pressure and touch the soil with your finger *(above)*. If the soil crumbles, it probably has a good, loamy texture, ideal for root development and drainage. If the soil fails to hold together and feels gritty, it is too sandy. If the soil remains in a tight, sticky mass and retains the imprint of a fingertip when touched, it has too much clay. Soils that are high in sand or clay require amendments *(page 21)*. To determine the type and amount of amending needed, go to step 2.

2 **Doing a settling-out test.** Calculate the proportion of sand and clay particles in the soil by using the difference in their weights. Fill a wide-necked, 1-quart glass jar with water to exactly 2 1/2 inches from the top, and add 1 tablespoon of commercial water softener. Using a trowel, dig soil from at least 2 inches below the surface of your garden, remove any twigs or stones and add the soil to the jar *(above)* until the water level rises to exactly 1/2 inch below the top of the jar; you will have added exactly 2 inches of soil. Cap the jar and shake it vigorously for about 60 seconds to mix the soil and water.

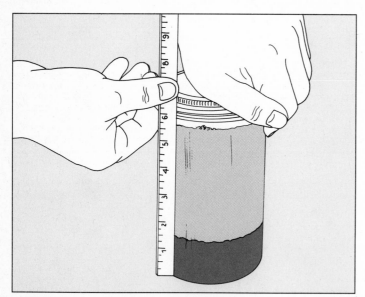

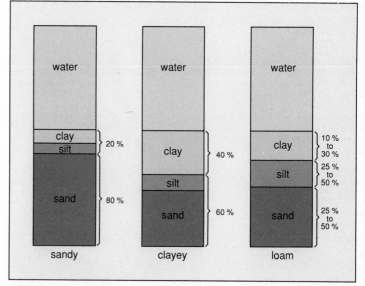

3 **Assessing soil composition.** Set the jar on a level surface and time the rate at which the soil settles out. Measure and note the height of the layer of soil that has settled out after 20 seconds, and again after 2 minutes *(above)*. The first measurement is principally sand, and the second measurement, minus the first, is slightly smaller-grained silt. The remaining soil suspended in the water is primarily clay; it may take several days to settle out. To calculate the quantity of clay more quickly, subtract the height of the sand and silt combined from 2 inches (the total amount of soil added in step 2). Figure the percentages of sand and silt in the soil by dividing each measurement by 2 inches, then multiplying by 100.

4 **Determining soil class.** The jars pictured above broadly illustrate the breakdown of sandy, loamy and clayey soils after settling-out tests. Soil that is more than 80% sand or 40% clay must be amended. The amounts of sand and clay in loamy soil may vary, depending on whether it is sand loam or clay loam. The ideal garden soil has 25 to 50% sand and 10 to 30% clay, with plenty of organic matter. To bring sandy or clayey soil closer to this ideal, review the chart on page 21. Add 2 to 4 inches of amendment in spring to mildly clayey or sandy soil, and cultivate it *(page 19, step 2)*. To amend a poorer soil more deeply, change the soil bed structure *(page 28)*.

MULCHES AND SOIL AMENDMENTS

PRODUCT	USE	CHARACTERISTICS	REMARKS
Agricultural by-products: Corncobs or cornstalks; cocoa bean, cottonseed, buckwheat or peanut hulls; seaweed	M, A	Cocoa bean hulls slightly acid; buckwheat hulls make an attractive mulch for a flower garden; if salty, seaweed must be washed before application	Grind or chop corncobs or cornstalks; add nitrogen-rich material such as blood meal or compost before adding cobs; cover cottonseed hulls with thin layer of another mulch to prevent blowing away. As mulch, apply 2 to 4 inches deep except for corncobs, which should be 6 inches deep
Straw, hay, salt-marsh hay	M, A	Light and porous; hay may contain weed seeds; alfalfa hay has a high nitrogen content	Excellent for vegetable and flower gardens. Salt hay good for new lawns. Before adding straw, add nitrogen-rich material such as cottonseed meal or compost. As mulch, apply hay or straw 6 to 8 inches deep and salt-marsh hay 4 to 6 inches deep
Farm animal manure: Poultry, swine, cattle, horse, sheep	M, A	Excellent source of organic matter; may be salty and have strong odor	Less poultry manure is required than other types because of its high nitrogen content. Compost (p. 22) before using. Apply as mulch 1 to 2 inches deep
Compost	M, A	Excellent source of organic matter; variable composition depending on contents; decomposes quickly	Materials must be well decomposed before application (p. 22). Apply as mulch 1 to 2 inches deep
Crushed rock or stone chips	M	Water penetrates easily; has no nutritional value	Used as decorative mulch. For best weed control, apply over polyethylene, 1 to 2 inches deep
Aluminum foil or foil-backed paper	M	Reusable mulch; may inhibit aphids and other insects; water does not penetrate; no nutritional value; may burn leaves	Apply foil side up in summer to keep ground cool; stake down or cover with thin layer of other mulch to prevent blowing away
Hardwood ashes	M	Excellent source of potash; alkaline, so avoid contact with acid-loving plants; potash will leach away in rain	Test soil pH and add only to acid soils. Apply as mulch 2 to 3 inches deep
Lawn clippings	M, A	If packed down water may not penetrate; add organic matter and micronutrients; decomposes quickly	Allow to dry or compost before applying as mulch 2 to 3 inches deep. Apply less if green. Do not apply if recently treated with herbicide
Leaves	M, A	Light and porous	Apply dried and shredded (p. 133) as mulch 3 to 4 inches deep. Excellent winter mulch when mixed with straw or hay and applied 8 to 12 inches deep
Paper (including newspaper, but not glossy or color pages)	M, A	Water may not penetrate easily; adds organic matter and trace nutrients; slightly alkaline	Shred or tear to improve water penetration and aid decomposition, or moisten newspaper and lay out flat 5 to 6 pages thick. Cover with another mulch to prevent blowing away
Peat moss	M, A	Light and porous; not suitable for arid climates; excellent source of organic matter; acidic; expensive; may form crust over soil; decomposes slowly	Good for acid-loving plants, kitchen gardens, flowers and new lawns. Apply 2 to 3 inches deep. Turn under to help aerate clay soil or to improve water retention of sandy soil. Excellent winter mulch
Polyethylene sheets (clear or black)	M	Reusable; water does not penetrate; has no nutritional value	Apply over moist ground in spring to warm the soil; use with young transplants (p. 41). Use black to control weeds; stake down or cover with thin layer of other mulch to prevent blowing away
Sand	A	Must be medium- or coarse-grained; used to improve soil with a high clay content; has no nutritional value	Best used mixed with one part peat moss and two parts cultivated soil to one part sand
Wood by-products: Ground bark, pine needles, sawdust	M, A	Add organic matter and nutrients; ground bark and sawdust may inhibit water penetration if not cultivated periodically; slightly acidic, may require the addition of lime	Use nitrolized sawdust or ground bark, or first apply nitrogen-rich material such as manure, or soybean or cottonseed meal. Apply as mulch 2 to 4 inches deep

Choosing mulches and amendments. Your choice of mulches and amendments will be limited by what is available locally; check the yellow pages for suppliers such as lumber companies, dairy farms, and quarries. The primary difference between mulches and amendments is that mulches are laid on the ground around plants, and amendments are worked into the soil. Even so, most organic mulches can be turned in to the soil at the end of a gardening season, becoming amendments. Mulches are applied once plants are about 6 inches high; they prevent soil erosion, discourage weed growth and water evaporation, and moderate the effects of weather. To determine how deep a summer mulch should be, consult the "Remarks" column. For a winter mulch, choose one that is light and porous and apply it a couple of inches deeper. To calculate the required volume of mulch in cubic feet, multiply its depth in inches by the soil area in square feet and divide by 12. Amendments improve soil texture, drainage and fertility. For beds that will grow shallow-rooted plants, or for minor adjustments in soil texture, work amendments into the ground to a depth of 6 to 8 inches (page 19, step 2). Otherwise, restructure the soil bed (page 28). In sandy soil, the addition of fine-textured decomposed organic materials such as manure, ground bark, peat moss or sawdust will help slow drainage and increase the nutrient value of the soil. The primary role of an amendment in clay soil is to improve drainage and aeration. Working sand into the earth may be all that is needed, although any soil, including loamy soil, will benefit from the addition of organic materials.

MAINTAINING COMPOST

Pipe

1 **Building a compost pile.** The pile shown here should decompose for three months before the compost is ready to be applied as an amendment or a mulch. Choose a spot for the pile close to the garden. Using a spade, pile plant matter 6 to 8 inches deep in a square area 6 feet by 6 feet and slightly concave in the center; maintain this shape as you build it. The smaller the pieces of material used, the faster the decomposition. Use carbon-rich matter such as dried twigs, wood chips, lawn clippings, hay, straw, leaves and other plant parts and vegetable kitchen waste. Avoid material that is diseased or pest-infested or that has recently been treated with a herbicide. Do not use meat scraps, bones or fat. Cover this first layer with a second layer, 2 inches deep, of nitrogen-rich material such as farm animal manure and hay. To speed up decomposition, sprinkle on two or three trowel-fuls of organic nitrogen, such as blood meal. Add a third layer of topsoil, about 1/4 inch deep, and then sprinkle a bit of alkaline material such as lime or wood ashes on top. Moisten the pile with water. Repeat this layering process until the pile stands between 3 and 5 feet high *(far left)*. Insert a 5-foot iron pipe into the middle of the compost pile as a thermometer *(near left)*.

2 **Aerating the compost.** Periodically check the pipe thermometer by touching it; after about two weeks, if the compost is decomposing properly, the pipe will start getting warm, until it is too hot to hold comfortably with your hand. Then the pipe will begin to cool; when it does, aerate the compost: Use a garden fork to turn the pile *(left)*, making sure the outer layer of the compost moves into the center so that the compost decomposes evenly. After aerating, moisten the pile and reshape it, maintaining a slight dip in the center. Keep checking the temperature over the next few weeks; the pipe will heat up again but not as much as the first time. About 6 weeks after the compost pile was first built, aerate it a second time. If the temperature of the pipe fails to increase at the beginning, or within two or three days after the compost was first aerated, cover the pile with a polyethylene sheet for a week or so to help heat it up; weigh down the corners with large stones or bricks *(inset)*. Apply compost as an amendment or a mulch when it has become dark and crumbly and smells earthy. Any materials that are not fully decomposed should be returned to the pile.

GATHERING A SOIL SAMPLE

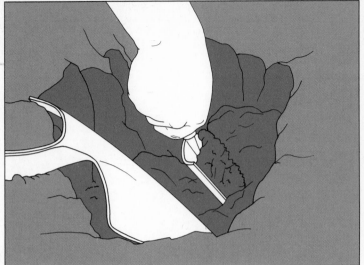

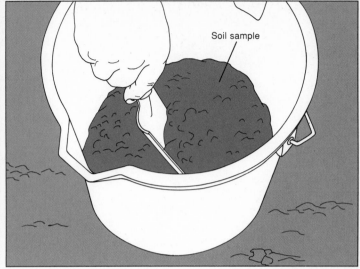

Soil sample

Preparing a soil sample. If you intend to send your soil sample to a lab to be tested, consult them regarding the steps to take for gathering a sample. To test soil pH or fertility at home, use a soil test kit available at a nursery or garden supply store. Check the directions supplied by the manufacturer; if they differ from the procedures outlined in this chapter, follow the manufacturer's directions instead. A typical kit for soil testing includes all the necessary equipment (syringe, test tube, and test solutions and powders) for testing both soil pH and levels of soil nutrients such as nitrogen, phosphorus and potassium. To gather a sample for the typical test kit used in this chapter, mark the bound-aries of the area you are testing and use a clean spade to dig a hole in the soil within the test area. In general, dig 8 to 12 inches deep when testing soil pH or soil phosphorus or potassium; in a lawn, 4 inches deep is enough. When testing soil nitrogen, however, dig down at least 2 feet. Then use a clean trowel to scoop a thin slice of earth off the wall of the hole, from the bottom up *(above, left)*. Scrape off any soil removed from the top 1/2 inch of the hole with a clean spoon. Deposit the remaining soil in a clean plastic bucket. Repeat this procedure five or six times at different sites within the test area, then mix the soil thoroughly into a representative sample *(above, right)*. Remove any stones or debris.

TESTING SOIL pH

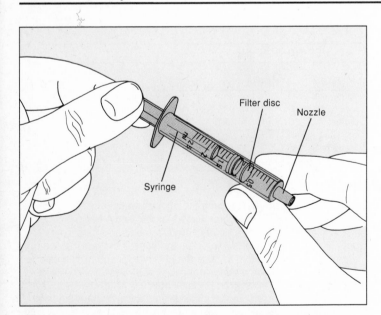

Filter disc

Nozzle

Syringe

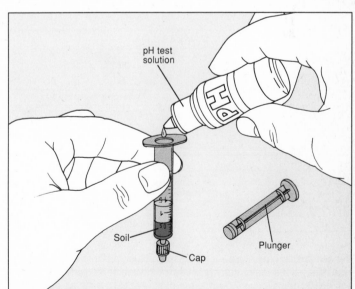

pH test solution

Soil

Cap

Plunger

1 Setting up. Gather a representative soil sample *(top)*. Take the cap off the nozzle of the syringe and pull out the plunger. Align a filter disc over the mouth of the syringe and use the applicator to push it out of the perforated sheet and down *(above)*, lodging it flat across the bottom of the syringe. Press the cap tightly onto the nozzle.

2 Adding test solution. Using a clean spoon, fill the syringe to the 0.5 ml mark with soil from the sample. Add pH test solution to the 2 ml mark on the syringe *(above)*. Insert the plunger into the top of the syringe just far enough to seal off the opening. Holding the plunger in place with a finger, shake the syringe vigorously for about 30 seconds to mix the soil and test solution together thoroughly. With a finger still supporting the plunger, turn the syringe nozzle up, and allow the soil to settle out.

TESTING SOIL pH (continued)

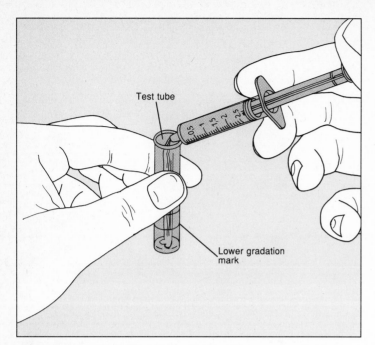

Test tube

Lower gradation mark

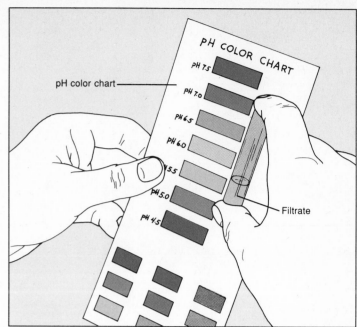

pH color chart

Filtrate

3 **Squeezing out filtrate.** Pull the cap off the nozzle. Rest the tip of the nozzle on the mouth of the test tube and push down firmly on the plunger to squeeze out as much filtrate as possible *(above)*. Fill the test tube to the lower gradation mark. If necessary, extract additional filtrate by releasing the plunger, allowing it to rise in the syringe, and then pushing it back down again. Take a pH reading immediately once the filtrate reaches the mark.

4 **Taking a pH reading.** Match the color of the filtrate with a color on the pH chart to determine the soil pH *(above)*, estimating between two pH levels if the color of the filtrate falls between two colors on the chart. Wash and dry the syringe, cap, plunger, applicator and test tube. For greatest accuracy, repeat steps 1 through 4 several times with the same soil sample, and average the pH readings. Remember to wash and dry the testing equipment thoroughly after each test. Adjust soil pH as described below.

ADJUSTING SOIL pH

SOIL pH AND NUTRIENT AVAILABILITY

Major nutrients	pH 4 •	pH 5 •	pH 6 •	pH 7 •	pH 8
Nitrogen (N)					
Phosphorus (P)					
Potassium (K)					
Micronutrients					
Calcium					
Magnesium					
Iron					
Manganese					
Boron					

ADJUSTING SOIL pH

Material	pH change	Sandy	Loam	Clayey
Dolomitic or calcic limestone	+1/2 unit (0.5 pH)	1-2 lb.	2-3 lbs.	4-5 lbs.
	+1 unit (1.0 pH)	2-3 lbs.	4-5 lbs.	*
Flowers of sulphur or iron sulfate	-1/2 unit (0.5 pH)	1/4-1/2 lb.	1/2-1 1/2 lb.	1-2 lb.
	- 1 unit (1.0 pH)	1/2-1 lb.	1-3 lb.	2-4 lbs.

Amounts listed are pounds per 100 square feet
* Do not add more than 5 lbs. of lime or sulphur in one application

Adjusting soil pH to improve fertility. The acidity or alkalinity of the soil affects a plant's ability to absorb nutrients. As shown in the chart above, the major nutrients are most available to plants within a soil pH range of 5.5 to 7.0. In areas of high rainfall, such as the northeastern and northwestern United States, soils tend to be more acidic, and potassium may be less available. In contrast, soils in the more arid southwest are likely to be alkaline, and thus iron, for example, may be unavailable. Within the microclimate of your own garden there may also be variations; the soil around a house with a concrete foundation may be alkaline, for example, due to seepage of lime from the concrete. Avoid applying fertilizers without first testing the pH of your soil *(page 23)* and adjusting it as required *(right)*.

Adding pH adjustors. Compare the pH test reading for the soil sample with the pH level recommended for the plants being grown; most soil test kits include a list of pH requirements for many common plants. Evaluate soil texture *(page 20)* and consult the table above for the amount of lime needed to raise the pH level, or sulphur needed to lower it. Also review the amendment chart *(page 21)* for a choice of organic materials to modify the pH level of your soil. It may take several years before the soil reaches the desired level; change the level by no more than one pH unit (1.0) at a time, and wait at least a month before retesting soil pH and reappling the adjustor. The majority of plants prefer a slightly acidic soil within a pH range of 5.5 to 7.0. Notable exceptions include rhododendrons and azaleas, which prefer levels as acidic as 4.5 to 5.0, and delphiniums, which thrive in soil as alkaline as 8.0. Lime and sulphur are available in various forms at garden supply stores and nurseries. Spread them evenly over the ground and cultivate them under *(page 19)*. Adjustors are best applied in the fall.

TESTING SOIL FERTILITY

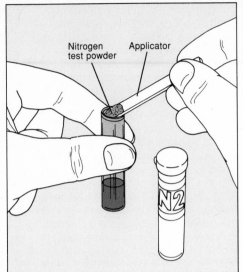

Nitrogen test powder   Applicator

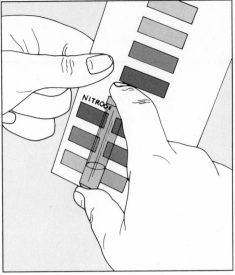

1 **Testing for nitrogen.** Gather a soil sample, fill the test syringe to the 1 ml mark with soil and add nitrogen test solution. Let the soil absorb the test solution. Fill the test tube with filtrate to the lower gradation mark *(page 24, step 3)*, then add 1 level scoopful of nitrogen test powder *(far left)*. Snap on the cap and shake. Let the mixture stand for 5 minutes. Compare the color of the filtrate with the colors on the nitrogen-level color chart to determine whether the soil nitrogen is high, medium or low *(near left)*. Thoroughly wash and dry the test equipment used. Repeat the test three times; if your results vary widely, consult your local extension service to test your soil. Leach *(page 19)* soil that is high in nitrogen, and apply a nitrogen fertilizer *(page 26)* if the level is low.

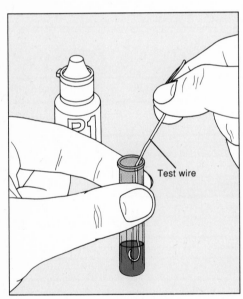

Test wire

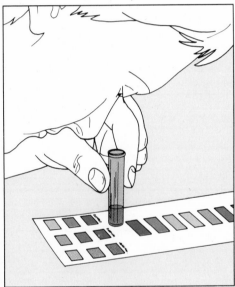

2 **Testing for phosphorus.** Follow steps 1 through 3 for testing soil pH *(pages 23-24)*, adding phosphorus test solution instead. Then polish the last inch on one end of the phosphorus test wire with emery paper. Bend this end into a loop and stir the filtrate vigorously for 15 to 20 seconds *(far left)*. Hold the test tube 1/2 inch above a white area of the test card, near the phosphorus-level color chart. Looking down through the test tube *(near left)*, compare the color of the filtrate with the colors on the chart to determine whether the soil is high, medium or low in phosphorus. Thoroughly wash and dry the test equipment. Repeat the test three times; if your results vary widely each time, consult your local extension service to test your soil. Apply a phosphorus fertilizer *(page 26)* if the soil is low in phosphorus.

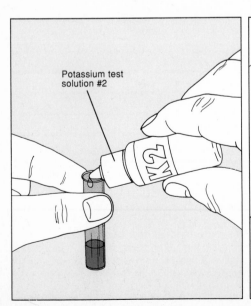

Potassium test solution #2

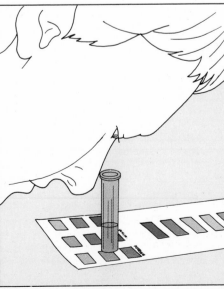

3 **Testing for potassium.** Follow steps 1 through 3 for testing soil pH *(pages 23-24)*, this time adding potassium test solution #1. Then add potassium test solution #2 up to the higher gradation mark on the test tube *(far left)*. Snap on the cap and swirl gently for 15 to 20 seconds. Let the mixture stand for 5 minutes. Place the bottom of the test tube over each circle of the potassium-level chart in turn, and look down through the test tube *(near left)*. If only the black rectangle is visible, the soil is high in potassium. If the dotted rectangle can also be seen, the soil is medium in potassium. If all the rectangles are visible, the soil is low in potassium. Thoroughly wash and dry the test equipment. Repeat the test three times; if your results vary widely each time, consult your local extension service to test your soil. Apply a potassium fertilizer *(page 26)* to the soil if the level is low.

CORRECTING SOIL NUTRIENT DEFICIENCIES

Nitrogen
Promotes rich green foliage in plants. When deficient, leaves turn pale green or yellow. When in excess, plants are easily broken by the wind and become vulnerable to cold and disease.

Potassium
Contributes to overall healthy growth and can help counteract an excess of nitrogen. When deficient, yellow spots or streaks may appear on leaves and their margins may dry up.

Phosphorus
Essential for root growth and seed, blossom and fruit production. When deficient, plants stop growing and their leaves may become purplish-red.

Micronutrients
Include calcium, magnesium, iron, manganese, and boron. Symptoms of deficiency may be confused with nitrogen deficiency. Consult the cooperative extension service before treating; micronutrients can be toxic if overapplied.

Understanding a plant's nutritional needs. The three major plant nutrients are the chemical elements nitrogen (N), phosphorus (P) and potassium (K). Other elements, including calcium and iron, are required in smaller amounts, and are known as micronutrients. As described at left, each nutrient promotes the health of a specific plant system. All three major nutrients must be available in balanced amounts to encourage the overall health of the plant. This balance may be varied, however, to promote certain types of growth. For example, since phosphorus promotes root growth, adding a transplanter-solution fertilizer, which is high in phosphorus, helps a transplant reestablish its root system. Of all the elements, nitrogen is most likely to require supplementation. It leaches easily and is frequently in short supply in the soil, and when applied in some forms it can escape as ammonia or nitrogen gas. Work nitrogen well into the soil immediately after application.

SOIL NUTRIENTS

NUTRIENT	CHARACTERISTICS
NITROGEN (N)	
Ammonium nitrate	Fast release; high burn potential
Ammonium sulfate	Fast release; high burn potential; may harm beneficial soil bacteria; may acidify soil
Blood meal	Organic; slow release; low burn potential; long-term source of P
Sodium nitrate	Fast release; low burn potential
Urea	Organic; available in several forms; may be fast or slow release; low or medium burn potential
PHOSPHORUS (P)	
Ammonium phosphate	Also contains N; fast release; high burn potential
Bone meal	Organic; slow release; low burn potential; recommended for bulb planting
Phosphate rock	Mineral source of P; is released faster when finely ground; best applied a month or two after soil is amended with animal manure
Superphosphate	Treated with sulfuric acid; medium release; low burn potential
POTASSIUM (K)	
Potassium chloride	Also called muriate of potash; fast release; high burn potential; may acidify soil
Potassium nitrate	Also contains N; fast release; high burn potential
Potassium sulfate	Fast release; medium burn potential; may acidify soil
Granite dust	Mineral source of K; slow release; best applied with amendments such as ashes, manure or compost

Choosing a fertilizer. When only one nutrient is deficient, as indicated by a soil fertility test *(page 25)*, it is generally more efficient to apply a fertilizer that responds specifically to that deficiency. The chart above lists commercially available sources of nitrogen, phosphorus and potassium. For quick results, choose a fast-release fertilizer, applying it carefully following the instructions on the package label; it can burn plant tissue. Many fast-acting fertilizers are available in liquid form; fertilizers applied dry are usually slow-release. Many of the nutrient forms above are present in compound fertilizers, occasionally accompanied by micronutrients. A "complete" fertilizer contains all three major nutrients. Their proportions are expressed by a number, such as 10-10-10 or 5-52-10, referred to as the N-P-K rating. When the proportions are roughly equivalent, the fertilizer is "balanced." Consult your local garden nursery to choose the appropriate fertilizer formulation.

APPLYING FERTILIZER TO THE SOIL

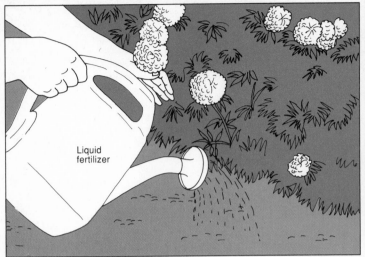

Applying fertilizer. If you recently adjusted the soil's pH level *(page 24)*, wait a month before applying fertilizer. Choose an appropriate fertilizer *(page 26)* according to the fertility test results *(page 25)*. Follow the instructions on the package label, taking care not to apply too heavily or too often. Keep in mind that most fertilizing needs can be met by the regular application of organic amendments *(page 21)* such as animal manure, peat moss or compost. In general, prepare a commercial liquid fertilizer for application by dissolving or diluting the fertilizer in a watering can, as instructed on the label. Use a clean stick to mix the fertilizer and water together thoroughly. Pour the liquid around plant bases, avoiding contact with the foliage *(above, left)*. If applying fertilizer in its dry form, push aside any mulch and use a trowel *(above, right)* or your hand to sprinkle the fertilizer in a thin band around the base of the plant, at least 4 inches away. Work it gently into the ground with a cultivator *(page 19, step 1)*. Carefully monitor your progress to prevent overfertilizing one area. Soak dry fertilizer into the root zone of the plants using a garden hose or a sprinkler. Replace the mulch, adding more if necessary.

EVALUATING SOIL DRAINAGE

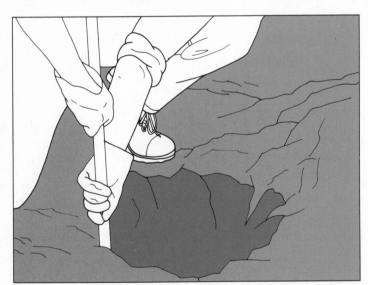

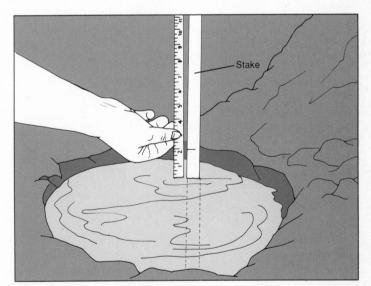

1 Digging the hole. Test the soil moisture *(page 18)* and water if dry. The next day, use a spade to dig a hole about 3 feet deep *(above)* and go to step 2 to evaluate soil drainage. If the walls of the hole reveal contrasting layers, soil of a different texture from another location may have been added to the garden as fill material. First cultivate the soil *(page 19)* to mix the layers before testing soil drainage. If the spade hits a layer of bedrock or subsurface compaction, try to dig another hole; if this is blocked, consider raising the soil bed *(page 28)* before next planting season. If the area is large, such as a kitchen garden, change the soil structure *(page 28)* after harvest, or install a drainage system *(page 30)* now.

2 Rating water droppage. If water seeps into the hole, raise the soil bed *(page 28)*; or install a drainage system *(page 30)*. Otherwise, drive a 4-foot-long stake into the bottom of the hole and fill the hole with water. Mark the water level on the stake. Allow the hole to drain for one hour and measure the drop in water level *(above)*. Drainage of 1 inch per hour is excellent. If the water drops faster than 3 or 4 inches per hour, or only 1/2 inch per hour, evaluate soil texture *(page 20)* and amend *(page 21)* accordingly. If the water level drops less than 1/4 inch, soil drainage is poor; determine the extent of the problem by evaluating nearby sites. If the area is small, raise the soil bed *(page 28)*; if the area is large or the hole failed to drain at all, install a drainage system *(page 30)*.

RAISING THE SOIL BED

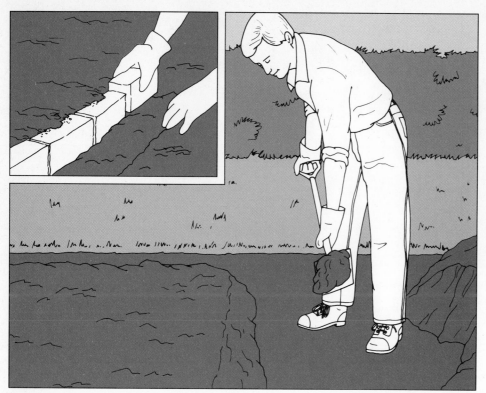

Building a raised bed. Raise a garden bed 4 to 6 inches with garden soil and bricks. In the spring, transplant any perennials *(page 55)* growing in the bed. To calculate the required volume of soil in cubic feet, multiply the desired depth in inches by the bed area in square feet, and divide by 12. Purchase good garden soil from a reliable garden nursery and consider having it delivered by truck if more than a few bags are required. Spread the soil evenly over the ground surface with a spade *(left)*, add an inch or so of organic amendment *(page 21)* and cultivate *(page 19, step 2)*. About 6 inches in from the edges of the raised bed, use a rake to push back the soil, carving out a shallow, uniform trough. Lay a border of bricks in the trough. Align the bricks on their sides, sliding each brick back and forth until it closely butts the one next to it *(inset)*. Enclose the entire bed. Tamp down the margin of soil around the outside of the bricks to keep them from falling over. If necessary, add a second row of bricks on top of the first, positioning them on their broad sides for greater stability.

CHANGING SOIL BED STRUCTURE

1 Removing soil. Evaluate soil texture *(page 20)*. If high in sand or clay content, or if the root zone of your plants is deeper than 8 inches or if you hit subsurface compaction when you were testing soil drainage *(page 27)* or cultivating *(page 19)*, change the structure of the soil bed.

Choose an appropriate soil amendment *(page 21)*. In general, the soil should be amended to the depth of the plant roots; study the soil cross-section *(page 16)* to learn the range of root-zone depths for plants, and consult your extension service for variations in your area. To amend a large area, consider hiring a landscaping firm to have it done professionally. Work during the dormant season, and transplant any perennials *(page 55)* or young trees or shrubs *(page 106)* that may be in the way. To determine the amount of amendment you need in cubic feet, multiply half the root-zone depth in inches by the soil-bed area in square feet, and divide by 12. Unless amending a very small area, use a wheelbarrow to move the dirt and pile it nearby *(left)*. Discard any debris or rocks larger than 1 1/2 inches in diameter. Then go to step 3. If your spade continually hits subsurface compaction as you dig, go to step 2.

CHANGING SOIL BED STRUCTURE (continued)

Compacted soil

2 **Breaking up subsurface compaction.** A hard surface beneath the topsoil may be either bedrock or subsurface compaction. If bedrock, choose another site for your garden. If subsurface compaction, break it up. Using a garden fork, force the tines as deeply as possible into the compacted layer *(far left)*, pushing down with the weight of both feet if necessary. Repeat every few inches, breaking the compacted soil into chunks. Use a hoe *(near left)* or a pointed spade to shatter the chunks into loose soil. Lift out any rocks larger than 1 1/2 inches in diameter; get help to lift large rocks. If you cannot break up the compaction, consult a professional landscaper about having it broken up with a jackhammer. Once you have broken through to the desired root-zone depth, dig out the soil and pile it with the upper layer of loose soil.

PEAT MOSS

3 **Amending the soil.** Using a spade, add the amendment to the pile of soil removed from the bed. Mix the amendment and soil together thoroughly with a garden fork *(left)*, and break up any lumps. If you mix them in small portions, be sure to maintain a ratio of 1 part amendment to 2 parts soil. Then use a spade to fill the hole with this mixture and rake the surface level. You will probably have some amendment/soil mixture left over. If you removed many large rocks, or amended with a light and porous material such as peat moss, the level of the amended bed may settle below that of the surrounding area. Observe the bed for several days, especially if it rains heavily, and top up the level with the leftover mixture if necessary.

INSTALLING A DRAINAGE SYSTEM

1 **Making a sump.** Depending on the soil type, one drainage pipe will drain an area about 8 feet wide; 4 feet along each side of the pipe. If the area you are draining is wider, or the pipe is longer than 100 feet, consider having the system installed professionally. Consult utility companies before digging. Choose a site for an outfall, or sump, to which the pipe can drain excess water. If there is no convenient low spot in the garden to serve as a natural outfall, make a sump by using a spade to dig a hole 3 to 4 feet deep and about 3 feet across *(above).*

2 **Digging a trench for the drainpipe.** Mark a guideline for digging the trench using stakes and string, keeping the trench as straight and short as possible while avoiding rocks or plants. Beginning at the outfall or sump, dig the trench 8 inches wide, using a square spade to keep the edges straight and even *(above).* Start the bottom of the trench 1 foot shallower than the sump, and slope it upward very slightly as you dig away from the sump.

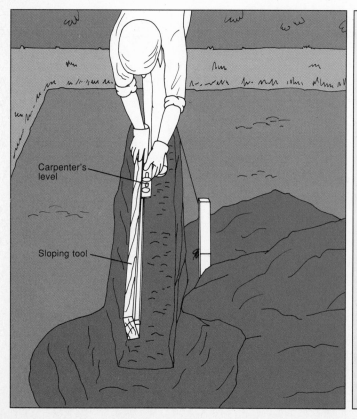

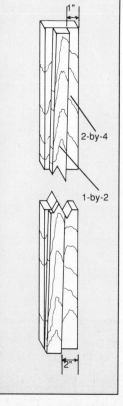

3 **Checking the trench slope.** For every 8 feet in length, the trench must gradually slope downward 1 inch toward the sump. Measure the slope of the trench using a carpenter's level and a homemade tool constructed from a 1-by-2 and a 2-by-4, each 8 feet long *(inset).* Nail the 1-by-2 along the broad side of the 2-by-4, angling the 1-by-2 so that one end is 2 inches up from the bottom corner of the 2-by-4, and the other end is 1 inch up from the opposite bottom corner *(inset).* Place the tool on the floor of the trench with the end that is 2 inches up positioned nearest the outfall or sump. Rest the carpenter's level on the 1-by-2; if the bubble centers, the trench has the proper slope *(left).* If the bubble fails to center, remove or add soil to the trench floor until it does. If the trench is longer than 8 feet, repeat this measuring and adjusting along its entire length.

Sand

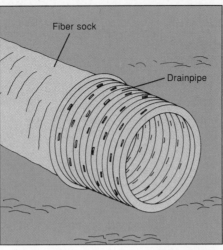

Fiber sock

Drainpipe

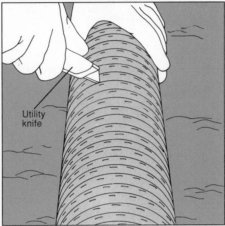

Utility knife

4 **Filling the trench with sand.** Once the trench is completed and its slope corrected, check whether the sump depth must be increased; if the trench is longer than 8 feet, use a spade to remove more dirt from the sump until it is at least 1 foot deeper than the shallow end of the trench. Order sufficient drain rock from a local nursery, garden supply center or construction material outlet to line the sump and backfill the trench, estimating about 8 to 10 cubic feet for the sump and about 3 to 4 cubic feet for every 8-foot length of trench. Also order enough sand to line the bottom of the trench to a depth of 2 inches, figuring about 2 cubic feet for every 8-foot length of trench. First fill the sump with 10 to 12 inches of drain rock. Then spread the sand in the trench *(far left)*, maintaining the slope using the carpenter's level and homemade tool *(step 3)* to adjust it if necessary. Buy flexible, perforated plastic drainpipe 3 or 4 inches in diameter and a bit longer than the trench at a local construction material outlet or garden supply center. If your soil has a high clay content, choose the type wrapped in a fiber sock *(near left, top)*. If the drainpipe is too long, use a utility knife to cut it to length, pressing the tip of the blade through the wall to begin and then slicing around the drainpipe back to the starting point *(near left, bottom)*.

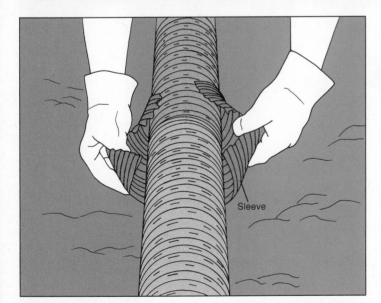

Sleeve

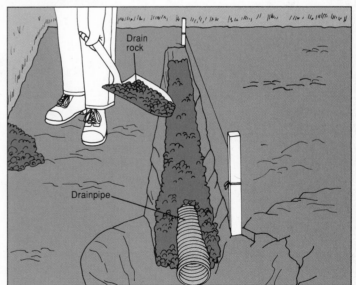

Drain rock

Drainpipe

5 **Connecting lengths of drainpipe.** If pieces of drainpipe need to be connected to reach the full length of the trench, use a short length of drainpipe as a sleeve. Slit the sleeve lengthwise with a utility knife. Pry open the sleeve and align two sections of drainpipe end to end inside, as close together as possible *(above)*. Release pressure on the sleeve; it will wrap the connected pieces to hold them together. Then rotate the sleeve so that the cut side faces downward.

6 **Backfilling the trench.** Lay out the drainpipe along the bottom of the trench. Use a shovel to backfill the trench and sump with drain rock to a depth of 4 inches over the drainpipe. Cover the sump with a sheet of polyethylene, roofing paper or other waterproof material to prevent heavy rains from overfilling the sump. Cover the drain rock with the soil removed until the trench is almost full. Soak the soil thoroughly to help it settle, then continue backfilling the trench to a level slightly higher than the surrounding soil.

KITCHEN GARDENS

A kitchen garden burgeoning with ripe, succulent vegetables, fruits and herbs is for many homeowners the ultimate expression of satisfying domesticity. The work of planning and caring for such a garden is more than compensated for by the luxury of fresh produce a stone's throw from the back door.

In the winter, design your garden based on a realistic assessment of the time and energy you are able to spend gardening. Expect to spend at least half an hour every couple of days during late spring and summer tending a typical vegetable garden like the one illustrated below. Before planting, consult a reputable gardening guide and talk with neighboring gardeners and nursery professionals. To learn how to cope with particular problems confronting local gardens, contact your Cooperative Extension Service.

When you are ready to plant, read the Soil Management chapter *(page 16)* and prepare the soil carefully. A loamy soil, rich in organic matter and free from rocks and debris, is ideal for vegetables. Most crops flourish in a soil within a pH range of 5.5 to 7.0. Buy only certified disease-free seeds. Examine nursery transplants carefully for evidence of insects and disease before buying them; select stocky, robust plants with rich green foliage and without flowers or fruit.

Once the seeds and plants are in the ground, your job of policing the garden begins, mostly in the form of defending it

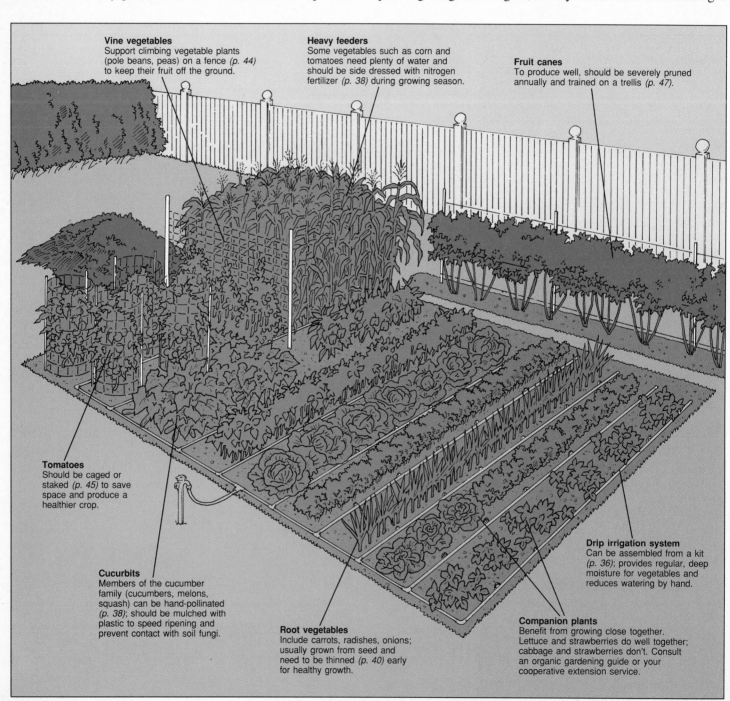

Vine vegetables
Support climbing vegetable plants (pole beans, peas) on a fence *(p. 44)* to keep their fruit off the ground.

Heavy feeders
Some vegetables such as corn and tomatoes need plenty of water and should be side dressed with nitrogen fertilizer *(p. 38)* during growing season.

Fruit canes
To produce well, should be severely pruned annually and trained on a trellis *(p. 47)*.

Tomatoes
Should be caged or staked *(p. 45)* to save space and produce a healthier crop.

Cucurbits
Members of the cucumber family (cucumbers, melons, squash) can be hand-pollinated *(p. 38)*; should be mulched with plastic to speed ripening and prevent contact with soil fungi.

Root vegetables
Include carrots, radishes, onions; usually grown from seed and need to be thinned *(p. 40)* early for healthy growth.

Drip irrigation system
Can be assembled from a kit *(p. 36)*; provides regular, deep moisture for vegetables and reduces watering by hand.

Companion plants
Benefit from growing close together. Lettuce and strawberries do well together; cabbage and strawberries don't. Consult an organic gardening guide or your cooperative extension service.

against the environment and arresting the spread of pests and diseases. Don't wait until harvest for bitter leafy or root vegetables to tell you that your garden wasn't irrigated enough or adequately protected against the burning sun. Learn what your plants need and act on it. For instance, most vegetables require about 1 to 2 inches of water a week. Splashing the leaves with the spray from a hose or sprinkler system can encourage the spread of disease; consider saving watering time by laying down a soaker hose, digging water furrows *(page 35)* or installing a drip irrigation system *(page 36)*, all of which will ensure that water reaches the critical root zone. Then, to regulate soil moisture and temperature while cutting down on weed growth and discouraging insects, maintain an adequate mulch *(page 38)*. Finally, protect plants, particularly younger ones, from harsh wind, sun, rain and frost: Choose from among an array of covering materials and erect a tunnel *(page 43)* over vulnerable garden rows.

Even a well-maintained garden can fall victim to an unhospitable environment—the Troubleshooting Guide below details likely symptoms and lists their possible causes. The Pests and Diseases chapter *(page 112)* will help you diagnose and treat specific ills. Read Tools & Techniques *(page 129)* for advice on pesticidal control procedures and good horticultural practices.

TROUBLESHOOTING GUIDE

continued ▶

SYMPTOM	POSSIBLE CAUSE	PROCEDURE
Garden doesn't thrive due to environmental stress: Seeds don't germinate, foliage dull, plants wilt and die, fruit poor	Soil too moist due to excessive watering or rainfall	Check soil moisture *(p. 18)* □○ and decrease watering
	Soil structure poor	Evaluate soil texture *(p. 20)* □○ and amend *(p. 21)* ◨○; reseed *(p. 39)* ◨◑
	Soil draining poorly	Evaluate drainage *(p. 27)* ◨○, raise soil bed *(p. 28)* ◨◑, change soil bed structure *(p. 28)* ◨◑ or install a drainage system *(p. 30)* ■●; reseed *(p. 39)* ◨◑
	Soil too dry	Check soil moisture *(p. 18)* □○ and increase watering; mulch *(p. 38)* □○; consider furrow watering *(p. 35)* □○ or installing a drip irrigation system *(p. 36)* ◨◑
Seeds don't germinate	Seeds old or require longer germination time	Check seed packets for issue date and germination time; if seeds older than 2 years, reseed *(p. 39)* ◨◑ with new seed
	Seeds sown too early; low soil temperature slowing germination	Ask cooperative extension service when to sow; reseed *(p. 39)* ◨◑ in warmer weather
	Heavy rains or excessive watering have washed seed away; birds are eating seeds	Reseed and add a row cover *(p. 39)* ◨◑
	Crusted soil inhibiting sprouting	If soil dry, keep moistened with mist spray from hose or sprinkler and wait for germination. If soil moist, cultivate *(p. 19)* ◨○ and reseed *(p. 39)* ◨◑ with soilless mix
	Seed-rotting fungi flourishing in wet soil	Check soil moisture *(p. 18)* □○ and decrease watering. If wet soil persists, evaluate soil drainage *(p. 27)* ◨○, raise soil bed *(p. 28)* ◨◑, change soil bed structure *(p. 28)* ◨◑ or install drainage system *(p. 30)* ■●; reseed *(p. 39)* ◨◑ with fungicide-treated seeds
	Seeds sown at wrong depth	Reseed *(p. 39)* ◨◑ at depth recommended on seed packets
Spindly growth; flowers sparse and may drop	Sun blocked by tree or shrub	Prune tree or shrub *(p. 94)* ◨○; in future, choose planting site with a minimum of six hours sun a day
	Seedlings overcrowded	Thin to proper spacing *(step 5, p. 40)* □○, and weed *(p. 35)* □○
	Vegetables overcrowded or unsupported	Erect a support fence *(p. 44)* ◨○ for climbing peas, beans and cucumbers. Cage *(p. 45)* ◨○ or stake *(p. 45)* ◨○ tomatoes. Weed *(p. 35)* □○ and mulch *(p. 38)* □○
	Temperature too high or too low	When below 55°F, install a protective tunnel *(p. 43)* ◨◑ over shorter vegetables (tomatoes, peppers, eggplant); when above 85-90°F, mulch *(p. 38)* □○
Pale green or yellow leaves	Soil pH unsuitable; nitrogen deficiency	See Pests and Diseases *(p. 119)*; test soil pH *(p. 23)* ◨○ and amend if necessary
	Vegetable planted too deeply	Replant at correct depth *(step 5, p. 42)* ◨○

DEGREE OF DIFFICULTY: □ **Easy** ◨ **Moderate** ■ **Complex**
ESTIMATED TIME: ○ **Less than 1 hour** ◑ **1 to 3 hours** ● **Over 3 hours**

TROUBLESHOOTING GUIDE (continued)

SYMPTOM	POSSIBLE CAUSE	PROCEDURE
Dry, curling leaves with brown margins	Salt accumulated in soil; pesticide spray on foliage; potassium deficiency	See Pests and Diseases *(p. 119)*
Leaves turn brown; plants wilt and die	Dehydration by sun, heat or wind	Mist foliage with hose or sprinkler, install a protective tunnel *(p. 43)* □◑ over surviving plants, do furrow watering *(p. 35)* □○ or install drip irrigation system *(p. 36)* ■●. If crop destroyed, reseed *(p. 39)* ◪○ or replant *(p. 41)* ◪○
	With blackened growing tips: Plant injured by frost	Install a protective tunnel *(p. 43)* ◪◑ for nights averaging less than 59°F. When unexpected frost is forecast, cover plants *(p. 13)* ◪○. If crop is destroyed, reseed *(p. 39)* □○ or replant *(p. 41)* ◪○
	Foliage damaged by contact with fertilizer; soil overfertilized	Leach soil *(p. 19)* □○; in the future, fertilize correctly *(p. 38)* □○
	Stems or roots damaged by transplanting	Replant correctly with new transplants *(p. 41)* ◪○
Leafy and root vegetables are going to seed (bolting)	Temperature too high	Mulch *(p. 38)* □○ and install a protective tunnel *(p. 43)* ◪◑
Few blossoms, poor vegetable and fruit production	Excessive application of nitrogen fertilizer	Test soil nitrogen *(p. 25)* ◪○ and leach soil *(p. 19)* □○; avoid overfertilizing in the future
	Cane fruits and strawberries overgrown or unpruned	Renovate overgrown strawberry beds *(p. 46)* ◪○; train and prune cane fruit correctly *(p. 47)* ◪○
Tomatoes and members of cucumber family have no fruit or produce poorly	Insect pollinators reduced due to excessive rainfall or pesticides	For tomatoes, gently shake plants daily to pollinate; for cucumber family, hand pollinate *(p. 38)* ◪○
Poor bean and cucumber crop	Fruit harvested too late	Harvest crop as soon as it ripens or further fruiting will be inhibited
Plants and vegetables are being eaten	Birds; rabbits	Install a protective tunnel *(p. 43)* ◪○ over shorter plants; install repellant devices *(p. 136)* □○ around taller plants
Seedlings collapse and die; stem bases rotted	Damping-off disease	See Pests and Diseases *(p. 113)*
Young plants collapse and die; stem bases chewed or severed	Cutworms	See Pests and Diseases *(p. 113)*
Discolored leaves, may be curled and distorted; growth stunted	Mosaic virus, aster yellows or curly top virus	See Pests and Diseases *(p. 113)*
Leaves turn yellow and wilt from bottom up; root vegetables rotten or eaten	Stem, crown or root rot, borer insects, wilt disease, maggots, wireworms, nematodes; if cabbage family, may be clubroot	See Pests and Diseases *(p. 114)*; for clubroot *(p. 123)*
Holes in leaves, buds, flowers and fruit, eaten by visible insects; silvery trails	Beetles, caterpillars or other visible insects	See Pests and Diseases *(p. 116)*
	Slugs and snails	See Pests and Diseases *(p. 113)*
Leaves, buds, flowers streaked and flecked; colonies of tiny insects on tender growth; plants look sooty	Aphids, whiteflies or leafhoppers	See Pests and Diseases *(p. 118)*
Brittle, yellow, dusty-looking leaves	Spider mites	See Pests and Diseases *(p. 118)*
Leaves and vegetables spotted and discolored	Bacterial or fungal diseases including downy mildew and powdery mildew; also sunscald or blossom end rot	See Pests and Diseases: for leaf symptoms *(p. 120)*; for vegetable symptoms *(p. 122)*
Rusty-looking blisters on underside of leaves	Rust	See Pests and Diseases *(p. 121)*
Pale, papery patches or winding trails on leaves	Leafminers	See Pests and Diseases *(p. 121)*

DEGREE OF DIFFICULTY: □ Easy ◪ Moderate ■ Complex
ESTIMATED TIME: ○ Less than 1 hour ◑ 1 to 3 hours ● Over 3 hours

WEEDING THE GARDEN

Dandelion weeder

Scuffle hoe

Weeding a vegetable patch. Consult the weed gallery *(page 76)* or a local library for books that will help you identify troublesome weeds. Regular weeding will reduce the possibility of weed seeds sprouting. Weed only when the soil is moist; if necessary, water the garden the night before. To remove shallow-rooted annual weeds, use a sharp-bladed scuffle hoe *(left)*. Move the hoe in a steady back-and-forth motion to cut through the top 1/2 inch of soil as you walk forward from one end of a row to the other. When weeds are in very close proximity to garden plants, pull them up by hand. To remove long-rooted perennial weeds, use a dandelion weeder to dig up the entire root system. Take hold of the base of the weed with one hand. With the other, drive the blade down into the soil beside the weed. Lever up the root as you pull the weed foliage up and out of the soil *(inset)*. Compost the weeds *(page 22)* and lay down an organic mulch *(page 38)*. In the future, before planting widely-spaced transplants, cover the soil bed with a plastic mulch *(page 41)*.

FURROW-WATERING VEGETABLES

Garden hoe

Dam

Furrow

Digging and watering the furrows. Furrow watering wastes less water than overhead sprinkling. It not only allows you to irrigate deeply, but it also reduces the risk from fungal and bacterial diseases that can be spread by water splashing from plant to plant. Use a garden hoe to dig furrows early in the growing season, before roots have spread. Pull one corner of the hoe blade through the soil, parallel to each row of plants, making a V-shaped furrow 4 to 6 inches deep and 3 to 4 inches from each row *(far left)*. Close each end of the furrow with a 6-inch pile of soil. Tamp down the furrow walls with the back of the hoe to keep the earth from falling in. Lay a hose in one end of a furrow and slowly fill it with water. When it is full, water the other furrows, in turn. Allow the water to soak into the soil. If a furrow is very long, water may not flow uniformly from one end to the other. In this case, break the furrow into shorter segments by making dams with pieces of board pushed upright into the soil across the furrow *(near left)*. Water each segment as described above. Tamp the sides of the furrow walls periodically with the back of the hoe to keep them from eroding.

INSTALLING A DRIP IRRIGATION SYSTEM

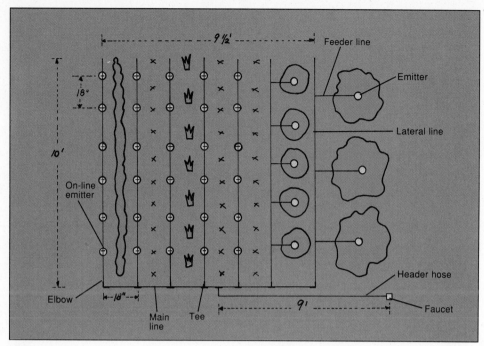

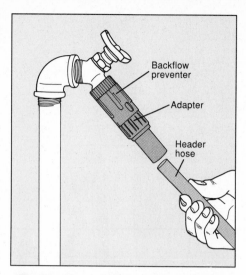

1 **Estimating your needs.** Install a drip system to provide constant, effortless irrigation, especially where the climate is arid and where water is expensive or in short supply. Drip-system kits are widely available; choose one that fits your garden's needs. Once set up, the drip system will include a header hose that carries water to a main-line hose, which in turn feeds lateral lines stretched along each row *(step 6)*. To estimate how much hose is necessary, sketch the layout and dimensions of your garden, then work out a plan for the system *(above)*. The hose length must equal the sum of the row lengths, garden width, and distance from garden to faucet, plus several extra feet. To determine the number of drip emitters required, evaluate the texture of your garden's soil *(page 20)* and calculate one emitter for every 12 inches of sandy soil, 18 inches of loamy soil, or 24 inches of clay soil. Count the number of connectors (tees and elbows) needed at joints.

2 **Hooking up to the water source.** To install the system, work from the faucet out to the end of the garden. Most systems provide several parts that control the flow of water through the hose network. The model shown here has a filter washer to prevent clogging of the system, a pressure regulator to reduce the standard residential water-supply pressure, a backflow prevention device to keep water from backing up into your drinking water, and an adapter to connect these parts to the hose. Follow the kit directions for assembly. Screw the assembly onto the faucet, then insert one end of the header hose into the adapter *(above)*.

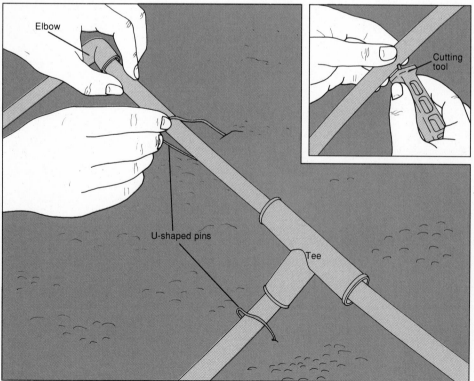

3 **Assembling the hose.** To organize the hose network for a typical vegetable garden, first make a header line: Roll out the hose from the faucet to the middle of one side of the garden that is perpendicular to the plant rows. Cut the hose with a utility knife. To make the main line, unroll more hose along the side of the garden and cut it to length. Cut up the remaining hose to make the lateral lines: Lay the hose from the main line along a plant row and cut it to the length of the row. Repeat for every row. Connect the header and laterals to the main with tee and elbow joints according to kit directions. Make U-shaped pins for holding down the hose by cutting a coat hanger into 8-inch pieces with wire cutters. Bend each piece and press it over the hose every 2 feet *(left)*. Most kits come with patented tools for making emitter holes in the lateral lines. The tool shown *(inset)* has a tiny circular cutting point that is twisted back and forth like a cookie cutter to cut a small hole in the hose wall. Space the holes according to your garden's soil type *(step 1)*; but if the plants are far apart, cut one emitter hole for the base of each plant.

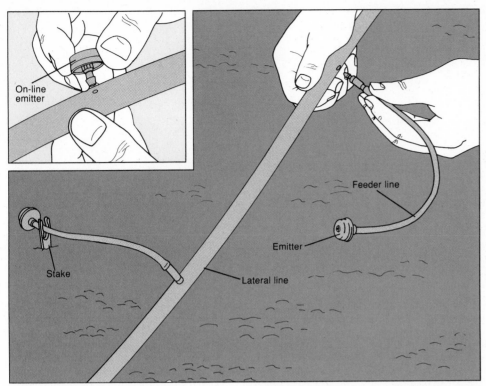

4 **Connecting the emitters.** Follow kit directions to determine what size emitters to install. The most commonly used have a capacity of 1 gallon per hour. If a lateral line lies within 1 foot of a plant row, insert on-line emitters directly into the holes you cut in step 2. Wiggle the barbed end into a hole until it snaps into place *(inset)*. If a lateral line is farther than a foot away from a plant row, attach feeder lines to the emitters. Assemble the 1/4-inch tubing, barbed connectors and feeder-line support stakes; these either come with the kit or can be bought separately. Cut a piece of tubing to reach from the lateral line to the plant row. Insert the connector into one end of the tubing and snap the emitter on the other. Then fit the connector end into the hole in the lateral line *(left)*. To support the emitter above ground and near the base of the plant, push a support stake into the ground and snap the end of the feeder line into the opening at the top.

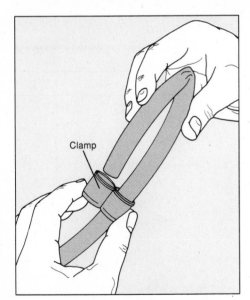

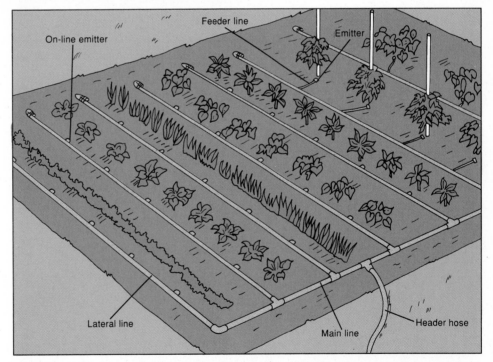

5 **Flushing and closing the system.** To keep the emitters from clogging later, turn on the water and flush the system of dirt or bits of plastic that may have entered during assembly. Turn off the water and finish the installation by clamping off the open ends of the lateral lines. Some kits provide figure-eight clamps, like the one shown here. Slide one side of the clamp back along the end of a lateral line. Bend the end back tightly to kink it, then slide the other side of the clamp back up over the kinked end *(above)*.

6 **Checking and maintaining the drip system.** The illustration above shows a typical drip system laid out in a vegetable garden. Turn on the water and inspect the system. Tighten or replace leaking tees, elbows and clamps. Plug unwanted holes or accidental punctures in the hosing with the plugs provided in the kit. Replace emitters that do not drip. Follow kit directions for watering times based on your system size, soil type and weather conditions. For example, in mid-summer heat, some kits recommend watering every other day, for three or four hours. Maintain the system properly: Periodically check and clean the filter, and check the emitters monthly to make sure they aren't clogged. Unclamp the lateral lines and flush the system yearly. In cold-winter areas, drain the lines and fittings in the fall.

FERTILIZING AND MULCHING THE GARDEN

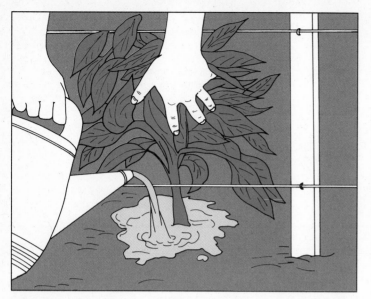

Straw mulch

1 Side-dressing with fertilizer. Vegetables with a long growing season, such as peppers, and heavy nitrogen feeders such as corn, often benefit from fertilizing to boost growth or remedy soil deficiencies. Consult the cooperative extension service for the timing, frequency and amount of fertilizer for a particular crop. In general, fertilize when seedlings are 3 to 4 inches tall, or when transplants have been in the ground for two to three weeks. Using a water-soluble 10-10-10 fertilizer, dissolve 1 tablespoon per gallon of water in a watering can and apply it directly around the base of each plant *(above)*.

2 Applying an organic mulch. Mulch to control weeds, conserve soil moisture or keep soil cool in hot weather. Mulch when plants are 4 to 6 inches tall, allowing soil to warm sufficiently in northern regions and before soil becomes too hot in southern regions. Weed before mulching *(page 35)*, and consult the mulching chart *(page 21)*. Lay a mulch of straw or hay 6 to 8 inches deep under the vegetables, leaving a bare space around each stem *(above)*. Do not mulch more deeply, since rotting mulch can be detrimental to plants. As the mulch compacts and decomposes, add more to maintain a constant depth.

HAND POLLINATING MEMBERS OF THE CUCUMBER FAMILY

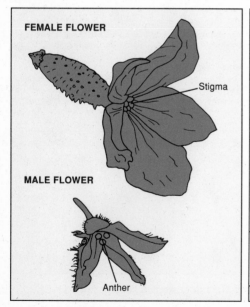

FEMALE FLOWER

Stigma

MALE FLOWER

Anther

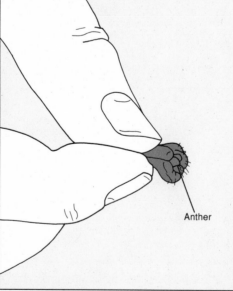

Anther

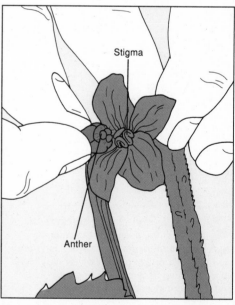

Stigma

Anther

Pollinating a female cucumber flower. When the population of insect pollinators is low, pollination may not occur, and fruit and vegetable flowers will drop. Members of the cucumber family (known as cucurbits), including cucumbers, squash, zucchini, and melon, can be hand pollinated successfully. On a cucumber, identify the female flowers *(above, left)* by the tiny, immature fruits at the base of their blossoms. Male flowers are smaller, less numerous and lack any fruit. The flowers of other family members can be similarly identified. Gently pinch off a

male flower and peel back its petals to expose the tiny cushion-like anther inside, at the base of its blossom *(above, center)*. Hold a female flower that is just opening in one hand and, with the other, press the exposed anther of the male lightly against the stigma at the base of the female blossom *(above, right)*. Apply the anther to the stigmas of other flowers until no pollen remains on the anther. Then find another male flower and continue until all female flowers have been pollinated.

RESEEDING VEGETABLES

1 **Preparing seed furrows.** When seeds fail to germinate, reseed your garden properly. Review the Soil Management chapter *(page 16)* and improve the soil if necessary; the best soil for a kitchen garden is rich and loamy with a pH of 5.5 to 7.0. Buy only certified disease-free seed from a reputable garden nursery. If you've had problems with damping-off or other seed-rot fungi, buy seeds treated with fungicide, distinguished by their pink coloring. Study the information on the seed packets carefully for directions on when, how deep and how far apart to sow the seeds. To mark the seed rows, set up parallel guidelines with small stakes and string. Run the strings north-south to ensure uniform sunlight for all seedlings. Space them according to the recommendations on the seed packets. Some tiny seeds require no furrow and can be sown directly onto the soil *(step 2)*. Make furrows for larger seeds with a garden hoe: For small seeds to be planted 1/2 to 1 inch deep, make a shallow furrow by laying the hoe flat beneath the string and pressing down on the handle gently with your foot *(far left)*. For larger seeds to be planted deeper than 1 inch, make a V-shaped furrow by pulling the corner of the hoe blade through the soil in line with the string guide *(near left)*.

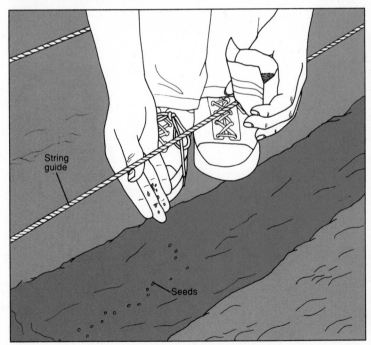

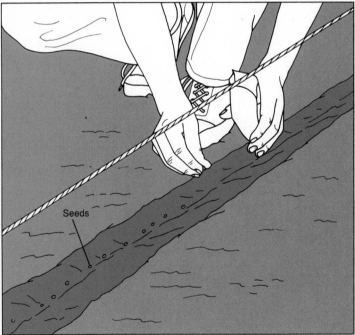

2 **Sowing seeds.** Sow seeds evenly. To aid germination and reduce the amount of thinning *(step 5)* needed, avoid sowing too deeply or thickly. If the seeds were treated with fungicide, wear gloves. Broadcast tiny, light-loving seeds, such as lettuce, directly on the soil surface beneath the string guide *(above, left)*. Sow small seeds, such as onion, by lightly tapping seeds out of the packet, three or four at a time, into a furrow, moving steadily from one end of the furrow to the other. Sow large seeds, such as peas and beans, by placing them one at a time in the furrow at a recommended distance apart, usually from 1 to 6 inches *(above, right)*. After sowing, store any leftover treated seed out of children's reach.

RESEEDING VEGETABLES (continued)

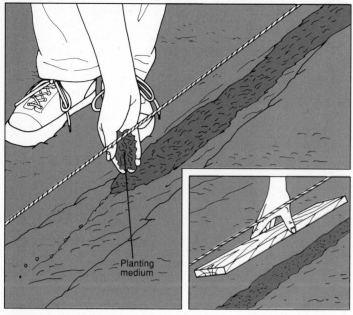

Planting medium

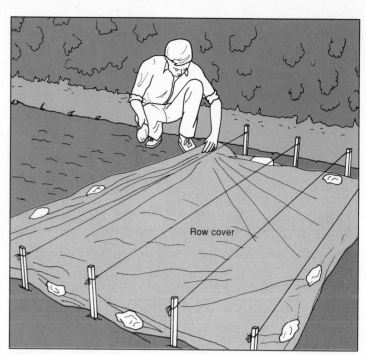

Row cover

3 Covering seed rows. In order to germinate, seeds need to be covered to protect them from light. If your soil is loamy and crumbly, use it to cover the seeds. Otherwise, use a soilless planting medium such as fine sand, peat moss, sifted compost or vermiculite mixed with soil. To cover seeds sown on the surface, sprinkle 1/2 inch of soil or rooting medium evenly over them. Then lay a flat board on top and gently press it down to bond the surface soil or medium to the soil beneath *(inset)*. Cover seeds in furrows by completely filling the furrow *(above)*, then gently tamping down the soil or medium with the back of a hoe blade.

4 Protecting the seedbed. Perforated polyester row covers facilitate seed germination by conserving soil warmth and moisture. As plants grow, the cover provides ample ventilation and light, as well as bird and insect protection. Buy a cover a few feet wider and longer than the seedbed. Lay it over the bed and anchor the edges with rocks *(above)*. As plants sprout, move in the edges, removing rocks if necessary, to let the cover float over the plant tops. Roll back the cover to thin *(step 5)* or weed *(page 35)* as required.

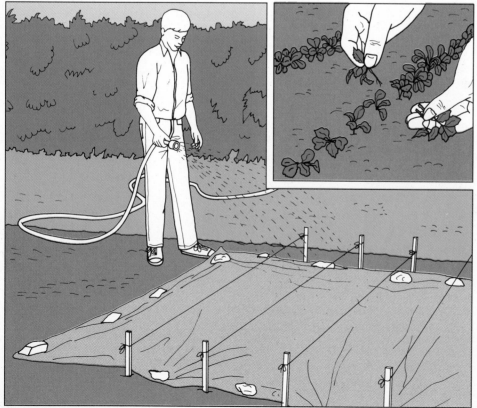

5 Caring for the seedbed. To prevent seeds from drying or soil from crusting, water a newly planted seedbed once a day in the early morning or, in hot, dry weather, twice a day. Avoid watering in full sun. Using a mist nozzle attachment on the hose, give the seedbed a fine spraying, never a strong stream of water that might drown seeds or wash them away. Water directly on the perforated row cover *(left)*. Keep the soil moist but never soggy. Check soil moisture daily *(page 18)* and adjust your watering accordingly. When seedlings have reached about 1 to 2 inches tall, and true leaves (those characteristic of the plant variety) begin to emerge, roll back the row cover and start to thin the plants. Check the seed packets or a planting guide for the recommended distance between the seedlings—crowding weakens them. Thin by pinching seedlings between thumb and index finger, pulling them gently out of the soil to avoid disturbing neighboring roots *(inset)*. Thin a bit every few days, always removing the least healthy-looking plants, until you achieve the recommended spacing. When plants requiring insect pollination start to flower, remove the cover completely and lay down an organic mulch *(page 38)*.

REPLANTING WITH NURSERY TRANSPLANTS

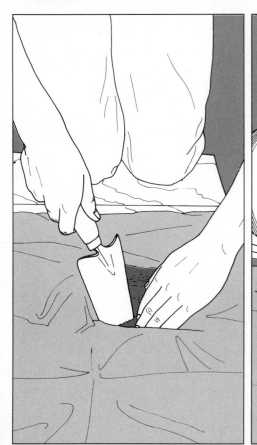

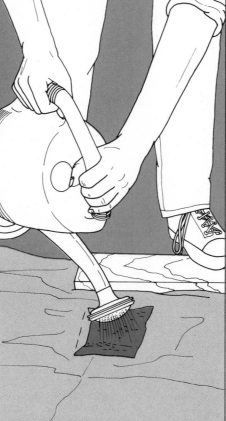

Plastic mulch

1 **Laying a plastic mulch.** Review the Soil Management chapter *(page 16)* and improve the soil if necessary; the best soil for a kitchen garden is rich and loamy with a pH of 5.5 to 7.0. Consider installing a drip irrigation system *(page 36)*. To prepare planting holes for all transplants, go to step 2. Most require mulching *(page 38)* after planting. However, for tomatoes, peppers or other widely spaced plants, first lay an opaque plastic mulch over the planting bed to conserve soil moisture, prevent weeds and keep the fruit of low-lying plants from rotting on the soil. In northern short-summer areas, use black plastic to help heat the soil and improve the growth of warm-season crops like tomatoes. In hot southern areas, use white plastic to reflect sun, reducing soil heat and water loss. Lay the mulch in wide strips. Anchor one end of a strip with rocks, stretch it tightly over the ground, then anchor the other end *(left)*. Continue placing strips until the entire bed is covered. Anchor or bury the sides to keep the wind from blowing it away. To plant through the layer of plastic mulch, cut holes in it. Calculate the number, size and spacing of planting holes that you need. Then use a utility knife to slit an X in the plastic at each planting location. Tuck the cut edges under the surrounding plastic to expose the soil beneath the mulch *(inset)*.

2 **Preparing planting holes.** One or two days before planting flats of vegetables, separate the young plants and their root balls by "blocking" them with a sharp knife: Cut through the packed soil around each plant deeply enough to sever any entwined roots. Plant on a calm, overcast day or in the late afternoon or early evening, to avoid transplant shock caused by heat and sun. A few hours before transplanting, water the plants well. Buy liquid starter fertilizer that is high in phosphorus (5-52-10 is ideal) and dilute it with water in a watering can as directed on the product label. You will need about one cup of solution for every planting hole. To dig planting holes, use a hand trowel. If you laid a plastic mulch, scoop aside the soil through the holes and pack it underneath the edges of the plastic *(far left)*. In general, make holes as deep as the transplant containers, except for holes for tomatoes, peppers, eggplant and members of the cabbage family, which should be slightly deeper. Dig the holes wide enough to fit your hand cupped around the root ball. Fill each hole with one cup of the starter fertilizer solution *(near left)*, and let the solution soak into the soil.

REPLANTING WITH NURSERY TRANSPLANTS (continued)

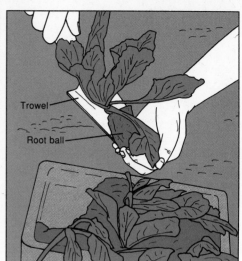

3 **Preparing transplants.** Before setting out a peat-potted plant, remove the bottom of the pot and tear off the upper edge at the soil line *(above, left)*. To remove a plant from a plastic pot, slide one hand over the top so that the stem is between your fingers. Turn the pot over and tap the bottom with the other hand until the root ball slides out *(above, center)*. To set out a blocked plant from a flat, cut down around it gently with the tip of a hand trowel and lift it, cradling the root ball against the trowel with the other hand *(above, right)*.

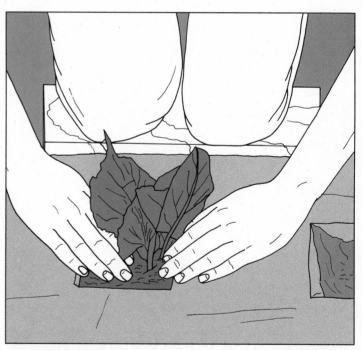

4 **Setting out transplants.** Simply lower a peat-potted plant into its planting hole. Be careful when putting a transplant with an exposed root ball into the ground; cup the plant in your hands *(above)* and slip it gently into its hole. With one hand, keep it upright. With the other, fill the hole with soil around the root ball, no higher on the stem than the original soil level. When filling in the hole around a peat-potted plant, make sure all peat material is covered with dirt; exposed peat acts as a wick, drawing moisture up out of the soil.

5 **Packing down transplants.** Smooth the soil around the transplant, then press down gently to remove air pockets that may slow root growth *(above)*. Don't pack too tightly or you will compress the root ball and inhibit air and water intake. When all transplants are in the ground, water them thoroughly. Check soil moisture *(page 18)* periodically over the next few weeks and, when needed, water to a depth of 6 inches; let the soil dry slightly between waterings. Install a protective tunnel *(page 43)* over cool-season vegetables such as lettuce and cabbage that are planted in a hot climate; over warm-season vegetables such as tomatoes and peppers that are planted while nights are still cool or there is still a risk of frost; or over any plants if the garden is in a windy location. Protect transplants against cutworms by installing protective collars *(page 136)*.

INSTALLING A PROTECTIVE TUNNEL

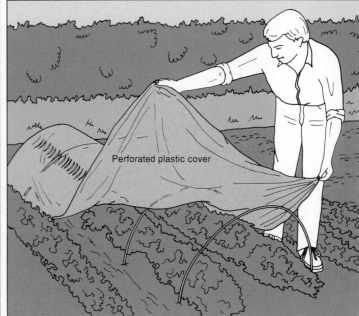

1 **Installing the hoops and cover.** A protective tunnel shields young plants and any short plants from frost, sun, wind and birds, and helps reduce insect problems. Buy a prepackaged kit, or make your own tunnel with wire and a protective covering of the appropriate material to meet your needs: Select slitted clear plastic, shown here, to protect against cold and frost; woven fabric against wind and sun; or plastic netting against birds. All three are set up the same way. To cover two rows at a time, buy enough 8- or 9-gauge

wire, precut into 8-foot lengths, to make hoops every 4 feet along the plant rows. Buy a cover at least 6 feet wide for two rows. The cover should equal the length of the rows, plus 12 feet. The extra is draped over the ground on each end of the tunnel *(step 3)*. To make a support hoop, bend the wire into an arch and push its ends into the soil 1 1/2 feet deep on opposite sides of the plant rows *(above, left)*. Install a hoop every 4 feet. Lay the plastic at one end and unroll it, pulling it across the tops of the hoops to the other end *(above, right)*.

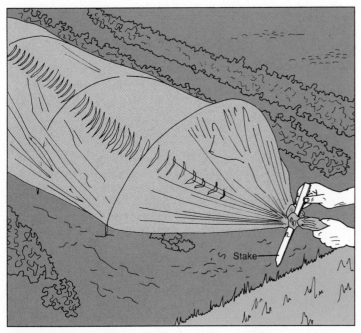

2 **Staking the ends.** Position the cover so that it drapes onto the ground evenly at both ends of the tunnel. At one end, gather the cover into a tight bunch and tie a loose knot. Insert a 12-inch stake through the center of the knot and tighten the knot around the stake *(above)*. Drive the stake into the ground with a mallet. Repeat at the other end, pulling the knotted end of the cover down firmly to tighten it over the hoops before driving in the stake.

3 **Burying the edges.** To keep the cover in place and provide maximum plant protection, bury its edges. Working around the perimeter of the tunnel, push the edge of the cover into the soil, then firmly press it down with your hands or feet to keep it buried. On hot, sunny days, pull out the stakes at the ends and roll up the plastic to make an open-ended tunnel. Remove the tunnel if the plants grow too tall, or when insect-pollinated plants start to flower.

SUPPORTING CLIMBING AND CRAWLING PLANTS ON A FENCE

Stake

Twist tie

1 Staking a net fence. Support climbing peas, pole beans and cucumbers on a fence to save space, to grow better-formed and faster-ripening fruit, and to reduce soil-related insect and disease problems. Erect the fence when the vegetables are planted, or before the vines grow longer than 18 inches and become thoroughly entwined. Buy two 6- to 8-foot angle-iron stakes of the type used for fencing, pierced with support holes. Also buy a piece of heavy plastic netting with a 4-inch-square mesh, 1 foot wider than the length of the vegetable row. Position a stake at each end of the row; wedge them into the soil by hand and then use a heavy mallet to drive them about 2 feet deep *(left)*. Attach the net to the stake at one end of the row, looping a twist tie through the top hole in the stake and around the edge of the net *(inset)*. Continue down the stake, fastening the net with a twist tie at each hole.

2 Tightening and trimming the net. When the net is securely tied to the first stake, unroll it over to the second stake. Pull the net taut *(left)* and tie it to the second stake as you did to the first. Use shears to trim off any extra netting on the side, and trim the bottom a few inches above the ground. Train young plants as they grow by pushing their tendrils and growing tips onto the net. To train older plants on the fence, gently unwind and separate the vines from one another on the ground; don't pull them apart. Lift each vine separately and loosely weave it up through the net *(inset)*, tightly enough to keep it from falling, but not so tightly that you snap the stem.

CAGING TOMATOES

Stake

Concrete reinforcing wire

Tying wire caging to stakes. Cage tomatoes to save space, reduce cracking and sunscald, and avoid soil-related insect and disease problems. Install ready-made cages for newly planted tomatoes; if the vines were left to sprawl over the ground, construct your own cages. All tomato varieties can be caged as long as they can be easily gathered into a cage 2 feet in diameter. To cage one tomato plant, buy three 4-foot stakes and a sheet of 5-foot-wide concrete reinforcing wire 7 feet long, from a home renovation center or fencing supplier. Wear gardening gloves to protect your hands. With a heavy mallet, drive the stakes 18 inches into the ground and 2 feet apart, forming a triangle around the plant. Tie one end of the wire sheet to one of the stakes with strong cord. Then bend the wire around the second and third stakes, tying it securely to each in turn. Be careful not to pin down any leaves or stems of the tomato plant with the bottom edge of the wire sheet. Bend the last section around until it touches the first stake *(far left)*. Secure it by wrapping the protruding horizontal wires of one edge around the vertical wire edge of the other *(near left)*. The tomato plant will grow up the inside of the cage on its own.

STAKING AND TRAINING TOMATOES

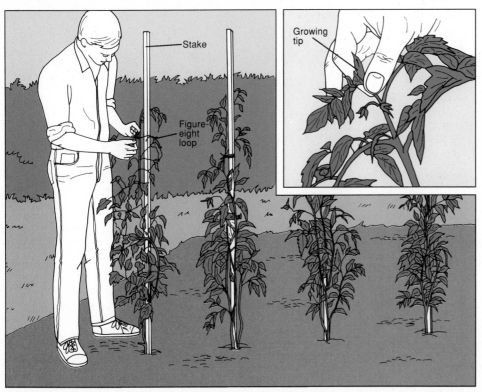

Stake

Figure-eight loop

Growing tip

Supporting and pruning tomatoes. Caging *(above)* provides good support for both types of tomato plant: determinate and indeterminate. However, an indeterminate variety may simply be staked instead. To distinguish an indeterminate tomato plant from the determinate type, notice that the terminal bud (at the tip of a stem) sets leaves on the former, and flowers on the latter. Stake young tomatoes when transplanting, or when the plants are shorter than 3 feet and have no more than two main stems. Push a 6-foot-long metal stake into the soil as far as possible, then drive it to a depth of 1 foot with a mallet. Tie the tomato stem to the stake at 1-foot intervals, looping twist ties in a figure eight *(left)*. To control sprawling growth, prune staked tomatoes by pinching off young shoots, or suckers, that emerge where a leaf stem joins the main stem. Train staked tomatoes to produce just two stems for increased yield and sunscald protection: Allow one sucker near the stem base to develop into a second stem that you can tie to the stake; pinch off all other suckers. In cold-winter areas, pinch off the growing tips of the main stems before the first frost to allow all fruit to ripen *(inset)*. Check with the cooperative extension service for the correct timing in your area.

SUPPORTING BUSHY PLANTS

1 **Driving in support stakes.** Support bush snap beans, bush peas and pepper plants with a simple trellis to keep their branches from sagging in wind or rain or collapsing under the weight of heavy fruit. Drive a row of 3-foot-long, 1-by-2-inch untreated wood stakes along each side of a row of plants *(above)*. Using a mallet, drive the stakes 1 foot into the ground every 4 to 5 feet, 6 to 8 inches from the plant stems.

2 **Attaching trellis cords.** Tie a length of strong garden cord tightly to a stake at one end of the plant row, 8 inches above ground. Then run it under the overhanging branches along one side of the plant row, looping each stake 8 inches up as you go. Continue around the end of the row and back up the other side *(above)*. Tie the end of the cord to the last stake. As the plants grow, tie parallel lengths of cord to the stakes at heights of 16 and 24 inches.

RENOVATING STRAWBERRY PLANTS

1 **Thinning the bed.** Improve strawberry crops by renovating overgrown, one- to two-year-old plants right after final harvest. (Dig up and replace poorly-producing older beds). To renovate, remove three quarters of the plants, leaving only the healthiest to produce daughter plants for next year's crop: Dig up both large, old plants with woody crowns and small, young plants, using a hand trowel *(above)*. Leave only vigorous, medium-size plants in the bed, approximately 12 to 18 inches apart. Then cut off the tops of the plants 3 inches above the crown with pruning shears.

2 **Pruning strawberries.** When cut-back plants begin producing new leaves and runners during the summer, use pruning shears to cut off all but two to four new runners from each plant *(above)*. Prune off the growing tips of these runners just beyond the first daughter plant on each. When the new daughter plants root, four to six weeks later, sever the runners connecting them to their mothers and any other runners they produce. The renovated fruit-bearing plants will produce next year's crop. If the crop is good, try renovating again. Otherwise, dig up the bed and replace it the following year.

PRUNING AND TRAINING FRUIT CANES

1 Removing old canes in the fall. Increase the quality and production of cane fruit such as raspberries and blackberries by pruning the bushes properly. Identify the two types of canes growing on your bushes: Floricanes are the older canes that have borne fruit. They have lateral branches down most of their length. Primocanes are the newer canes that have not yet produced fruit. They have branches only near their tips. Begin pruning floricanes in early fall, after harvest, cutting them all back to ground level with pruning shears *(above)*, and compost them *(page 22)*.

2 Selecting new canes in the fall. Identify the healthiest of the primocanes now remaining on your bushes—those at least 1/2 inch in diameter. Select four to six of these per bush and cut back all the other canes to ground level with pruning shears. Compost the cut canes *(page 22)*. Tie the remaining canes to a trellis with twist ties or twine tied into figure-eight loops *(above)*. Tie red or yellow raspberry canes or trailing blackberry canes to parallel wires three and five feet high. Tie purple or black raspberry canes or non-trailing (erect) blackberry canes to a single wire 2 1/2 feet high.

3 Trimming new canes in the fall. The tied-up primocanes will become next season's floricanes. To encourage the growth of lateral branches that will eventually bear fruit, use pruning shears *(above)* to cut back the tops of these canes in the fall after they've been tied up, or early the following spring just as new growth appears. Trim back red or yellow raspberries or trailing blackberries to a height of 5 to 5 1/2 feet, and purple or black raspberries or erect blackberries to a height of 2 1/2 to 3 feet.

4 Selecting new shoots in spring. In spring, floricanes will bloom and set fruit, and new primocane shoots will emerge from the crown. On each bush, cut off all but four to six of these new shoots at ground level with pruning shears *(above)*. Let these remaining shoots continue growing. During the summer, when the primocanes of purple or black raspberries or erect blackberries reach 2 1/2 feet, snip off their growing tips. In early fall, when tied-up floricanes have finished fruiting, begin the pruning process again.

FLOWERS

Each flower garden is a unique blend of color and fragrance that faithfully reflects the imagination and care of its gardener. Most plants flower in order to procreate; those hybrid plants we refer to as "flowers" are breeds specially developed for their profuse and showy blossoms.

Before starting a flower garden, study reputable gardening manuals and talk with the professionals at your local Cooperative Extension Service, garden nursery and botanical garden, if your city has one. Choose species that thrive best in the space and light conditions of your garden. Even then, some recommended flowers may not thrive; you may need to transplant them *(page 55)* to find the right combination of shade, soil type and shelter from the elements. When choosing flowers, also consider the time you have to devote to gardening. A

casual arrangement of hardy standbys—daisies, marigolds, petunias—can be nearly maintenance free, while a hybrid rose bush will require diligent care to encourage blossoming and prevent disease.

Disease and insect infestation can be minimized by bringing the soil bed up to par before planting. Read the Soil Management chapter *(page 16)*; it contains instructions for improving soil texture and fertility as well as adjusting its pH. In general, flowers, like most garden plants, prefer a well-drained soil that is loamy, rich in organic material and has a pH of 5.5 to 7.0.

Most flowers are either annual or perennial. Annuals grow from seed, flower and die in one season. If their spent blossoms are dead-headed *(page 53)*, they will produce blossoms again and again throughout the growing season. In contrast,

Iris
Grow from perennial rhizomes or bulbs. Rhizomes need to be divided *(page 58)* when irises become overgrown or begin to die out in the center.

Bushy flower clumps
Position them behind a low-lying annual border and corral them *(page 62)* if they tend to sprawl.

Perennials
Some phlox and primroses, and irises and daylilies, return year after year. They generally blossom in the summer or fall and need to be divided *(page 56)* every three to four years.

Tall, single-stemmed flowers
Form a colorful backdrop against a wall or fence. Their tall stems make them flimsy and may require staking *(page 62)*, particularly if planted in a windy location.

Rose bush
A woody shrub, the hybrid rose requires special care because it is more susceptible to pests and diseases than other flowers.

Annuals
Grow and bloom profusely, but only for one season. They include pansies, petunias, some marigolds and asters. Their seeds may survive the winter, and grow back in spring.

Flower border
Best composed of continuously blooming annuals that grow close to the ground, such as marigolds, violets, sweet alyssum and wax begonia.

Mulch
Summer mulches are chosen for their ability to prevent evaporation of soil moisture and to discourage the spread of weeds. A porous winter mulch will help to insulate roots from freezing and thawing

Lawn edging
A plastic strip that keeps grass or ground cover from invading your garden. Unnoticeable when installed properly *(page 63)*.

perennials may bloom only once or twice in a season, but their root systems survive the dormancy period to flourish each year. In the case of perennial bulb-rooted plants, the roots store food during the dormant season; some types are best dug up and carefully stored during winter *(page 61)*. Keep in mind that flowers grown away from their native climate may change their life cycle; some southern perennials, for example, are considered annuals when grown in the north.

Keep a gardening journal to record your observations throughout the season. Remembering when certain flowers blossom will help you develop a balanced garden of annuals and perennials that will bloom continously from spring to autumn. Or noting that a certain flower grows tall or bushy by midsummer will alert you to the need for staking or corralling

it *(page 62)*. Regular weeding, watering *(page 51)* and mulching *(page 52)* are essential all season, but not all gardening chores are done while the flowers are in bloom; early spring and late autumn maintenance is described in Tools & Techniques *(page 134)*.

Study the Troubleshooting Guide below so you can spot and treat symptoms of ill health before they get too advanced. Pests and Diseases *(page 112)* offers specific remedies for disease- and insect-related symptoms. The Guide will also help you to recognize flowering patterns that can be modified to produce a more beautiful garden. For example, while the production of numerous small blossoms is not a symptom of ill health, you may wish to encourage fewer, showier blossoms by disbudding *(page 52)*.

TROUBLESHOOTING GUIDE
continued ▶

SYMPTOM	POSSIBLE CAUSE	PROCEDURE
Flowers wilted but foliage healthy and soil moist	Intense heat or wind	Plant will recover when temperature drops or wind dies down
Flowers wilted, leaves dry, brown and shriveled; buds fail to develop, or drop off	Lack of water	Water thoroughly (p. 51) □○ and mulch (p. 52) □○
	Soil too sandy	Evaluate soil texture and amend soil (p. 20) ◒○
Flower bed fails to thrive: Spindly stems, few blossoms, discolored leaves	Flowers need more sun	If tree or shrub blocks sun, prune it (p. 94) ◒◕; otherwise, transplant flowers to sunnier location (p. 55) ◒○
	Overwatering	Check soil moisture (p. 18) □○ and water correctly (p. 51) □○
	If water puddles on the ground, soil clay content may be too high	Evaluate soil texture and amend soil (p. 20) ◒○; while perennials are dormant at start of next growing season, dig up flowers (p. 55) □○ and change soil bed structure (p. 28) ◒◕
	Flower bed not draining properly	Evaluate soil drainage (p. 27) □○, raise soil bed (p. 28) ◒○ or install drainage system (p. 30) ■●
	Weeds competing for soil nutrients, sun and water	Weed (p. 51) □○ and mulch (p. 52) □○ flower bed
	Soil nutrient deficiency	See Pests and Diseases (p. 119). Test soil pH (p. 23) ◒○ and fertility (p. 25) ◒○ and adjust if necessary
Discolored, burned foliage; stunted growth	Fertilizer, road salt, pesticides	See Pests and Diseases (p. 119)
	Sunburn	Transplant flower to less sunny location (p. 55) ◒○
Seeds don't germinate	Dehydration	Check soil moisture (p. 18) □○ and water gently at low pressure
	Seeds old, diseased or inferior; seeds planted too soon or at wrong depth	Consult planting guide or Extension Agent for correct planting time in your area and reseed with certified disease-free seeds. Check seed packets for issue dates and planting depth.
Seedlings dying	Dehydration	Test soil moisture (p. 18) □○ and water thoroughly. Install a woven protective tunnel (p. 43) ◒○
Seedlings severed at soil level	Damping off; cutworms, slugs or snails	See Pests and Diseases (p. 113)
	Birds or animals eating seedlings	Install protective tunnel with netting (p. 43) ◒○
Few blossoms on an otherwise healthy plant	If foliage abundant, too much nitrogen fertilizer in soil	Leach soil (p. 19) ◒○
Blossoms numerous but small	Flowering energy of plant directed to too many buds	Disbud to promote fewer, larger blossoms (p. 52) □○

DEGREE OF DIFFICULTY: □ Easy ◒ Moderate ■ Complex
ESTIMATED TIME: ○ Less than 1 hour ◕ 1 to 3 hours ● Over 3 hours

TROUBLESHOOTING GUIDE (continued)

SYMPTOM	POSSIBLE CAUSE	PROCEDURE
Blossoms faded, new blossom production slow	Flower going to seed	Dead-head faded blossoms (p. 53) □○
Flower stems spindly, blossom production poor	Plant energy concentrated on vertical stem growth	Pinch flower stems in spring (p. 54) □○
Flower stems leaning or sprawling on ground	Stems too tall or weak to support flowers	Stake tall-stemmed flowers (p. 62) ▱○; corral tall, bushy flowers (p. 62) ▱○
Perennial stems straggly, blossoms small	Plant overcrowded	Thin stems in spring (p. 53) □○
Perennial clump dying out	Perennial is aging	Rejuvenate by division (perennial, p. 56; rhizomatous iris, p. 58) ▱○
Perennial clump taking over	Roots allowed to spread unchecked	Reduce by division (perennial, p. 56; rhizomatous iris, p. 58) ▱○
Annual flower spindly and weak in midseason	Stems not pinched back	Cut back foliage 50 percent (p. 54) □○ and add a complete fertilizer (p. 26) ▱○; in the future, pinch stems in spring (p. 54) □○
Rose canes growing from base of rose bush	Original root stock sending out suckers	Remove suckers (p. 59) □○
Rose shoots blackened, leaves discolored	Winterkill—damage caused by frost or cold	Prune damaged canes (p. 59) ▱○ in the spring; in the future, protect rose bush before winter (p. 60) ▱○
Flower type on rose bush has changed	Winterkill has destroyed hybrid rose; original root stock has taken over	Replace rose bush; in the future, protect rose bush before winter (p. 60) ▱○
Black or brown growths appear on rose canes	Fungal disease producing cankers	See Pests and Diseases (p. 128)
In spring, bulbs lie on top of soil or protrude from it	Bulbs planted too shallow in previous fall	Plant new bulbs at proper depth and time (p. 60) ▱○; mulch bulbs before winter (p. 61) □○
Bulbs don't blossom, but foliage healthy	Bulbs undersized	Plant larger bulbs (p. 60) ▱○; or wait 1 to 2 years for flowers to bloom when bulbs have grown larger
Bulbs produce smaller and fewer blossoms each year	Bulbs aging	Plant new bulbs (p. 60) ▱○
Bulbs do not sprout at all	Bulbs eaten by animal pests	Plant new bulbs (p. 60) ▱○ and protect planting site with chicken wire (p. 61) □○
	Leaves cut back before bulbs ripened in previous season	Plant new bulbs (p. 60) ▱○; allow foliage to turn yellow and wither before cutting back
	Half-hardy or tender bulbs left in ground over cold winter; hardy bulbs not mulched	Plant new bulbs (p. 60) ▱○; dig up and store half-hardy and tender bulbs over winter; mulch hardy bulbs (p. 61) ▱○
	Bulbs rotted due to poor drainage or compacted soil	Test soil drainage (p. 27) □○, change soil structure (p. 28) ▱◖ or install drainage system (p. 30) ■●; plant new bulbs (p. 60) ▱○
Grass intrudes into flower bed	Lawn overgrown	Install edging around edge of flower bed (p. 63) ▱○
Blossoms small and sparse, leaves mottled yellow	Mosaic virus, aster yellows or curly-top virus	See Pests and Diseases (p. 113)
Leaves yellow, wilt from bottom up; roots may be rotten or eaten	Stem, crown, root or bulb rot, wilt disease, nematodes; if roses, may be borer insects	See Pests and Diseases (p. 114)
Holes in blossoms, buds, leaves; plant eaten by visible insects	Beetles, caterpillars or other visible insects	See Pests and Diseases (p. 116)
Blossoms, buds, leaves distorted, leaves yellowing	Aphids, whiteflies, thrips, leafhoppers or spider mites	See Pests and Diseases (p. 118)
Leaves and stems spotted and discolored	Bacterial or fungal leafspot disease, rust or powdery mildew	See Pests and Diseases (p. 121)
Pale, papery patches or winding trails on leaves	Leafminers	See Pests and Diseases (p. 121)
White foam where leaves join stems	Spittlebugs	See Pests and Diseases (p. 126)

DEGREE OF DIFFICULTY: □ Easy ▱ Moderate ■ Complex
ESTIMATED TIME: ○ Less than 1 hour ◖ 1 to 3 hours ● Over 3 hours

WEEDING A FLOWER BED

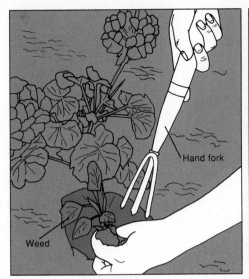

Weeding close to the roots. Weed a flower bed often to keep weeds from becoming established. The soil should be slightly moist; if necessary, water the bed the night before. Use a hand fork to loosen the soil around the weeds. Then insert the fork into the soil alongside a weed and rock it back and forth, gently tugging on the weed *(above, left)* with the other hand. Disturb the flower's roots as little as possible. If you encounter a weed that is difficult to pull out, it is probably a plant with spreading roots, such as crabgrass. In this case, use a weeding hoe *(above, center)* to chop off the weed at ground level. Repeat whenever the weed grows back; later, when annuals have died and perennials are dormant, use the hand fork to dig out the entire root system. If the weed roots are thoroughly entwined around the root system of a perennial, dig up the flower *(page 55)* and carefully disentangle the roots by hand *(above, right)*. Replant the flower *(page 55)*. If the flower bed was not mulched, consult the mulching chart *(page 21)* and apply the appropriate mulch *(page 52)*. If weed infestation gets out of hand, consider spot application of a herbicide *(page 77)*.

WATERING A FLOWER BED

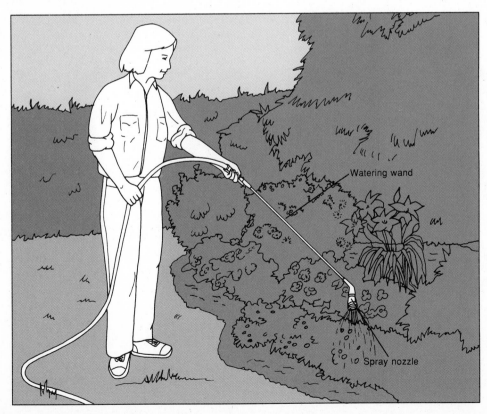

Watering a flower bed. To keep water from splashing on the underside of leaves and spreading soil-borne fungus diseases, use a hose and spray nozzle. Attach a watering wand to the hose when you need to reach deeply into an established bed *(left)*. Aim the nozzle around the base of the flowers, about 6 inches from the ground. Water deeply and thoroughly each time, allowing the soil to dry out between applications. Check soil moisture daily *(page 18)* and water whenever the soil feels dry and crumbly, but do not allow it to become bone dry. Water annuals to a depth of about 6 to 8 inches and perennials and roses to about 12 inches. Most flowers, when mulched properly *(page 52)*, do not require frequent watering except during periods of drought. Phlox is particularly sensitive to water loss and will signal the entire flower bed's need for water by wilting first.

Before planting in the spring, consider installing a drip irrigation system *(page 36)*. A sprinkler *(page 90)* will help save watering time in a large flower garden, and will prevent your having to walk on a seed bed. When using a sprinkler, water in the early morning to allow foliage to dry out before nightfall.

MULCHING A FLOWER BED

Grass clippings

Applying a mulch. Keep the flower bed mulched to discourage weeds, retain moisture and reduce fluctuations in soil temperature. Lay a summer mulch once the flower bed is well established. For a choice of mulches, consult the mulching chart *(page 21)*. If your lawn is well-maintained with a minimum of weeds, collect grass clippings after you mow, let them dry out and use them as a mulch. If herbicide was recently applied to your lawn, wait at least two weeks before using grass clippings as mulch. Lay the clippings 2 to 4 inches deep under the flowers *(left)* but only 1/4 inch thick around the base of the plant; if mulch is allowed to bury the stem, rot or fungus disease may set in.

GROOMING ANNUALS AND PERENNIALS

Central bud

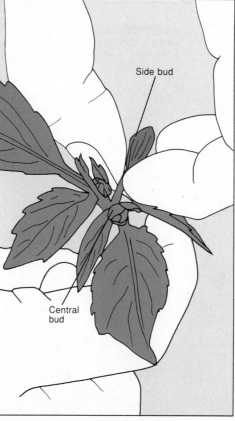

Side bud

Central bud

Pinching buds for bigger blossoms. To promote fewer, larger blossoms, disbud in the spring: Pinch off the smaller side flower buds between your thumb and forefinger, leaving the central bud to receive all the flowering energy that would otherwise have been diverted. Roses *(far left)*, peonies *(near left)* and chrysanthemums are three types of flowers that lend themselves well to this kind of grooming. The stems may not be strong enough to support the larger, heavier flowers that result from disbudding, and may require staking *(page 62)*.

GROOMING ANNUALS AND PERENNIALS (continued)

Pruning shears

Thinning stems for thicker growth. To encourage a perennial with a clump of stems, such as American phlox or shasta daisy, to grow bushier and produce bigger blossoms, thin the clump in the spring. When the shoots are about 5 inches tall, use pruning shears to cut off the weakest, least healthy-looking shoots at ground level *(left)*; leave at least four to six stronger-looking shoots to flourish. In time, new leaves will grow to fill the spaces in the clump created by thinning.

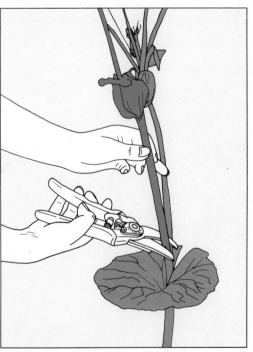

Dead-heading to prolong blooming. To prevent flowers from going to seed after they bloom, dead-head, or remove, their blossoms when they fade. Remove the spent flowers of a plant with tender green stems by pinching off the stem between thumb and forefinger just above the nearest set of leaves *(above, left)*. Use pruning shears to dead-head thicker-stemmed flowers at the same place *(above, center)*. In some cases this may mean cutting at the base of the plant *(above, right)*. Dead-heading annuals, and some perennials such as hosta, ligularia, marsh marigold and oriental poppy, will encourage them to reblossom the same season. Even flowers that will not produce another crop of blossoms, such as peonies and bearded irises, will grow stronger if their faded blossoms are removed.

GROOMING ANNUALS AND PERENNIALS (continued)

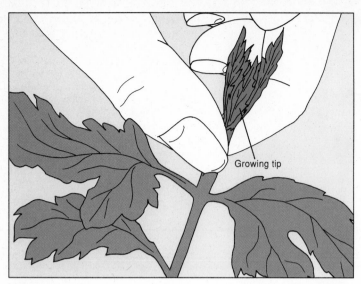

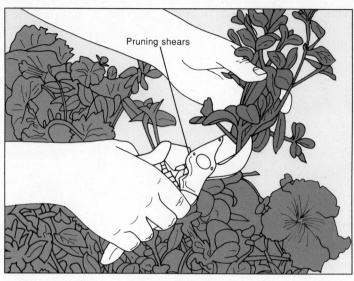

Pinching stems for more blossoms. If a particular annual or fall-blooming perennial is normally single-stemmed with few flowers, pinch off the growing stem tips in the spring to encourage branching. The bushier plant that results will produce more flowers. When an annual has produced its third or fourth set of leaves, pinch off its growing tip between thumb and forefinger just above the top set of leaves. On a perennial, pinch off the tips of shoots when they reach 6 inches long or when the plant reaches one quarter of its mature height *(above)*. Continue to pinch new shoots on a perennial until midsummer, leaving it enough time to develop flower buds for its fall blooming.

Cutting back to strengthen growth. When not pinched back in the spring, some annuals, such as petunias or zinnias, grow leggy and weak looking. To strengthen growth and flowering, use pruning shears to cut back the stems of annuals halfway, making sure the remaining portion of the stem has several leaves left on it *(above)*. To assist its efforts to bloom again the same season, apply a balanced liquid fertilizer *(page 27)* at the base of the plant. In the future, pinch back annuals earlier in the season.

WINTERIZING PERENNIALS

Preparing a perennial bed for winter. After the first frost, use pruning shears to cut the stems of perennial plants about 2 inches above ground level *(far left)*. Compost healthy stems and foliage *(page 22)*, and dispose of diseased plant parts. Apply a winter mulch to the perennial bed to stabilize soil temperature and protect the plant from alternate freezing and thawing. Shred dry autumn leaves with a lawn mower *(page 133)* and rake them 3 to 4 inches deep over the perennial bed *(near left)*. Evergreen branches with needles also serve as an excellent winter mulch, and can be laid down alone or on top of the leaves to keep them from blowing away. Consult the mulching chart *(page 21)* for other types of mulch. When spreading a mulch around an isolated perennial plant, cover as much of the ground as the plant foliage used to cover. In the spring, many organic mulches will be sufficiently decomposed to be tilled into the ground *(page 19)* as an amendment.

TRANSPLANTING ANNUALS AND PERENNIALS

1 **Digging up a flower for transplanting.** One or two days before transplanting, water the flower thoroughly. Consult a planting guide regarding the appropriate light and soil conditions for the flower. Read the Soil Management chapter *(page 16)* and improve the soil texture and fertility in the new location as required. Dig up the flower, using a garden spade *(above)* or a trowel, depending on the size of the plant. To avoid damaging the roots, dig around the plant no closer than the outer circumference of the leaves *(above)*. Lever the plant out of the soil and carry it *(inset)* to its new location.

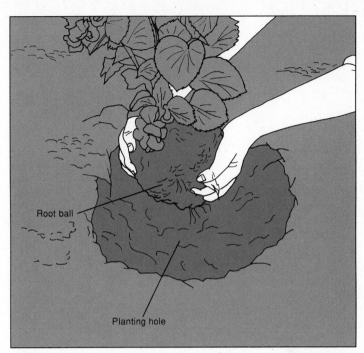

2 **Lowering the flower into the hole.** Using the spade or the trowel, dig a hole twice as large as the root ball of the transplant. If the soil feels dry, fill the planting hole with water and allow it to soak in. To lessen the shock of transplanting and to speed development, add a transplanter fertilizer with a rooting hormone *(page 26)*. Lower the root ball into the hole *(above)*, making sure that the top of the root ball is level with the ground.

3 **Replacing the soil.** Refill the planting hole with soil. Firmly tamp down the soil around the base of the plant to fill any air pockets that may dry out the roots. Then press down the soil with your foot. Finally, press a shallow depression into the soil around the flower below the outer edge of the foliage *(above)*.

4 **Watering.** Using a watering can *(above)* or a slow trickle from a hose, water the depression made in step 3. After a few minutes, check the soil moisture *(page 18)*. The soil should be moistened to a depth of 6 to 8 inches for a transplanted annual and 12 inches for a perennial. Trim back the foliage about 1 to 3 inches with hedge shears *(page 57)* or pruning shears. If there has been any serious root damage, the flower will immediately wilt. In that case, cut back the foliage halfway.

DIVIDING PERENNIALS

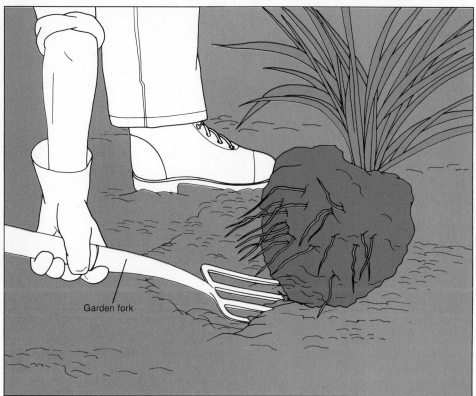

1 **Digging up a perennial plant.** Divide perennials to keep them healthy and control their growth, as well as to propagate them. Herbaceous perennials, such as daylilies, and certain asters and daisies, indicate their need for division when their centers die out. Other symptoms include a change in color; phlox may be in need of division if you notice it developing a magenta bloom. In general, divide when the plant is dormant: Divide spring-blooming perennials in the fall and fall-blooming perennials in the spring. In northern climates, however, division even of spring-blooming perennials is usually carried out in the spring, to give the roots a season to acclimatize before winter. If you divide in late fall, make sure to apply an adequate winter mulch *(page 54).*

Water the clump thoroughly two or three days before dividing it. If you intend to move the perennial, prepare the new hole in advance *(step 3).* Dig up the plant with a garden fork *(left)* or a spade. To avoid damaging the roots, cut the soil around the plant no closer than the circumference of the plant's foliage. Lever the plant out of the ground and set it down carefully. If you do not replant immediately, cover the roots with a damp piece of burlap.

Garden fork

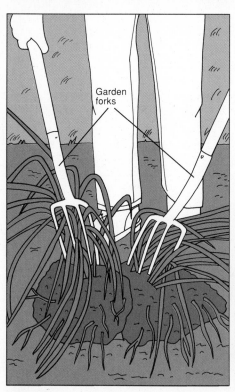

Garden forks

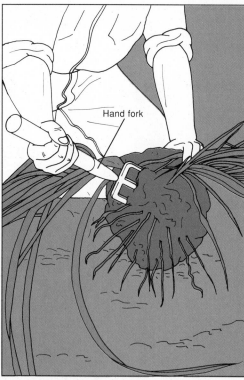

Hand fork

Roots

2 **Dividing the roots.** The roots of some perennials, such as phlox, veronica and shasta daisy, grow large, dense and tangled. To divide them, drive two garden forks, back-to-back, straight into the center of the clump. As you pull the handles away from each other, the root mass will divide in half *(above, left).* Continue to divide in this way until you have reduced the mass into manageable sections about 1 foot in diameter. Use your hands and a hand fork when the clumps get small enough *(above, center)* or on the smaller root clumps of blackberry lily and perennial coreopsis. Perennials with shallow roots, such as primrose and astilbe, can be pulled apart gently with your hands *(above, right).* Compost any dead portions of the plant *(page 22),* but if they show signs of disease, throw them out.

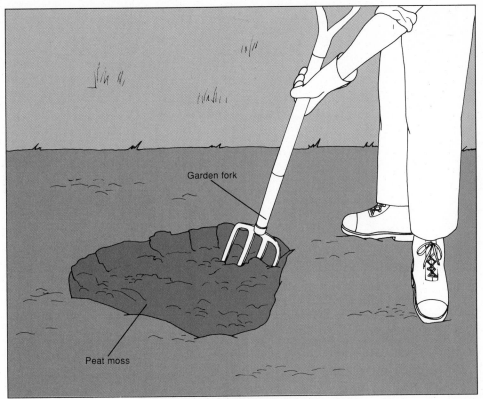

3 Preparing the planting site. Once perennials have been divided, they are often returned to their original hole. Because they have been absorbing nutrients from the planting site for several years, division is a good opportunity to cultivate and amend the soil. Use a garden fork to break up the soil in and around the hole, then till in some well-rotted compost and peat moss *(left)* as well as a high phosphorus, low nitrogen fertilizer *(page 26)*. If the soil is very poor (too clayey, for example) you can replace it entirely in the planting area.

If you are moving the perennial to a new location, consult a gardening guide and choose a site that meets the flower's soil and light needs. Read the Soil Management chapter *(page 16)* and improve the soil texture and fertility if necessary. Then use a garden spade to dig a hole twice the size of the root ball.

4 Replanting a perennial. Mound soil in the center of the hole. To prevent disease, dip the pruning shears into a solution of 1 part household bleach to 9 parts water, and trim and discard any dead or damaged roots *(inset)*. Leave only healthy white or yellowish roots. Dust the root ball with an appropriate fungicide *(page 137)*. Replant the perennial with its younger growth spreading outward and the top of the root ball level with the ground. Place the root ball in the center of the hole, gently draping the roots over the mound of soil. Refill the hole, pressing the soil firmly into place around the roots by hand *(above)* and then by foot. Finally, mold a slight depression around the base and water well *(page 55, step 3)*.

5 Cutting back the foliage. If you are dividing a perennial in the spring, trim back the young foliage 2 to 3 inches to compensate for root loss and transplant shock. If you are dividing perennials in the fall, cut back the foliage to 6 inches above ground level with hedge shears *(above)*. This will help the plant concentrate its growing energies on reestablishing its root system. After the first frost, cut back the foliage again, this time 2 inches above ground level, and lay on a winter mulch *(page 54)*.

DIVIDING RHIZOMATOUS IRISES

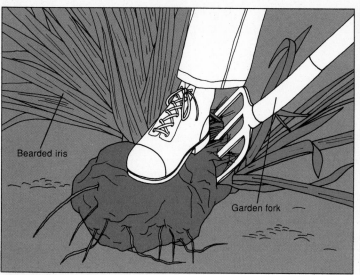

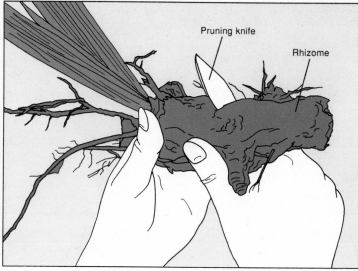

1 **Dividing an iris rhizome.** Both bearded and beardless irises must be rejuvenated by division every four to five years. In most cases, they can be divided in midsummer after they have bloomed. Prepare the planting site as described for perennials *(page 57)*. To dig up a clump of irises, use a garden fork to pry the clump out of the soil. To divide a bearded iris, use the same fork, stabilizing the clump with your foot *(above, left)*. Break the rhizome into smaller pieces, each with six to nine shoots. Before dividing the more delicate beardless iris, cut back its foliage to about 9 inches and then break its rhizome in smaller sections with a hand fork. Wash all the pieces of rhizome with water under low pressure. Use a pruning knife to cut every piece into smaller, healthy-looking sections about 2 to 3 inches long, each with one or two leaf fans *(above, right)*.

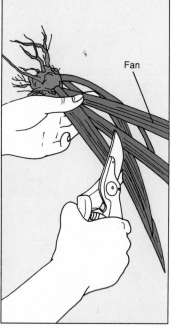

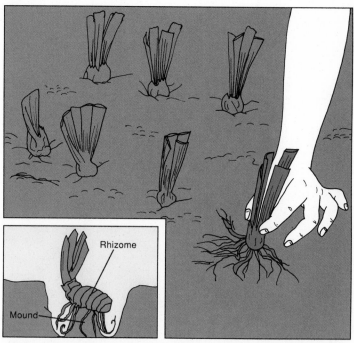

2 **Trimming roots and leaves.** Using pruning shears, trim the roots of each young rhizome to approximately 2 inches in length *(above, left)*. Trim the leaves to form a 2- to 3-inch fan *(above, right)*. Dust the entire surface of each rhizome with an appropriate fungicide *(page 137)* to inhibit disease and prevent rot. Compost *(page 22)* leaves, roots and dead rhizome sections unless signs of insect pests or disease are present. In that case, dispose of them in the garbage.

3 **Planting the young rhizome.** Prepare the planting site as described for perennials *(page 57)*. In general, plant bearded irises about 1 inch below the surface, with three to seven rhizomes in a clump; plant beardless irises about 2 inches below the surface, 15 to 18 inches apart. Use a trowel to dig the hole, pile a small mound of soil in the center and place the rhizome on it horizontally with its roots draped loosely over the sides *(inset)*. Scoop the soil over the rhizome and firm it down gently. Position rhizomes so their fans all face the same direction *(above)*. Water gently with a watering can or a garden hose with a spray nozzle, and lay down a mulch *(page 52)*.

CARING FOR ROSES

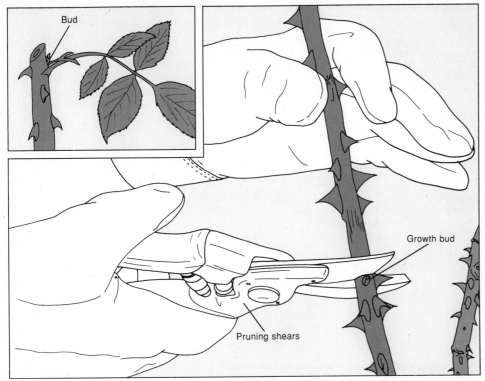

Bud

Pruning shears

Growth bud

Pruning dead, damaged or diseased canes. In the north, prune canes in spring after the risk of cold injury is past. Wearing gardening gloves, hold pruning shears with the cutting blade down. Cut the cane at an angle slightly above an outward-facing growth bud and at least 1 inch below the damaged area *(left)*. The angle must drop away from the growth bud *(inset)* so that water can run down from the bud. Examine the center, or pith, of the remaining portion of cane; if it looks brown or black, cut back some more until the pith looks healthy and white. Dispose of cut canes in the garbage; they take too long to compost.

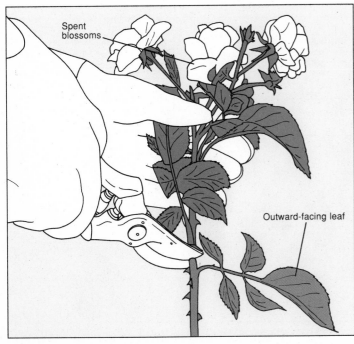

Spent blossoms

Outward-facing leaf

Sucker

Bud union

Dead-heading faded roses. As each rose fades, dead-head, or remove, it to promote blossoming throughout the flowering season. Use pruning shears to cut at a slight angle about 1/4 inch above the first outward-facing leaf stem that has five to seven leaflets *(above)*. If you want longer stems on your roses, particularly on hybrid tea roses, dead-head them by cutting the stem back to the second set of leaflets after the first cycle of blooming fades.

Removing suckers. Rose suckers are canes that sprout from the base of the bush. They grow fast, robbing the plant of nutrients. A sucker on a hybrid rose has leaves and blossoms that look different from those on the rest of the bush, and it originates in the root stock below the bud union (the swollen portion of the rose at or near ground level). To remove a sucker, wear gardening gloves. Grasp the sucker firmly and pull down hard, tearing the sucker off the root stock *(above)*. If the sucker is growing from beneath the soil, brush away the soil that covers the point where it is connected to the root stock and tear it or cut it with pruning shears.

WINTERIZING ROSES

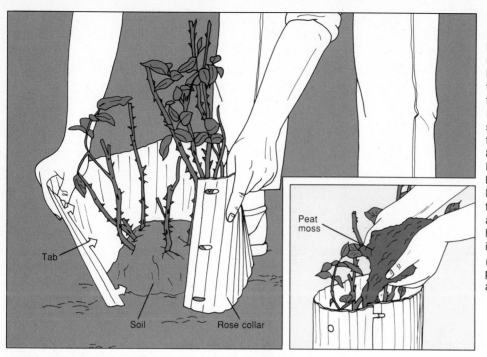

Winterizing roses. Stop disbudding roses *(page 53)* three to five weeks before the first hard frost, to give the plant a rest. The bud union of a rose (the swollen portion at ground level) must be protected against the cold. After the first frost, remove and compost *(page 22)* the summer mulch from the base of the rose. In the south, mound up disease-free cultivated soil, pine needles or straw around the base of the bush. In cold northern areas, pile soil 6 to 8 inches deep and then install a rose collar. Buy a plastic collar the right size for your bush, wrap the collar around the plant and lock the tabs *(left)*. If the collar won't fit around the canes, cut them back 10 to 12 inches above ground level. Once the collar is locked, hold it in place by mounding more soil around its base. Fill the collar with clean peat moss *(inset)*. In spring, when all danger of frost is past, remove the collar, peat moss and soil and prune any winter dieback *(page 59)*.

PLANTING BULBS

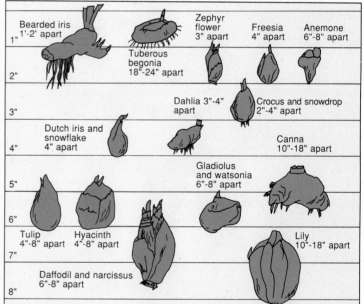

1"	Bearded iris 1'-2' apart		Zephyr flower 3" apart	Freesia 4" apart	Anemone 6"-8" apart
2"		Tuberous begonia 18"-24" apart			
3"			Dahlia 3"-4" apart	Crocus and snowdrop 2"-4" apart	
4"	Dutch iris and snowflake 4" apart			Canna 10"-18" apart	
5"			Gladiolus and watsonia 6"-8" apart		
6"					
7"	Tulip 4"-8" apart	Hyacinth 4"-8" apart		Lily 10"-18" apart	
8"	Daffodil and narcissus 6"-8" apart				

Planting bulbs. Select only healthy, firm bulbs for planting. Consult the cooperative extension service for specific instructions regarding the correct planting time in your area; hardy bulbs must be planted early enough to root before winter. Read a gardening guide to learn soil and light requirements for your bulbs. In general, bulbs demand well-drained soil and full sun, although some spring-blooming bulbs flourish in the shade. Evaluate the soil texture *(page 20)*; amend heavy clay soil or extremely sandy soil before planting *(page 21)*. Arrange the bulbs on top of the soil where you would like to see them grow. Using a trowel, dig a planting hole of the correct depth next to each bulb; consult the planting chart above as a guide to the planting depth of some common bulbs. A rule of thumb is to plant a bulb at a depth two-and-one-half times its diameter. Put a tablespoon of bone meal in each hole. Place a bulb that is rootless at planting time securely on the bottom of the hole *(inset)*, or one that has roots on a slight mound in the center *(page 58, step 3)*. Cover well with soil and press down firmly. Water with a sprinkler or a hose with a spray nozzle. Once the plants flower, water with a hose and watering wand *(page 51)*. Some bulbs benefit from a summer mulch *(page 52)* to retain soil moisture during dry season; some bulbs require a winter mulch *(page 61)* to protect them against alternate freezing and thawing. Check with a local garden nursery regarding the mulching needs of your bulbs.

SPECIAL SEASONAL CARE FOR BULBS

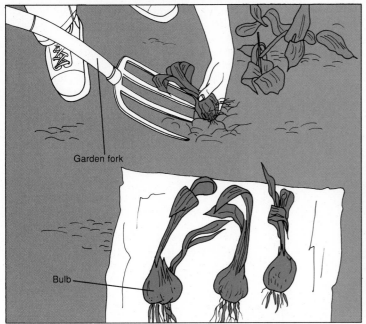

Garden fork

Bulb

Peat moss

Storing bulbs. Dead-head the blooms *(page 53)* after they have faded. When the foliage has turned yellow and withered, cut it back with pruning shears 1 inch above ground level. Hardy bulbs, such as narcissus, daffodil and crocus, can be left in the ground during a cold winter if mulched properly *(below)*. Half-hardy bulbs, such as gladiolus and canna, and tender bulbs, such as amaryllis and dahlia, must be dug up and stored during a cold dormancy period. To dig up bulbs, use a garden fork to lift them gently from the soil *(above, left)*.

Compost *(page 22)* any that feel soft or spongy or look unusually small. Lay the healthy ones on newspaper and let them dry for a day or two. Clean and protect the bulbs before storage: Pull off dead roots, foliage and stems by hand *(above, right)* and dust them with an appropriate fungicide *(page 137)*. Then place them loosely in labeled boxes so their sides don't touch. If the bulbs lack a protective skin, like dahlia or begonia bulbs, cover them with slightly moistened peat moss *(inset)*. Store bulbs in a cool place where the temperature will not dip below freezing.

Weight

Chicken wire

Mulch

Protecting bulbs in the ground. To keep animal pests from digging up bulbs that are in the ground during winter, lay a piece of chicken wire on top of the area. Mulching can be done before or after. Weigh down the chicken wire with bricks or stones *(inset)*. It can remain on the ground as long as the bulbs are buried.

After the first frost, particularly in areas where there is little snow, lay down a porous winter mulch. It will protect hardy bulbs and some half-hardy bulbs against the cold, and keep bulbs from flowering early in false spring-like weather and then dying when hit by a sudden freeze. Choose a porous mulch such as salt or marsh hay, prairie hay or evergreen boughs. Lay the mulch about 4 to 6 inches deep and leave it in place until true spring growing weather begins. Then remove the mulch and compost it *(page 22)*.

SUPPORTING TALL PLANTS

Staking tall, single-stemmed flowers.
Flowers such as delphinium and garden holly-hock may grow top-heavy and have a tendency to fall over unless supported. If possible, stake them when they are 6 to 8 inches tall so that their later growth will be strong and erect. Tuber and bulb flowers should have stakes installed before planting to prevent piercing the bulb. Select 1-by-2-inch wooden stakes for heavier stems, and bamboo stakes for lighter ones. The stakes should equal the flower's mature height. Sharpen one end of the stake with a utility knife. Position the stake 4 to 6 inches away from the flower and, using a mallet, drive it about 8 inches into the ground *(left)*. Wrap a twist-tie in a loose figure eight around the stem and stake near the top *(inset)*, and in two or three places below.

Corralling bushy flowers. Flowers that grow in tall bushy clumps, such as daisy and aster, can be supported by corralling. Each clump will require enough covered garden wire to encircle it twice, and four bamboo or plastic-covered metal stakes as tall as the flower's mature height. To make a corral, space the stakes around the flower clump, about 8 inches from the flower, and push them into the ground about 6 inches *(above, left)*. Twist the wire near the top of a stake and pull the wire around the clump, looping each stake several times *(above, right)*. When you reach the first stake again, twist the wire to it securely and cut it with heavy scissors or wire cutters. If the flowers have fallen over, lift them into the corral. Wrap wire around the stakes a second time three quarters of the way up.

EDGING A FLOWER BED

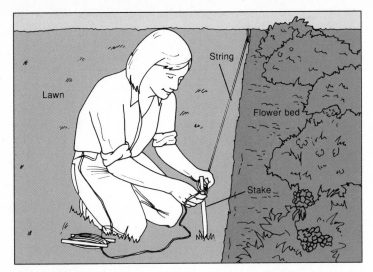

1 Defining the edge. Plastic lawn edging comes in a roll and is available at garden nurseries. Measure the length of the bed and buy enough to edge it, plus a bit more. If the border of the flower bed is straight, string the border to guide you when you cut the sod: Use a mallet to drive short stakes into the lawn at each end of the flower bed, 1 or 2 inches from the edge. Tie the string to the first stake, stretch it taut, and knot it to the stake at the other end *(above)*. More stakes may be needed if the bed is very long; drive in enough to keep the string secure and taut. For a curving border, unroll a garden hose along the lawn where you want to edge it.

2 Cutting a straight edge. Use a lawn edger with a blade in the shape of a half moon to cut a straight, clean edge. Using the string or hose to guide the position of the tool, drive the blade 2 to 3 inches into the lawn with your foot, at a slight angle toward the flower bed to allow extra space for the grass roots. Rock the blade side to side, to slice through the sod *(above)*. Repeat this cutting motion along the full length of the string or hose, making sure each cut overlaps the previous one.

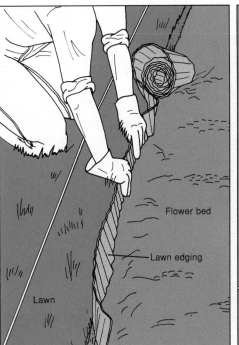

3 Disposing of sod. Remove the cut sod *(above)* and shake off the soil into the flower bed. Then place the sod upside down on your compost heap *(page 22)*. If the sod was recently treated with a herbicide, wait two weeks before composting it or dispose of it in the garbage.

4 Installing lawn edging. Push the edging into the soil along the edge of the lawn, flush with the height of the grass, unrolling it as you go *(above, left)*. Once the entire length of the bed is edged, use a spade to pile the soil in the flower bed against the edging, leaving about an inch of the top of the lawn edging exposed *(above, right)*. Trim any excess at the ends with heavy scissors. If the border length requires a second roll of lawn edging, install it the same way, overlapping the first strip by about 4 inches.

CLIMBING PLANTS

Glossy, green ivy blanketing an old brick wall, a fragile clematis framing a doorway, and the sweet smell of honeysuckle all recall earlier, simpler times. Climbing plants are still prized for their convenience and versatility. They are uniquely useful for softening a bleak house exterior or adorning an otherwise unsightly wall, and are relatively self-sufficient.

The classic climbing plants are those that cling independently to a brick or stone wall with adhesive discs or rootlets, and those that twine their tendrils, leaf stalks or stems around a slender column or string. Examples of these types are pictured below. Plants that are not natural climbers, such as the climb-ing rose, can be encouraged to "climb" by careful hand-twining or by tying with string or wire to a support. When transplanting *(page 68)*, or in some cases when pruning *(page 66)*, notice how your plant is secured in order to detach it with the least harm from its support.

Read the Soil Management chapter *(page 16)* for general instructions on watering, fertilizing and mulching. For proper maintenance, familiarize yourself with the growth habits of the climbers in your garden. If a plant flowers, for example, discover its blooming season for timely pruning *(page 66)*. Recognize signs of ill health before they become advanced.

Clinging vines
Fast-growing climbers such as Virginia creeper *(Parthenocissus quinquefolia)* cling with adhesive discs *(above)*; they may grow twice as fast as English ivy *(Hedera helix)*, which clings with rootlets *(below)*. Moisture in the discs or rootlets can damage wood siding.

Stem twiners
The stem winds itself around rain-spouts, wires, strings and trellises. Examples are Hall's Japanese honeysuckle *(Lonicera japonica halliana, above, right)* and Dutch-man's pipe *(Aristolochia durior, above, left)*. When transplanting, wrap the stem of a young counter-clockwise twiner such as honey-suckle, or a clockwise twiner such as Dutchman's pipe, in the proper direction; this encourages it to establish faster.

Tendril twiners
Have specialized structures that entwine a narrow support. The sweet pea *(Lathyrus odoratus, above, left)* needs horizontal as well as vertical supports for its tendrils. The tendrils of clematis *(above, right)* are modified leaf stalks that wind easily around vertical supports. Some tendril twiners also wrap their stems.

A list of symptoms particular to vines, with possible causes, is presented in the Troubleshooting Guide below. Some climbing plants can grow like ground cover, and others like shrubs; consult the Troubleshooting Guides in Ground Cover *(page 88)* and Trees and Shrubs *(page 94)*. Keep in mind that few gardening problems respond swiftly to a "quick fix." Particularly in the case of pruning, it may take months, even a season or two, before the full effects of a repair are evident.

Climbing plants generally are less vulnerable to pests and diseases than are flowers or vegetables. An occasional brisk hosing-down of the leaves will help to discourage invading insects. If you suspect that some pest or disease is affecting your plant and the symptom is not listed in the Troubleshooting Guide, consult Pests and Diseases *(page 112)*. When pesticidal control is recommended, study Tools and Techniques *(page 129)* for more information on pesticides and their application, and read the product label. Close all windows and doors if spraying plants that climb on or near your home. Some climbing plants, particularly kudzu, are considered weeds. Kill an unwanted climber with herbicide *(page 67)*, or consult your Cooperative Extension Service to learn the best way to destroy it.

TROUBLESHOOTING GUIDE

SYMPTOM	POSSIBLE CAUSE	PROCEDURE
New leaves smaller; older leaves turn yellow, may drop; plant growth slowed	Soil pH wrong for plant; nitrogen deficiency	See Pests and Diseases *(p. 119)*. Test soil pH *(p. 23)* ▪○ and adjust *(p. 24)* ▪○; test soil nitrogen level *(p. 25)* ▪○ and fertilize *(p. 26)* □○ or transplant *(p. 68)* ▪◐
Plant wilts, may turn brown and shrivel	Heat scorch or drought stress, due to insufficient watering or excessive moisture evaporation from leaves	Check soil moisture *(p. 18)* □○ and water correctly *(p. 51)* □○; in hot, dry or windy weather, mist plant to reduce its temperature; or transplant *(p. 68)* ▪◐
	Soil too sandy	Evaluate soil texture *(p. 20)* □○; amend soil *(p. 21)* □○ or transplant *(p. 68)* ▪◐
Leaves pale or yellow, may turn brown around edges and drop; roots may be rotted	Soil too moist due to excessive watering	Check soil moisture *(p. 18)* □○ and decrease watering *(p. 51)* □○
	Soil draining poorly; water overflowing from gutter or downspout	Evaluate soil drainage *(p. 27)* ▪○; transplant *(p. 68)* ▪◐ or install a drainage system *(p. 30)* ▪●
	Soil too clayey (high clay content)	Evaluate soil texture *(p. 20)* □○; amend soil *(p. 21)* □○ or transplant *(p. 68)* ▪◐
Recently transplanted plant wilts; buds or flowers drop	Roots damaged during transplanting	Cut back some of the branches *(p. 66)* ▪○; water thoroughly and often *(p. 51)* □○
Blackened stems; buds don't open; buds and flowers drop	Frost damage	Prune damaged stems *(p. 66)* ▪○; when cold snap is forecast, water thoroughly and mulch *(p. 21)* □○
Abundant foliage but few flowers	Too much nitrogen fertilizer used during growing season	Test soil nitrogen level *(p. 25)* ▪○ and avoid overfertilizing in the future; prune roots *(p. 67)* ▪○ to stimulate flower growth
	Flower buds accidentally pruned	Ensure proper pruning of flowering climbing plant *(p. 66)* ▪○
	Plant is too young or too old	Wait until young plant is old enough to flower. Prune roots on older plant to activate flower growth *(p. 67)* ▪○
Spindly growth, few flowers	Too little sunlight	Transplant to sunnier location *(p. 68)* ▪◐
Dense exterior foliage, interior stems bare	Insufficient air and light reaching inner branches and stems	Thin plant *(p. 66)* ▪○; consult a gardening guide for long-range pruning needs
Leaves yellow between veins (especially new leaves)	Alkaline soil (possibly due to lime seepage from concrete foundation) or iron deficiency	See Pests and Diseases *(p. 119)*. Test soil pH *(p. 23)* ▪○ and adjust *(p. 24)* ▪○, or transplant *(p. 68)* ▪◐ to more acidic soil
Stem and foliage overgrown and tangled	Neglect	Prune roots or stems *(p. 67)* ▪○; consult a gardening guide for long-range pruning needs; destroy vine if unable to control *(p. 67)* ▪○
Yellow leaves, may be mottled; growth stunted	Viral disease	See Pests and Diseases *(p. 113)*
Irregular holes in leaves	Caterpillars, earwigs	See Pests and Diseases *(p. 116)*
Colored flecks on leaves; may be curled or sooty	Aphids	See Pests and Diseases *(p. 118)*
Leaves mottled; bumps on stems; leaves drop	Scale insects	See Pests and Diseases *(p. 126)*

DEGREE OF DIFFICULTY: □ Easy ▪ Moderate ▪ Complex
ESTIMATED TIME: ○ Less than 1 hour ◐ 1 to 3 hours ● Over 3 hours

PRUNING CLIMBING PLANTS

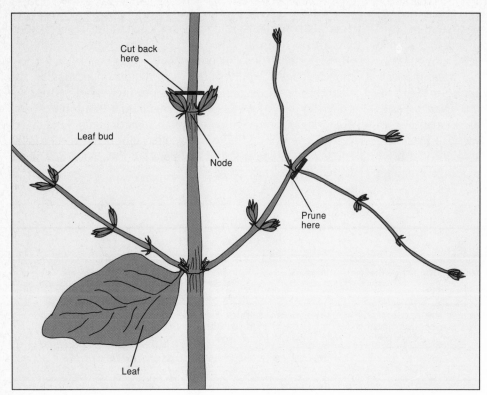

Cut back here

Leaf bud

Node

Prune here

Leaf

When and where to prune. When pruning, choosing the right location on the plant and the right time of year are essential. Whether pruning to promote or arrest growth, always execute the cut just above a growing point, or node. Cut back to a bud or branch pointing in the direction you wish the growth to go: To open a dense, twiggy vine, cut next to an outward-facing bud; to fill in a skimpy vine, cut back to an inward-facing bud. If extensive pruning of a flowering climbing plant is necessary, consult your cooperative extension service for information about the plant's blooming characteristics. In general, climbing plants that flower in the spring bloom on the previous year's growth; prune them after they bloom to give the new growth time to strengthen before winter. Those that flower in late summer or fall bloom on the present year's growth, and are best pruned in late autumn when the plant is dormant, or in early spring before new growth appears. If your climbing plant flowers in both spring and late summer or fall, prune lightly in the dormant season and more heavily just after the spring blossoming.

Lopping shears

Node

Thinning a climbing plant. Aggressive climbing plants such as trumpet vine (*Campsis*) or Japanese honeysuckle (*Lonicera japonica*) grow so vigorously that, if left untended, their dense foliage will slow air circulation and block light from reaching the inner branches. In general, thin a crowded climbing plant in summer; if the winters are severe, thin early enough for new growth to strengthen before autumn frost. Prune selectively, removing unhealthy stems where possible without damaging the rest of the plant. Cut off a slender branch at its point of origin *(inset)* using pruning shears. Cut a large stem (up to 1 1/4 inch in diameter) down to the ground with lopping shears *(above)*. If much thinning is necessary to open the plant to light, cut back *(right)* to prevent the plant from becoming straggly.

Cutting back to spur new growth. To encourage lateral buds to sprout new shoots, cut back part of the stem; use pruning shears to cut just above a node *(above)*. If the stems are green and slender, pinch them off between thumb and forefinger at the same place. On young plants, pinch off stem tips just above the growth buds to encourage branching. Similarly, to spur the end portion of a stem to grow longer, cut back some of the lateral buds or shoots. Beware of cutting back too extensively, or over time the plant's foliage will become heavy and dense; balance cutting back with light thinning *(left)*.

Pruning damaged stems and branches. Inspect a climbing plant regularly for signs of pests and disease. After a storm or sudden frost, check for broken or blackened stems. Using pruning shears, cut back to a healthy part of the stem (healthy wood is creamy green or white). Cut through the stem just above a leaf or bud and its node *(above)*, following the angle of the leaf or bud. Remove dead stems wherever possible without damaging the rest of the plant; they invite disease and attract pests. Dispose of diseased parts in a sealed garbage bag, and disinfect pruning shears with household bleach or rubbing alcohol.

Pruning roots. Sever some of the outer third of a climbing plant's feeder roots to curb growth or stimulate flowering. First, evaluate the texture of the soil *(page 20)* and the age of the plant. Prune the long, shallow roots of an older plant growing in sandy, loose soil at a distance of about 5 feet from the plant. In dense, compact soil, the roots should be cut about 3 to 4 feet away. If in doubt about the spread of the plant's root system, use a garden spade to dig a short trench about 6 inches deep, 3 feet from the main stem, and examine the roots. If they are thick and chunky, move farther away, until you find thin, whiskery roots. Then make several sharp cuts with the spade about 6 to 10 inches deep around the plant *(above)*.

DESTROYING A CLIMBING PLANT

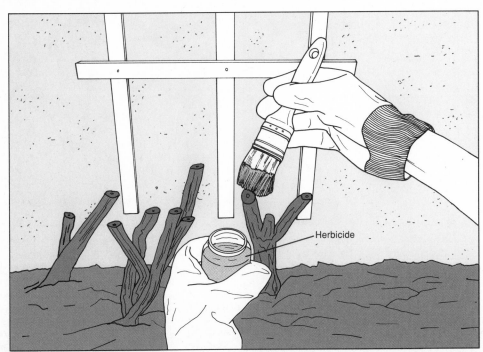

Applying herbicide to a vine. When buying herbicide, read the label to make sure it includes the name of the plant you wish to eliminate. Cut the stems to near ground level. Wearing neoprene gloves, carefully pour a tiny amount of herbicide into a clean jar and reseal the herbicide container. Dip the end of a narrow paintbrush into the herbicide and swab it over the cut ends of the stems *(left)*. Use up all herbicide remaining in the jar and store the herbicide container safely *(page 141)*. Wrap the paintbrush in newspaper and only reuse it and the jar if reapplications are necessary. Check periodically over the next few weeks to see whether new growth appears. If it does, wait for it to sprout four or five leaves before cutting it back and applying more herbicide. When the stems have stopped growing completely, dig them up and discard them.

TRANSPLANTING A VINE

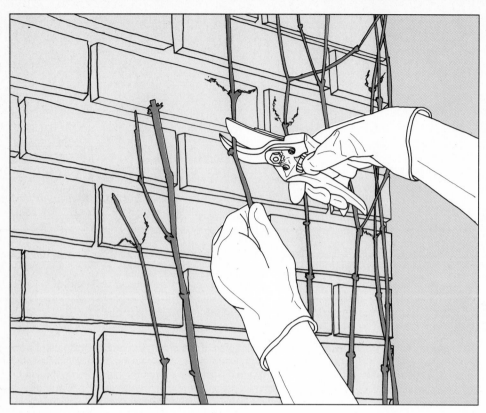

1 **Cutting back.** A climbing plant that took several years to become established is worth transplanting when its present environment is no longer healthy or desirable. Most perennial climbing plants are strong enough to relocate. However, many annuals are too delicate to move, as are some perennials such as allamanda (*Allamanda carthartica*) and several varieties of clematis. Before transplanting, check with your cooperative extension service to learn whether your climbing plant is hardy enough to withstand the shock of being moved. Transplant in cold weather when the plant is still dormant. In cold-winter climates, relocate your plant in early spring to give new growth a chance to strengthen before autumn frost. Never transplant on a hot, dry day; the root system will dry out.

Evaluate soil texture *(page 20)*, soil pH *(page 23)* and fertility *(page 25)* in the new planting spot and amend the soil as required. Before digging up a climbing plant, cut it down halfway or to eye level *(left)*. An especially vigorous vine may be cut back near ground level before moving; go directly to step 3.

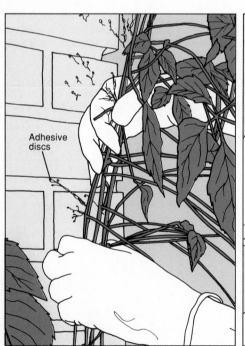

Adhesive discs

Tendril

Leaf stalk

2 **Detaching stems and branches.** Remove a climbing plant from its suppport carefully to minimize damage to stem, tendrils and leaves. Tug gently on a clinger, such as Virginia creeper (*Parthenocissus quinquefolia*), that uses adhesive discs to cling to a wall *(above, left)*. Unravel the tendrils of a twiner such as a cathedral bells (*Cobaea scandens, above, center*) or the leaf stalks of a clematis *(above, right)*. In some cases, the vertical support around which a plant stem twines may be moved with the plant attached. If not, unwind the stem carefully, noting whether it grows clockwise or counterclockwise. If the woody stems of a climbing plant such as honeysuckle (*Lonicera*) or wisteria are wedged tightly in the latticework of a trellis, removal may break the stems. Consult the cooperative extension service for advice.

3 **Digging up the plant.** Tie the plant's stems together loosely with garden cord or strips cut from nylon hose *(inset)*. Use a spade to dig up as much of the root system as possible. Find the extent of the roots by following the guidelines for pruning roots on page 67. Leave plenty of soil on the roots for protection; if the plant is big, you will need help to lift it. Lay the plant on a wet piece of burlap. Cut off damaged roots with pruning shears and then wrap the burlap around the root ball. Use a wheelbarrow to move a heavy plant to its new location.

4 **Replanting the root ball.** Evaluate and amend the soil in the new location *(step 1)*. Dig a hole about twice the size of the root system and equal in depth to the original hole. Unwrap the burlap from around the root ball and lower the plant into the hole. Cover the roots with the amended soil to the same level as in their previous location. Firm the soil around the stem *(above)*. Finish by watering at the base of the plant. Apply a transplanter solution *(page 26)* with a high phosphorus content (10/52/10), available from garden supply stores.

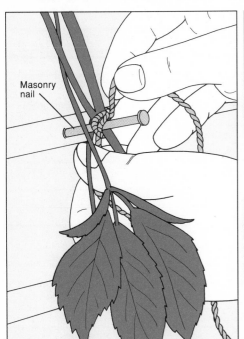

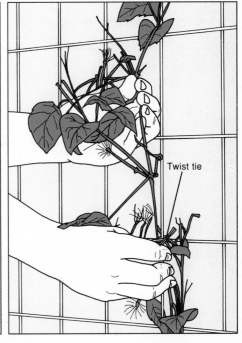

5 **Reattaching a climbing plant.** Untie the stems. To support a clinging plant on a brick or stone wall, hammer masonry nails into the mortar. Loosely tie the stems of the plant to the nails with string or strips of nylon *(above, left)*. When reattaching a plant that twines with tendrils *(above, center)* or leaf stalks *(above, right)*, install a slender vertical support, such as string or wire, for new growth to climb. In the meantime, tie the plant stem loosely to the support with twist ties. Wrap the stem of a stem twiner around its new support, in the same direction in which it originally twined. If necessary, use twist ties to help support its weight until it is reestablished. A slow-growing, woody stem twiner must also be tied to a trellis or arbor until new growth takes hold. Check the plant periodically over the next few days. If the leaves near the top begin to yellow and wilt, cut back slightly *(page 66)* to balance the root and stem growth, allowing the root system to regain its strength. Once the plant is established, remove the strings or twist ties.

LAWNS

Although a healthy lawn may appear to be a seamless carpet of uniform greenery, there are typically six grass plants growing every square inch. For the average American lawn of 10,000 square feet, this amounts to about 8 million plants.

The Troubleshooting Guide below lists the most common lawn problems and directs you to procedures for solving them. Fortunately, many problems can be simply resolved by mowing *(page 73)* and watering *(page 75)* and by fertilizing *(page 75)* when necessary. Mow the lawn when it is dry and keep the mower blades sharp *(page 74)*; blunt blades will injure the grass, making it more susceptible to disease. Find your lawn's grass type on page 72 and don't let your grass grow more than a third over its maximum height before cutting it.

A lawn signals its need for water by holding your footprints after you walk on it. If the grass is growing in sandy soil more frequent watering is called for than if the soil is clayey. Read the chapter on Soil Management *(page 16)* for more information on watering and soil texture. Also check to see that your sprinkler is distributing enough water equally to all areas of the lawn *(page 75)*. Too much traffic across the lawn will compact the soil. Aerate *(page 86)* on a regular basis and redirect traffic if the problem gets too severe.

Since weeds, pests and diseases are discouraged by healthy turf, their presence indicates an underlying weakness. Remove weeds as soon as you spot them. The weed chart *(page 76)* will help you to identify the unwanted plants in your lawn. If

TROUBLESHOOTING GUIDE

SYMPTOM	POSSIBLE CAUSE	PROCEDURE
Lawn uneven and thinning	Irregular maintenance or neglect	Mow lawn at correct height *(p. 73)* □◖; water lawn regularly *(p. 75)* □○; maintain program of fertilizing *(p. 75)* ◖◖
	Mower blade at uneven level	Adjust all four wheels to same height *(p. 73)* □○
	Grass type not suitable for soil and climactic conditions	Consult chart *(p. 72)* □○ and Cooperative Extension Agent for suitable grass type or mixture, and overseed existing lawn *(p. 87)* ◖◖
Grass intrudes into garden or over sidewalk	Lawn overgrown	Trim edges *(p. 73)* ◖○; install edging around garden bed *(p. 63)* ◖○
Ground cover invading lawn	Ground cover overgrown	Prune back stems and runners, and control growth by cutting through roots *(p. 91)* ◖○; install lawn edging *(p. 63)* ◖○
Patch of lawn scalped during mowing	High spot in lawn	Roll back sod and level soil *(p. 79)* ◖◖
Tips of grass blades turn brown after mowing	Dull lawn mower blade	Sharpen mower blade *(p. 74)* ◖◖; adjust blade height level *(p. 73)* □○
Grass losing resilience and turning brown at the tips	Insufficient moisture	Water lawn regularly to supplement rainfall *(p. 75)* □○
	Fast-draining sandy soil	Water lawn more frequently *(p. 75)* □○; overseed lawn with drought-resistant type of grass *(p. 87)* ◖●; evaluate soil texture *(p. 20)* ◖○, amend soil *(p. 82)* ■● and replant lawn with seed *(p. 85)* ◖◖, sod *(p. 83)* ◖◖, plugs or sprigs *(p. 81)* ◖◖
	Excessive thatch buildup	Dethatch lawn *(p. 86)* ◖◖▲; aerate lawn *(p. 86)* ◖●▲
	Soil compacted	Aerate lawn *(p. 86)* ◖●▲
Lawn pale and thin	Soil pH unsuitable or nutrient deficiency	Test soil pH and adjust *(p. 23)* ◖○; test soil fertility *(p. 25)* ◖○; maintain program of fertilizing *(p. 75)* ◖◖
	Excessive thatch buildup	Dethatch lawn *(p. 86)* ◖◖▲; aerate lawn *(p. 86)* ◖●▲
	Soil compacted	Aerate lawn *(p. 86)* ◖●▲
Several weeds in lawn	Normal condition	Identify weeds *(p. 76)* □○ and remove weeds by hand or spot-apply herbicide immediately *(p. 77)* □◖; water lawn regularly *(p. 75)* □○ and maintain program of fertilizing *(p. 75)* ◖◖
Lawn infested with weeds	Lawn neglected	Identify weeds *(p. 76)* □○; destroy weeds with broadcast application of herbicide *(p. 79)* □○; prepare small patch *(p. 80)* ◖○ or large area *(p. 82)* ■● for reseeding *(p. 85)* □● or laying sod *(p. 83)* ◖◖ or replanting with sprigs or plugs *(p. 81)* ◖◖; water lawn regularly *(p. 75)* □○ and maintain program of fertilizing *(p. 75)* ◖◖
	Water pooling in low spots	Identify weeds *(p. 76)* □○ and remove weeds by hand or spot-apply herbicide *(p. 77)* □○; roll back sod and fill in low spots *(p. 79)* ◖○
	Soil pH unsuitable for lawn or nutrient deficiency in soil	Test soil pH and adjust *(p. 23)* ◖○; test soil fertility *(p. 25)* ◖○ and apply recommended fertilizer *(p. 75)* ◖◖
Lawn thin and pale under tree	Insufficient light	Prune tree or shrub to admit light *(p. 94)* ◖◖ and overseed area with shade-tolerant grass type *(p. 87)* ◖◖, or mulch under tree *(p. 97)* □○ or plant shade-tolerant ground cover *(p. 93)* ◖○

DEGREE OF DIFFICULTY: □ Easy ◖ Moderate ■ Complex
ESTIMATED TIME: ○ Less than 1 hour ◖ 1 to 3 hours ● Over 3 hours

▲ Special tool required

hand weeding is insufficient, consult the herbicide chart *(page 78)* for a list of commonly available herbicides. To mix liquid concentrates of herbicides, read Tools & Techniques *(page 139)*. Spray on a calm day and carefully follow the instructions for safe application *(pages 77, 79)*. When insects or fungi have infested your lawn, match the symptoms with those in Pests and Diseases *(page 112)* and treat as described.

Once these problems are under control, evaluate the condition of the soil. Test soil pH *(page 23)* and fertility *(page 25)*. Most grasses grow best in a soil with a pH of 6.0 to 6.5. If soil nutrients are lacking, fertilize carefully *(page 75)*. If your lawn is prone to thatch, consider using an organic fertilizer such as manure, which contains organisms that break down thatch

buildup. Thatch is a layer of grass roots, stems and runners that develops between the leaf blades and the soil. A 1/2-inch layer can actually be useful, serving as an organic mulch, but too much thatch prevents water and nutrients from reaching roots while attracting insects and disease. Most grass types require dethatching in the spring *(page 86)* although warm-season grasses may need to be dethatched in the fall as well.

A long-neglected lawn may have to be torn up *(page 82)* and replanted. If you don't own the necessary tools, check local rental rates as well as the cost of having a professional landscaper or lawn service company do the job. It may be more convenient, and not much more expensive, to have the work done for you.

TROUBLESHOOTING GUIDE (continued)

SYMPTOM	POSSIBLE CAUSE	PROCEDURE
Grass pale, thinning and growing slowly	Nitrogen deficiency	Test soil pH and adjust *(p. 23)* ▢◯; test soil fertility *(p. 25)* ▢◯ and apply recommended fertilizer *(p. 75)* ▢◖
	Excessive thatch buildup	Dethatch lawn *(p. 86)* ▢◖▲; aerate lawn *(p. 86)* ▢◖▲
	Compaction	Aerate lawn *(p. 86)* ▢◖▲
Bare patches in lawn	Excessive traffic	Redirect traffic with sidewalk or stepping stones; cultivate patches and reseed or resod *(p. 80)* ▢◖ or replant with plugs or sprigs *(p. 81)* ▢◖
Grass brown and straw-like	Excessive fertilizer or herbicide application	Water well to leach soil *(p. 19)* ▢◯ and overseed *(p. 87)* ▢◖; remove sod and prepare the bed *(p. 82)* ■◖ for seeding *(p. 85)* ▢◖, or replant with sod *(p. 83)* ▢◖ or with plugs or sprigs *(p. 81)* ▢◖.
	Warm-season grass going dormant	Leave alone or overseed with compatible cool-season grass *(p. 87)* ▢◖
	Grass going dormant due to insufficient moisture	Water regularly and deeply to supplement rainfall *(p. 75)* ▢◯; overseed *(p. 87)* ▢◖
Tiny mounds of soil on lawn	Earthworms	Rake soil, but leave earthworms alone
Grass yellowed in small patches	Dog urine	Water lawn well to leach soil *(p. 19)* ▢◯; overseed area *(p. 87)* ▢◯; spread commercial animal repellant or fence in lawn if problem is persistent
Bands or patches of mushrooms in lawn	Rotting wood in soil below	Roll back sod *(p. 79)* ▢◖ to dig up and remove wood
Dead patches in lawn. Grass blades may be chewed off at soil level	Sod webworms, chinch bugs, or white grubs	See Pests and Diseases *(p. 123)*; if chinch bugs, dethatch lawn *(p. 86)* ▢◖▲
Mounds of earth and tunnels, or chewed patches of grass	Moles, gophers, skunks or other animals feeding on grubs	See Pests and Diseases *(p. 123)* to control white grubs, and *(p. 116)* to control Japanese beetle grubs
Bare patches, and caterpillars feeding on grass blades	Armyworms	See Pests and Diseases *(p. 124)*
Holes in grass blades, grubs in lawn	Japanese beetles	See Pests and Diseases *(p. 116)*
Lawn thinning, browning and dying in patches	Fungal diseases	See Pests and Diseases *(pp. 124-125)*
Donut patches in lawn, green on the inside, dead and brown on the ouside	Fusarium blight	See Pests and Diseases *(p. 124)*
Thin, pale grass blades covered with orange powder	Rust	See Pests and Diseases *(p. 125))*
Small, bleached spot with reddish edges in lawn	Dollar spot	See Pests and Diseases *(p. 125)*
Small dead patches in lawn, pink or red fungal threads on grass blades	Red thread	See Pests and Diseases *(p. 125)*

DEGREE OF DIFFICULTY: ▢ Easy ▢ Moderate ■ Complex
ESTIMATED TIME: ◯ Less than 1 hour ◖ 1 to 3 hours ◖ Over 3 hours ▲ Special tool required

GRASS CHART

TYPE	SEEDING DENSITY (lbs. per 1000 sq. ft.)	MAXIMUM MOWING HEIGHT	CHARACTERISTICS
Kentucky bluegrass	2 to 4	1 1/2" to 2 1/2"	Hardy, cool-season grass. Used extensively. Color differs with variety. Forms dense turf. Planted by seeding or sodding. Drought-tolerant. Medium disease resistance.
Perennial ryegrass	6 to 10	1 1/2" to 2 1/2"	Rapidly growing, cool-season grass. Color differs with variety. Planted by seeding or sodding. Medium drought and disease resistance. Often mixed or used for overseeding.
Tall fescue	8 to 10	2" to 3"	Low-maintenance, cool-season grass. Medium to dark green color. Planted by seeding or sodding. May form clumps if not heavily seeded. Good drought and disease resistance.
Fine fescue	2 to 4	1 1/2" to 2 1/2"	Cool-season grass. Medium green color. Fine texture, open turf. Planted by seeding or sodding. Often mixed with bluegrass. Good shade tolerance. Medium drought and disease resistance.
Bahia grass	4 to 5	2" to 3"	Hardy, low-maintenance, warm-season grass. Light green color, coarse texture. Planted by seeding, sodding, sprigging or plugging. Poor salt tolerance. Excellent drought resistance. Medium disease resistance. Prone to forming excessive thatch.
Bermuda grass	2 to 4	3/4" to 1 1/2"	Hardy, warm-season grass. Dark green to bluish color. Planted by seeding, sodding, sprigging or plugging. Establishes and grows rapidly. Medium disease resistance. Excellent drought resistance. Prone to forming excessive thatch.
St. Augustine grass		1 1/2" to 2 1/2"	Warm-season grass. Dark green to bluish color. Coarse texture, dense turf. Planted by sprigging, plugging or sodding. Good shade and salt tolerance. Medium drought resistance. Poor disease resistance. Prone to forming excessive thatch.
Centipede grass		1" to 2"	Low-maintenance, warm-season grass. Color differs with variety. Planted by sprigging, plugging or sodding. Establishes and grows slowly. Medium disease and drought resistance. Winter dormancy begins early. May form thatch; do not over-fertilize.
Zoysia grass		1/2" to 1"	Hardy, warm-season grass. Planted by sprigging, plugging or sodding. Establishes and grows very slowly. Good salt and shade tolerance. Medium disease resistance. Good drought resistance. Prone to forming excessive thatch.

When choosing a grass for your lawn, take into account the climate and soil, the amount of traffic the lawn will receive and the maintenance the grass type requires. Each type of grass listed above has several varieties. You can purchase a pure variety or a blend of types. A blend is designed to grow better in varying conditions, such as periods of drought and rain, or mixed shade and sun. You can order grass seed mixed to your needs. Consult your Cooperative Extension Service to learn the best types for your area. Cool-season grasses withstand winter cold but are not suited to long, hot summers.

Warm-season grasses withstand hot, dry summers but become dormant and turn brown in winter. To maintain a green lawn year-round, overseed a warm-season grass with a cool-season grass (page 87). Grasses are sold as sod, seed, sprigs or plugs, depending on how the plant establishes its roots. In general, cool-season grasses are seeded (page 85) or sodded (page 83) and warm-season grasses are plugged or sprigged (page 81). Keep your lawn mowed to within the heights listed on the chart. During periods of extreme heat or drought, allow the grass to grow slightly higher.

MOWING AND TRIMMING A LAWN

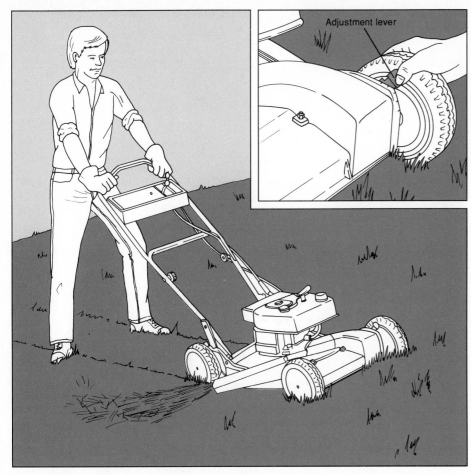

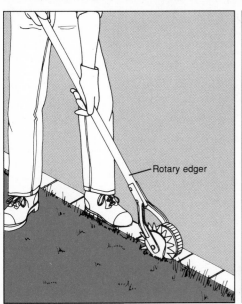

1 **Adjusting the mowing height.** Mowing a lawn as short as the grass will tolerate keeps growth thick and vigorous, and discourages the growth of broad-leafed weeds. To set the mowing height, adjust the blade height levers at each of the lawn mower's wheels *(inset)*. Place the mower on a driveway or sidewalk and push each lever to the setting recommended for your grass type *(page 72)*. If the height is not indicated on your lawn mower, test the adjustment by mowing a small area of grass, then use a ruler to measure from the soil to the tip of the blade. For mowing ground cover, set the mower blade at its highest position. For grass that has grown more than an inch too high, mow the lawn twice— once at the highest setting, then once again at its proper height. Mow only when the grass is dry. Before mowing, remove all rocks, sticks and objects from the lawn. Mow the lawn in parallel rows that overlap by about one quarter. To prevent ruts and stripes, alternate the mowing pattern at a right angle each time you mow. Short clippings add nutrients if left on the lawn. For long clippings, use a catcher bag or rake them up. Add clippings to your compost or use them as garden mulch. When cutting on a slope *(left)*, mow across the slope, beginning at the bottom and working up the slope in parallel rows. Cut as closely to trees and shrubs as possible without injuring them, then trim *(step 2)*. Disconnect the spark plug *(page 74)* before storing the mower.

2 **Trimming edges.** Use a rotary edger to cut away grass encroaching on a sidewalk or driveway. Keeping the wheels on the hard surface, roll the edger back and forth a few inches at a time, cutting through the sod with the notched blade *(above, left)*. If the sod is tough to cut, use a lawn edger *(page 63)*. To trim grass against a fence or house foundation, use a power string trimmer *(above, center)*. Wear shoes and long pants, and put on protective goggles. Consult the owner's manual for operating instructions. Hold the trimmer firmly with both hands and, using a sweeping motion, move the rotating string slowly into the uncut grass from the mowed area, working toward the left whenever possible. If the grass or weeds are very thick and high, cut them down in layers, a section at a time. Lengthen the string as it wears. To prevent damage to trees and shrubs, use grass shears *(above, right)* to trim long grass.

SHARPENING THE LAWN MOWER BLADE

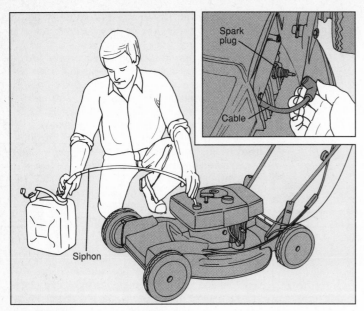

Spark plug

Cable

Siphon

1 **Emptying the gas tank.** Inspect and sharpen the blade of a rotary lawn mower, shown here, at least once a year. First, pull the cable off the spark plug *(inset)*. On some models, the spark plug may be hidden inside the housing; consult your owner's manual. Before turning a gas mower on its side, empty the gas tank (and the oil tank, in the case of a four-cycle engine). Working away from the grass in a well-ventilated area, remove the gas cap. Place one end of the siphon hose into the tank all the way to the bottom, and the other end into a gas can. Pump the siphon bulb until the gas flows through the tube *(above)*, and drain the tank completely.

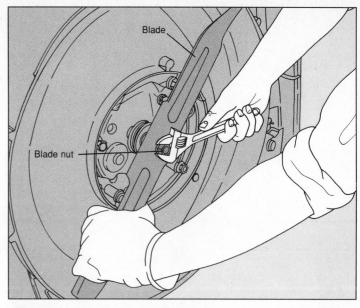

Blade

Blade nut

2 **Removing the blade.** Rest the lawn mower on the side recommended by the owner's manual. To remove a rotary blade, hold one end of the blade with a gloved hand or a rag to keep it from turning. Use an adjustable wrench *(above)* or a socket wrench to loosen the nut or nuts securing the blade to the shaft. Scrape off any accumulated grass clippings with a flat stick and wipe the blade clean with a cloth. Inspect the blade for nicks or cracks. If it is severely damaged, take it to a professional for sharpening or replacement. If the grass blades are ragged and brown after mowing, the blade is dull; sharpen it *(step 3)*.

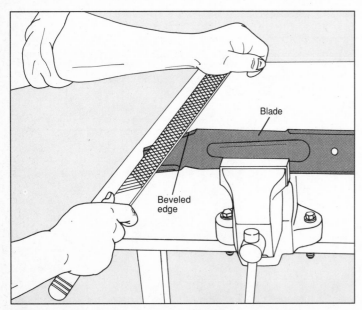

Blade

Beveled edge

3 **Sharpening the blade.** Secure the blade in a bench vise with the beveled edge of one side facing you. Clean off the flat side of the blade by scraping the edge of a file across it once or twice. Then sharpen the bevel: Lay the file against the bevel, holding it at the bevel's original angle (about 25 degrees). Push the file away from you at an angle *(above)*, along the entire edge of the bevel, exerting strong pressure. Pull the file back without applying pressure, and repeat for several strokes. When the beveled edge looks shiny, pass the file once across the flat underside to remove the burr from the edge. Sharpen the other end the same way.

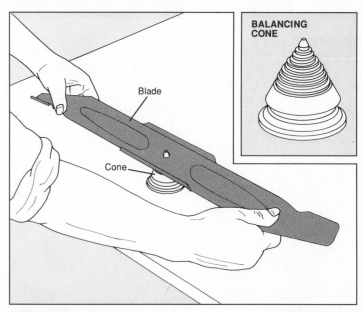

BALANCING CONE

Blade

Cone

4 **Balancing the blade.** An unbalanced blade will damage the mower engine and cut the grass poorly. To determine whether you have sharpened the blade equally on both sides, buy an inexpensive balancing cone *(inset)* at a hardware store. Place the blade on the cone *(above)* and check that the blade balances evenly. If it tips heavily to one side, secure the blade in the vise and file it some more on the heavy side. Once the blade is sharpened and balanced, reinstall it on the mower shaft, bevel side toward the mower. Grease the nut and screw it on tightly; replace any nuts that have stripped threads or have been removed more than four times.

WATERING A LAWN

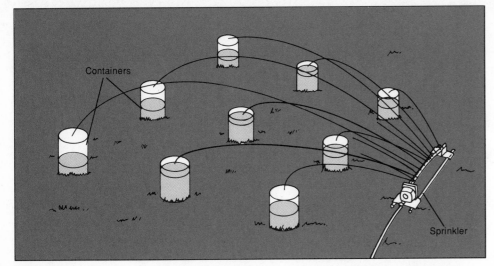

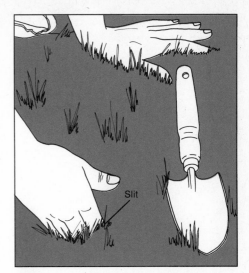

1 **Testing sprinkler efficiency.** Water early in the morning or at night, when there is no wind and no hot sun. Place the sprinkler in an open area of the lawn and turn it on to determine the extent its spray covers. Then turn off the sprinkler and place about 6 to 9 empty cans at various locations within the area *(above)*. Turn on the sprinkler for an hour, then measure the depth of water in each of the cans. An efficient sprinkler will deliver about 1 inch of water in an hour, evenly distributed among the cans. If the water is distributed unevenly, the sprinkler holes may be blocked or the hose adapter dirty. Scrub them with a vinegar-and-water solution, and turn the sprinkler back on to flush it. Replace the sprinkler if it is extremely inefficient. If the water puddles and fails to drain away, wait 24 hours, then aerate or dethatch the lawn *(page 86)*, or evaluate soil drainage *(page 27)*.

2 **Checking water penetration.** Wait 15 to 20 minutes after watering, then use a trowel or spade to cut through the grass and into the soil below at least 8 inches. Push the trowel back to open a slit wide enough to insert your fingers *(above)*. The soil should be moist, but not wet, to a depth of at least 6 inches, in order to provide enough water for the root zone. Adjust watering time to achieve proper penetration.

FERTILIZING A LAWN

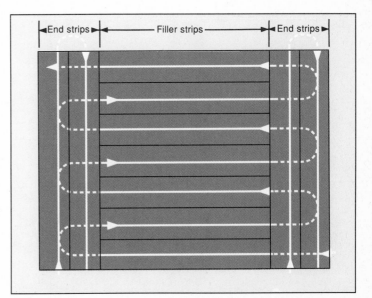

1 **Calculating the fertilizer needs of your lawn.** Most lawns do well with three or four applications of fertilizer per year. The proportion of nutrients should vary according to grass type, age and season; consult your local Cooperative Extension Service for advice. To determine the amount you need, figure the size of the lawn in square feet. A drop spreader *(above)* will ensure even coverage of the lawn, but also makes it easy to apply too much. Set the distributor gauge carefully, and walk fast enough that you don't spread the fertilizer too heavily. To use a broadcast spreader, see page 85. Avoid applying lawn fertilizer containing herbicide near tree roots.

2 **Applying granular fertilizer.** Begin by spreading a strip of fertilizer along one end of a dry lawn. Pull the lever to open the hopper, walk at a normal pace, and close the hopper at the end of the strip to avoid double application. Then turn around, open the hopper again and spread a second strip parallel to the first, using the wheel marks left on the lawn as a guide. Do not overlap fertilized areas. Cover the other end of the lawn with two parallel strips the same way. Finally, cover the lawn in between with filler strips at a right angle to the end strips *(above)*, closing the hopper when turning around over the end strips.

A ROGUES' GALLERY OF WEEDS

GRASS-TYPE WEEDS

Crabgrass. Annual that forms dense patches, smothering lawn. Small, pale-green leaf blades. Spreads by seeds, which develop from July to October. Widespread.

Barnyard grass. Annual with coarse, dark leaves and purplish stems. Spreads by seeds, which develop on stems from July to September. Can be hand-pulled *(page 77)*. Widespread.

Bermuda grass. Warm-season perennial with narrow leaves on 1-foot stems. Turns brown during winter dormancy. Spreads by seeds and overground or underground runners. Widespread.

Quack grass. Perennial with narrow, bluish leaves that grow on tall stems. Spreads by seeds and rapidly-growing underground runners. Seedheads develop on stems from May to September. More common in the North.

Nutsedge. Perennial with yellow-ish leaves. Spreads by seeds and underground runners. Purple or yellow seedheads develop on stems from July to September. Widespread.

Johnsongrass. Perennial with leaves up to 2 feet long. Spreads by seeds or underground runners. Purple seedheads develop on tall stems from June to October. More common in the South.

BROAD-LEAFED WEEDS

Mouse-ear chickweed. Creeping perennial with hairy, dark leaves 1/2 inch long. Spreads by seeds and by overground runners. Seeds germinate throughout growing season. White flowers produce seeds from April to October. Widespread.

Spotted spurge. Annual with red-dish patch on upper surface of small leaves; stems contain milky sap. Spreads by seeds that are produced by pink flowers and germinate throughout growing season. Can be hand-pulled *(page 77)*. Widespread.

Plantain. Rosette-shaped per-ennial with oval leaves 2 to 10 inches long. Spreads by seeds; roots regenerate. White flower stalks produce seeds from May to October. Widespread.

Dandelion. Rosette-shaped perennial with jagged leaves, milky sap in stems and deep taproot. Spreads by seeds; taproot regenerates. Yellow flowers transform into white puffballs contain-ing seeds. Can be hand-pulled *(page 77)*. Widespread.

Black medic. Creeping annual with hairy stems. Spreads by seeds and runners. Yellow flowers produce black seed pods from May to September. Can be hand-pulled *(page 77)*. Discourage by improving nitrogen content of soil *(page 26)*. Widespread.

Curly dock. Rosette-shaped perennial, reddish leaves and deep taproot. Spreads by seeds; taproot regenerates. Reddish flowers pro-duce seeds from June to Septem-ber. Can be hand-pulled *(page 77)*. Widespread.

Identifying and controlling weeds in a lawn. A weed is any plant that grows where it is not wanted. Pictured above are some common broad-leafed and grass-type weeds. Most spread by seeds that may lay dormant for years. Perennials and some annuals also spread by various runners and stems. If you cannot identify a weed, consult your local Cooperative Extension Service for identification, in order to choose an effective control method. Pull out weeds by hand *(page 77)* as soon as they appear; they rob the lawn of water, sun, and nutrients.

Use the tool and method suitable for removal of the weed's entire root system to avoid resprouting. A herbicide may also be used *(page 78)*, but apply it carefully to avoid damaging surrounding plants. Always read the label to ensure that the herbicide is effective against the weed you are killing. Attack weeds in the spring and early summer, before they have a chance to develop deep, complex root systems, or go to seed and reproduce.

REMOVING WEEDS BY HAND

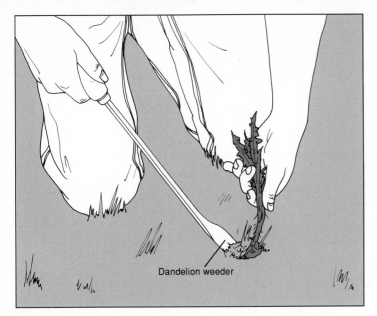

Removing tap-rooted weeds. Weed in early spring, while roots are young and small. Water the lawn the day before to soften the soil. Hold the base of the weed to one side. Push a dandelion weeder down beside the root as deeply as possible. Then pull gently on the plant while levering it up with the weeder *(above)*. If the root breaks, dig down with the weeder to remove all pieces, to prevent resprouting.

Removing shallow-rooted weeds. Annual weeds, and those that send out runners, can be pulled up by hand. Water the lawn the day before to soften the soil. Loosen the soil around the roots with a weeding fork *(above)*, and use it to gently lever up the weed and its roots. Make sure you leave no root fragments behind. Do not compost weeds that have seeds.

SPOT APPLICATION OF HERBICIDES

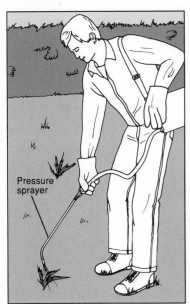

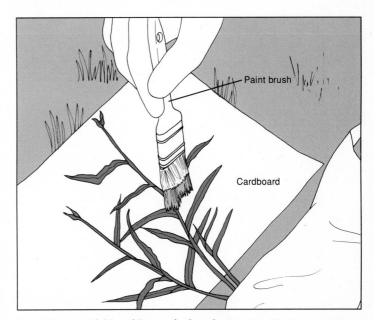

Spraying herbicides on weeds. First identify the weed by consulting the weed gallery *(page 76)* or the Cooperative Extension Service, then choose the appropriate herbicide *(page 78)*. Spray broad-leafed weeds individually to avoid stressing the lawn. Mix the herbicide and load it into the tank *(page 139)* of a pressure sprayer *(above, left)*, or buy a pre-mixed solution in a disposable spray bottle *(above, right)*. Wear rubber gloves and protect nearby plants with a piece of cardboard. Adjust the nozzle and direct a fine spray 2 inches from the weed, coating it lightly with herbicide; avoid letting it drip on the grass. Dispose of leftover solution and clean the applicator *(page 141)*.

Applying herbicide with a paintbrush. First identify the weed by consulting the weed gallery *(page 76)* or the Cooperative Extension Service, then choose the appropriate herbicide *(page 78)*. Wearing rubber gloves, carefully pour a tiny amount of herbicide into a clean jar. To treat a grass-type weed, place a piece of cardboard under it to protect the lawn. Use a paintbrush to spread the herbicide sparingly on the entire weed *(above)*. For broad-leafed weeds, paint 50 percent of the leaf surface with a selective herbicide such as 2,4-D *(page 78)*. Dispose of leftover herbicide. Wipe the herbicide off the paintbrush, wrap it in newspaper and reuse it and the jar only for reapplying herbicide.

HERBICIDES

NAME	TYPE	REMARKS
Ammonium sulfamate	Post-emergent, non-selective, systemic.	Kills unwanted trees, woody plants and vines including hard to control species like poison ivy, poison oak and kudzu. Use during spring and fall. Paint recently cut stumps *(p. 67)*; spot-treat *(p. 77)*.
2,4-D	Post-emergent, selective, systemic.	Use on lawns to kill plantain, dandelion and curly dock. When used in combination with mecoprop and dicamba it will kill spotted spurge, black medic, mouse-ear chickweed, plantain, dandelion, curly dock. Use during spring and fall. Do not use on bentgrass, St Augustine grass or centipede grass. Spot-treat *(p. 77)* or broadcast *(p. 79)*.
DCPA (Trade name: Dacthal)	Pre-emergent, selective.	Use in lawns, flower or vegetable gardens to kill germinating seeds of grasses including barnyard grass, crabgrass and johnsongrass. Kills seedlings of some broad-leafed weeds such as spotted spurge and mouse-ear chickweed. May be available mixed with fertilizer. Apply before weed seeds germinate in the early spring or late fall. Broadcast *(p. 79)* or sprinkle granular form as directed on product label.
Dicamba	Post-emergent, selective, systemic.	When used alone, requires a permit; consult local Cooperative Extension Service. Available in combination with 2,4-D and mecoprop for home lawn use. Kills many broad-leafed weeds in lawns including spotted spurge, black medic, mouse-ear chickweed, plantain, dandelion and curly dock. Use during spring or fall. Spot-treat *(p. 77)* or broadcast *(p. 79)*.
Glyphosate	Post-emergent, non-selective, systemic.	Will kill most vegetation; do not spray when breezy. Use in lawns to kill grass-type weeds including crabgrass, barnyard grass, nutsedge, johnsongrass, bermuda grass, and quack grass; broad leafed weeds including dandelion, plantain, mouse-ear chickweed, spotted spurge, black medic and curly dock. Also used to kill woody plants such as poison ivy and poison oak. Timing of application depends on weed; read product label. Spot-treat *(p. 77)* or broadcast *(p. 79)*.
Mecoprop	Post-emergent, selective, systemic.	When used alone, requires a permit; consult local Cooperative Extension Service. Available in combination with 2,4-D and/or dicamba for home use on lawns to kill mouse-ear chickweed, dandelion, plantain, spotted spurge, curly dock and black medic. Use during spring or fall. Spot-treat *(p. 77)*; or broadcast *(p. 79)*.
Methanearsonates (MSMA, DSMA)	Post-emergent, selective with some systemic effect that kills grasslike weeds.	Sometimes combined with 2,4-D. Use in lawns to kill crabgrass. Do not use on St. Augustine, carpet and centipede grass. Use during spring or fall. Spot-treat *(p. 77)* or broadcast *(p. 79)*.
Siduron	Pre-emergent, selective.	Use on cool-season grass lawns *(p. 72)* to kill seedlings of grass-type weeds such as crabgrass, barnyard grass. Do not use on warm-season grasses *(p. 72)*. May be available mixed with fertilizer. Apply before weed seeds germinate in the early spring or late fall. Sprinkle granular form as directed on product label or broadcast *(p. 79)*.
Triclopyr	Post-emergent, non-selective, systemic.	Will kill most vegetation; do not spray when breezy. Use on woody plants and vines including poison ivy, poison oak and kudzu. Paint onto freshly cut stumps *(p. 67)* or spot-treat *(p. 77)*.

The best defense against weeds is a healthy, well-tended lawn. However, herbicides may be needed to control numerous or persistent weeds. Herbicides can be spot-applied *(page 77)* if individual weeds need to be controlled, broadcast *(page 79)* when large infestations must be eliminated, or sprinkled onto the soil in granular form. Apply post-emergent herbicides when weeds are established and growing. Use pre-emergent herbicides in early spring or late fall to eliminate germinating seeds before they can get a foothold. Systemic herbicides like glyphosate course through the weed, killing the roots as well as the leaves and stems. Non-systemic herbicides defoliate the weed by chemically burning the leaves and stems, injuring the plant beyond the point of recovery. Selective herbicides target a specific type of weed. Non-selective herbicides kill weeds as well as desirable plants and must be used carefully. Always read the instructions on the product label before using any herbicide.

If your plants are suffering from drought stress or lack of nutrients, water *(page 75)*, or fertilize *(page 75)* several days before applying a post-emergent herbicide. Always apply post-emergent herbicides to dry plants; rainfall or watering within 24 hours of application will lessen the herbicide's effect. Since herbicide activity is usually increased when the temperature is high, do not apply when the temperature exceeds 80°F. Take particular care to apply non-selective herbicides on a windless day to ensure that the herbicide does not drift onto other plants, trees or shrubs.

Before applying herbicides, consult the safety tips on page 8. Wear protective clothing such as rubber gloves, a long-sleeved shirt and rubber boots and use a face shield or goggles to protect your eyes from spray mist. Keep children and pets away from treated areas. Never spray into ponds, streams or pools. Store all herbicides in a safe place and do not reuse equipment for any other purpose.

SPRAYING HERBICIDE OVER A LARGE AREA

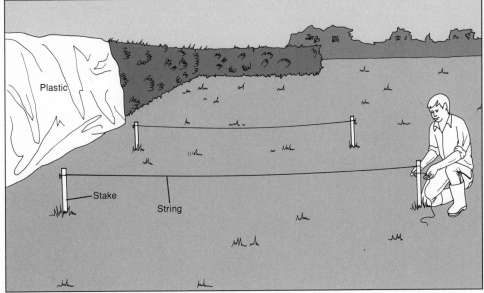

Sectioning and spraying the lawn. Cover nearby plants with sheets of plastic, and spray on a calm day in early morning. Set up two parallel guidelines of stakes and string to divide the lawn into sections *(above, left)*, ensuring complete coverage and guarding against double application. Mix the herbicide according to label directions. Load a pressure sprayer *(page 139)* or hose-end sprayer *(page 140)*, and adjust its spray to cover the width between the string guidelines. Wear long pants, waterproof shoes and rubber gloves. Stand inside the sectioned-off area and, walking backward, spray side to side in a sweeping motion *(above, right)*. After spraying the area between the string lines, leapfrog one set of stakes over the other to mark off the adjoining unsprayed area, and repeat. When you have completed spraying the entire lawn, put up a sign warning people to keep off the lawn for 24 hours, or the time period indicated on the herbicide label. Clean the sprayer and store it safely *(page 141)*.

ROLLING BACK AND REMOVING SOD

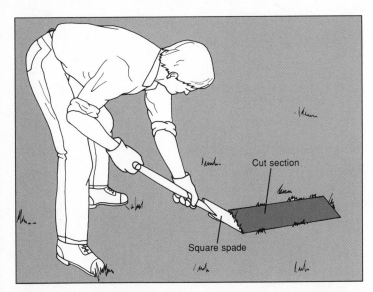

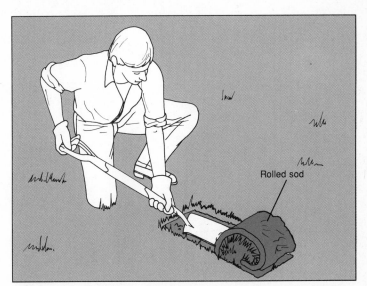

1 Cutting the sod edges. Water the area a day before cutting the sod to moisten the soil. Using a spade with a sharp, square blade, cut straight down through the sod to a depth of 2 inches, outlining a long rectangular section the width of the spade blade. If you are not moving the section of sod, but just rolling it back to perform a soil test or level out bumps, cut through only one of the narrow ends, so you can roll the sod back after completion. To start rolling the sod, push the spade blade at a 45-degree angle under the narrow end *(above)*, and cut through the roots of the grass about 1 inch deep.

2 Rolling back the sod. Push the spade horizontally under the sod as far as it will go, severing the roots 1 inch deep. As you cut the sod, roll it back, taking care not to break it or cut through it from underneath. Cut and roll the sod in this manner until you have completely separated the marked-off section. Cover the rolled-up sod with wet burlap to keep it from drying out. Test or repair the soil as required. Before replacing the sod, water the soil with a high-phosphorus fertilizer solution *(page 26)* to encourage root growth. Unroll the sod over the soil and tamp it down. Fill the cracks around the edges with soil, and water the sodded area to a depth of 6 inches.

PREPARING A SMALL PATCH FOR RESEEDING OR REPLANTING

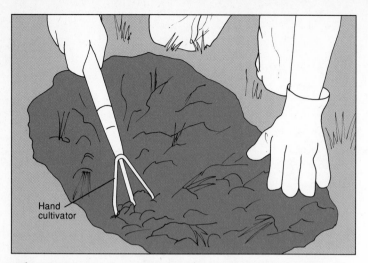

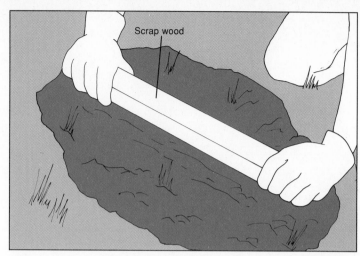

1 **Cultivating the soil.** Remove dead turf by rolling back the sod *(page 79)*. If you are resodding the area, use a sharp knife to square off its sides. Pick out roots, stones and other debris. Then use a cultivator *(above)* to dig up all weeds and their roots, and to loosen the soil to a depth of 4 inches. If the soil is heavily compacted, break it up with a garden fork. Evaluate the soil texture *(page 20)* and amend if necessary. Add topsoil if needed to raise the area to the surrounding soil. Water the soil with a high-phosphorus fertilizer solution *(page 26)* to encourage root growth.

2 **Leveling and firming the soil.** Use a scrap of 2-by-4 to firm and level the soil in the patch *(above)*. First locate high and low spots with your hands, and spread the soil evenly. Then tamp it down, leaning heavily on the 2-by-4 to make a flat, smooth surface. If seeding, plugging or sprigging, the soil should be level with the surrounding soil. Add more topsoil if necessary. If laying a patch of sod to repair the spot, tamp the soil lower than the surrounding soil by about 3/4 inch, or by the thickness of the replacement sod.

RESEEDING A SMALL PATCH

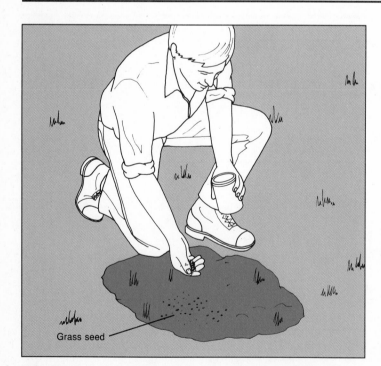

1 **Reseeding the patch.** Lightly rake the surface of the patch to loosen the soil to a depth of 1/4 to 1/2 inch. Sprinkle seed on a small area by hand *(above)*. Be sure that the seed used is the same species as the surrounding lawn. Each grass type requires a specific amount of seed per square inch, detailed on the seed label; if in doubt, try to spread about 18 seeds per square inch. If there are patches of thin grass around the area being repaired, sprinkle some seed over these areas as well.

2 **Tamping the surface.** To protect the seeds from birds and wind, gently spread a thin layer of soil over them with the top edge of a rake. Then use the rake to tamp the soil firmly over the seeded area *(above)*. Water the patch to a depth of 1/2 inch with a very fine spray, and keep the soil moist for two weeks, until the seeds have had a chance to establish roots. For sandy, fast-drying soils, apply a 1/2-inch mulch of peat moss to help retain moisture and discourage weeds.

REPLANTING A BARE PATCH WITH PLUGS

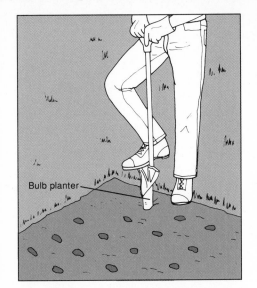 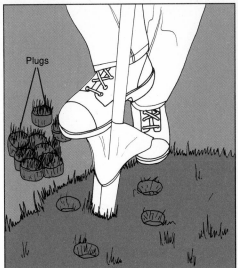 

1 **Cutting holes for planting.** Purchase plugs of warm-season grasses from a nursery, or cut your own plugs from an established lawn or from a piece of sod *(step 2)*. Using a plug-cutting tool or a bulb planter *(above)*, cut evenly spaced holes 6 to 12 inches apart over the area to be planted. (Holes spaced 12 inches apart may take up to 5 months to fill in.) The holes should be as deep as the plugs, usually 2 inches.

2 **Cutting and planting the plugs.** Before cutting plugs, water the sod or lawn well. Step on the foot bar of a bulb cutter, pushing it into the lawn about 2 inches, or into sod to its full depth. Cut plugs from sod *(above, left)* as close together as possible to avoid wasting the sod. Cut plugs from a lawn about 18 inches apart, to avoid damage to the lawn. Insert each plug into a hole *(above, right)* and step on it to set it firmly in the soil. Crumble clumps of dirt from the plug holes and scatter them over the ground. Plant the plugs in one 4-foot-square section at a time, and water each section well within one hour of planting. Keep the soil moist for two weeks, until the roots are established, then return to a regular watering schedule.

PLANTING A BARE PATCH WITH SPRIGS

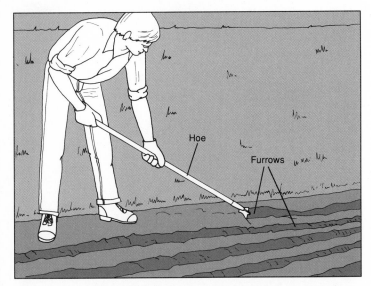 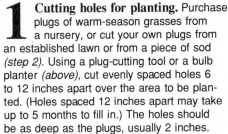 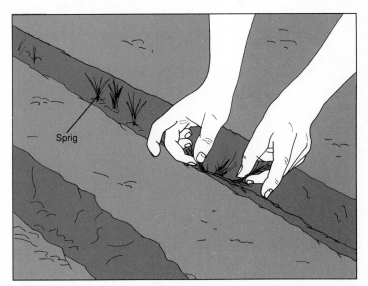

1 **Furrowing the soil.** Grass types that spread by means of underground runners can be planted by sprigging, using individual grass plants. Buy sprigs of the same grass type as the lawn at a nursery, or make your own by carefully pulling apart a section of sod cut from another area of the lawn *(page 79)*. Protect the sprigs by covering them with wet burlap. Prepare the planting area *(page 80)*, adding soil and amending if necessary. Then use a garden hoe to make parallel, V-shaped furrows about 3 inches deep and 4 inches apart *(above)*. To prevent trampling the furrows in a large area, prepare and plant them two at a time.

2 **Planting the sprigs.** Set the sprigs in the furrows, about 6 inches apart or as recommended by the nursery, with their green shoots pointing up *(above)*. Press soil firmly around their stems. Then push the furrows back down around them, taking care to leave the shoots exposed. If purchased sprigs were packed in peat moss, use it to mulch around the transplants. Apply a complete fertilizer such as 10-10-10, and moisten the soil to a depth of 3 inches with a fine spray. Keep the area moist until the sprigs are well-rooted—about two weeks—then return to a normal watering schedule.

REPLANTING A LARGE AREA OF GRASS

1 **Tearing up the sod and cultivating the soil.** Spray severely weed-infested lawns with glyphosate *(page 79)* to kill off all vegetation, and wait 15 days. To remove old grass and turn over the soil in a large area, rent a power tiller. A rear-tine model *(left)* is best for tearing up tough sod. Ask the rental agency to install blades that will cut through grass, and have them teach you how to start and stop the machine. See Tools & Techniques *(page 132)* for general operating instructions. Water the area the day before to make it moist, but not wet. Start tilling in an area away from the house, driveway or trees; move closer to them when you have become familiar with the action of the tiller.

Wear sturdy shoes or boots, long pants and gloves. Start the tiller, making sure the tines are up off the grass and the speed is low. Then lower the tines into the ground. The machine will lurch into motion as the revolving tines dig into the sod. Walk slowly, letting the machine move at its own pace. Cut through the lawn from end to end in parallel rows, 3 to 4 inches deep. Go over the lawn a second time at a right angle to the first, tilling as deeply as possible (about 8 inches) to leave clumps the size of a fist. Go over it a third time only if necessary.

2 **Raking up the clumps.** Use a garden rake to break up soil clumps and to gather grass clumps left on the surface *(above)*. Bag grass for disposal if the lawn was diseased or if you applied herbicide, otherwise compost it. Clumps of grass turned under will decompose, adding nutrients to the soil. Remove stones and other debris turned up by the tiller. Leave the area alone for a week to allow the grass and weeds to die out. Dig up any newly-sprouted weeds with a hoe and dispose of them.

3 **Working in amendments.** Test the soil pH, fertility, texture and drainage *(page 16)* and amend as required. It may also be necessary to add a new layer of topsoil. Work the amendment into the pile of topsoil, then spread it evenly over the surface *(above)*. Turn the amended mixture in to the new lawn bed with the power tiller. Using a drop spreader *(page 75)*, apply a high-phosphorus fertilizer such as 5-15-10 over the soil to ensure good root development, or use a fertilizer formula that will correct any deficiencies indicated by testing.

 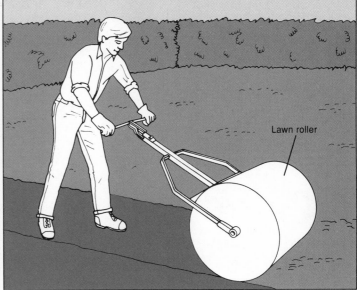

4 Smoothing the soil bed. Use the rake to spread and level the soil, sloping it slightly away from the house *(above, left)*. Take care not to create any high or low spots. Use a long, straight board to check for flatness across the surface. Rent a lawn roller and fill it one-third to one-half full of water. Roll the area from one direction, and then at a right angle to it *(above, right)*. Rolling does not just firm the soil, it also makes high and low spots more obvious. Remove soil from high spots and add it to low spots. Rake the area smooth, then roll it again with the roller empty of water. If you are replanting with sod *(below)*, the level of the soil should be 3/4 inch below the level of the driveway or sidewalk. If reseeding, see page 85; if sprigging or plugging, go to page 81.

REPLANTING A LAWN WITH SOD

 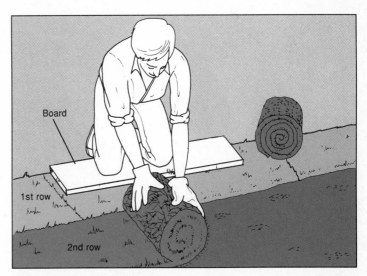

1 Laying the first row. Though expensive, sod provides an instant carpet over a bare space and is the surest way of establishing a lawn in shade. Consult the grass chart on page 72, and purchase sod from a reputable nursery. Protect the new sod from sun and wind by laying wet burlap over it until you are ready to install it. Lay all the sod on the day of delivery. Lay the first row along a straight driveway or sidewalk *(above)*, or use stakes and a string to provide a guideline. Without breaking or stretching the sod, unroll strips and lay them end to end, butting closely. To trim excess length, see step 3.

2 Laying succeeding rows of sod. Kneeling on a board on the first row of sod, butt a strip of sod snugly against the first row. Stagger its position so that its end lines up at the midpoint of the first strip of sod *(above)*, creating a brick-wall pattern. Continue placing strips end to end, butting them firmly against each other and the first row. Move the board as you go; it helps tamp the roots into the underlying soil. Begin watering the new sod within 15 minutes after the first strip is laid, completely soaking it with at least 1 inch of water. (This is most easily done with a soaker hose.) If laying sod on a steep slope, you may need to secure the strips with stakes, which are left in until the sod roots are established in the soil.

REPLANTING A LAWN WITH SOD (continued)

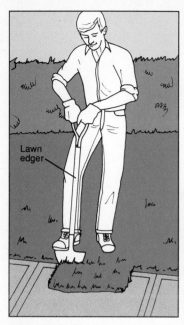

Lawn edger

Utility knife

Lawn roller

3 **Trimming sod.** Avoid wasting sod. At the end of a row, trim off any excess, and use it to start the next row. Position the blade of a lawn edger along the line to be cut. Step on the edger *(above, left)* to force it into the sod, and rock it sideways to cut through. Curved pieces and end pieces too small to be used can be trimmed off with a utility knife after all the sod is laid. Lift up the sod and slice through it *(above, right)*, much like trimming a carpet.

4 **Tamping the sod with a lawn roller.** Kneeling on a board while laying the sod *(step 2)* has already helped to tamp down the sod. To establish root contact with the soil and to smooth out small bumps and air pockets, go over the freshly sodded lawn with an empty lawn roller *(above)*. (A small roller may need the weight of some water.) Roll the area from several directions. For a very small area, tamp the sod with a board and rubber mallet.

Topsoil

Crack

5 **Filling cracks and breaks.** Fill a bucket with topsoil, and check the sodded area for cracks, breaks and exposed edges. Spread soil into all seams between the rows of sod *(above)*, to keep the edges of the sod from dying due to moisture loss. In the future, whenever you spot an open seam, fill it with topsoil and keep it well watered.

6 **Restoring the grass texture.** Use a lawn rake to fluff up the grass blades *(above)*, breaking up and working in any small clumps of soil left from unrolling the sod. Then water the sod well, to a depth of 6 inches. Keep traffic off the lawn, and water deeply and frequently for the first two to three weeks until the sod is firmly rooted. Gradually taper off watering for the following two weeks, and return to a regular watering schedule about a month after sodding.

PLANTING A NEW LAWN FROM SEED

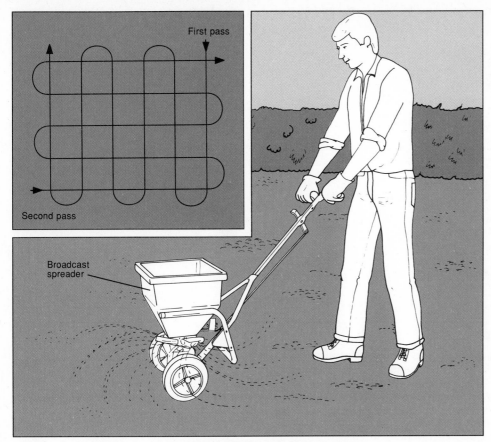

First pass

Second pass

Broadcast spreader

1 **Sowing seed.** Seed a new lawn in spring if possible, well after the risk of frost is past. Prepare the area *(page 82)*, and consult the grass chart *(page 72)* to choose an appropriate type. Figure the dimensions of the lawn in square feet, and read the instructions on the grass seed bag to determine how many square feet one bag will cover. Buy enough bags at once to seed the entire area. Use stakes and string to mark off an area that can be covered with one bag, and put one half the bag into a broadcast spreader. (To use a drop spreader, see page 75.) Starting 3 feet from the side of the marked area, push the broadcast spreader up and down the area in parallel rows about 6 feet apart *(left)*—the seed is thrown about 3 feet on each side of the spreader. Walk fast enough so that all the seed is distributed over the entire marked area in one pass. Note any corners the seed does not reach, and seed them by hand later. Repeat with the other half of the bag of seed, spreading these rows at a right angle over the first rows *(inset)*. Mark off and seed succeeding areas of the lawn the same way. Check from time to time that the coverage is even; most grasses are sown at about 18 seeds per square inch.

2 **Raking and mulching.** Lightly rake the seed under with a garden rake *(above)* to a depth of 1/4 to 1/2 inch. Work in a direction away from the raked area. After raking, use an empty lawn roller to tamp down the surface *(page 83)*. For sandy, fast-draining soils and warm climates, spread a thin layer of decomposable mulch that will retain moisture but allow light to pass through, such as clean straw or peat moss. A covering of cheesecloth or tobacco netting will keep birds from eating the seed.

3 **Watering and mowing.** After mulching, water with a fine spray, moistening the soil to 1/2 inch *(above)*. Water once a day, more often in hot weather, for the first two weeks. During the following two weeks, taper off watering until you reach a normal schedule *(page 75)*. Mow when the new grass has reached its highest recommended height *(page 72)*, first making sure that the mower blade is very sharp *(page 74)*. Leave the grass clippings on the lawn. Hand-pull weeds; do not apply herbicides before the fourth mowing.

AERATING A LAWN

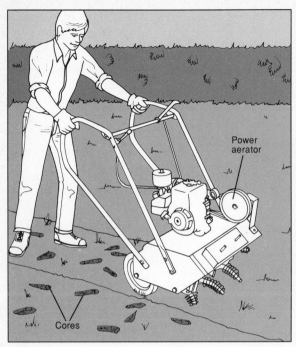

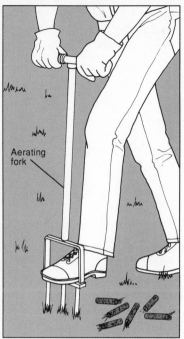

1 **Aerating a lawn.** Aerating opens small, deep holes through the sod into the soil, allowing air and water to penetrate a compacted or a heavily-thatched lawn. Water the lawn the night before to soften the soil. For a large area, such as an entire lawn, use a power aerator, available from a tool rental company. Have them teach you how to start and operate the machine. Check with your Cooperative Extension Service for the ideal aeration depth. Most power aerators will remove and toss aside small cores up to 2 inches deep. Some machines open up holes through a process called shatter-coring, which leaves no cores behind. Go over the entire lawn as you would with a lawn mower *(above, left)*. A power aerator is heavier, but don't try to push it; it runs forward at its own pace. To aerate corners or small areas, use an aerating fork. Step on the bar to push the tines their full depth into the soil *(above, right)*. When you pull out the tines, the cores will drop out. Aerate at intervals of 10 to 20 holes per square foot.

2 **Spreading an amendment.** Rake up sod and soil cores left on the lawn and compost them, or break them up in place. Shovel coarse sand mixed with peat moss over the aerated lawn *(above)*, or spread plain sand and fertilize afterwards *(page 75)*. Use the back edge of a garden rake to spread a 1/2-inch layer of the mixture over the lawn, letting it fall into the holes. Water the lawn to a depth of at least 6 inches.

DETHATCHING A LAWN

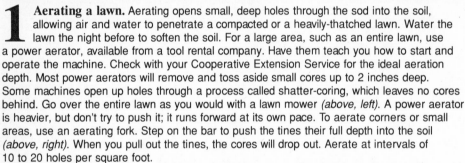

1 **Checking for thatch buildup.** Using a garden trowel, cut down through the sod and push it aside to open a slit in the lawn *(left)*. Look for a mat of densely intertwined roots, runners and stems *(inset)* between the grass blades and the soil level. A layer of thatch up to 1/2 inch thick can be beneficial, serving as a mulch to retain moisture and prevent weeds. But thatch thicker than 1/2 inch keeps moisture and air from reaching the roots, and encourages superficial root growth, making the thatch even worse and encouraging disease. Dethatch warm-season grasses *(step 2)* once or twice a year to prevent excessive thatch buildup. Thatch too thick to be cut through with a power dethatcher requires aeration *(above)*.

DETHATCHING A LAWN (continued)

2 **Dethatching the lawn.** Dethatching is best done in the spring, and again in the fall, if necessary. Special dethatching attachments are available for some lawn mowers. You can also rent a power dethatcher from a tool rental company. Have them teach you how to start and run the dethatcher; most are operated much like a lawn mower. Wear heavy shoes and long pants, and follow the safety precautions in the owner's manual. Adjust the cutting depth of the blades to cut through the entire thatch depth, plus 1/4 inch into the soil. Check the lawn after a few feet to make sure the depth setting is correct. Run the dethatcher slowly over the lawn *(above)* without forcing it. Follow the same pattern as for a lawn mower, but don't overlap the dethatching rows.

3 **Raking the lawn.** The dethatcher leaves behind a trail of thatch that it has pulled up. With a lawn rake, gather the mass of grass and roots into piles *(above)*, and dispose of it. To help prevent thatch, fertilize with a low-nitrogen fertilizer *(page 75)* and bag or rake up the clippings every other mowing. Or apply an organic fertilizer; its bacterial action helps break down thatch.

OVERSEEDING AN ESTABLISHED LAWN

Spreading the seed. To produce dense growth and discourage weeds in a patchy lawn, or to establish a temporary lawn cover over a dormant warm-season grass, spread seed over the established lawn. Buy seed that is compatible with the lawn's grass type. First mow the lawn as closely as possible by adjusting the lawn mower blade to its lowest setting *(page 73)*. Then use a power dethatcher *(above)* or a garden rake to scratch the soil, making shallow furrows for the seed. Rake off any debris left on the surface by the lawn mower and dethatcher. Spread a starter fertilizer *(page 85)* over the lawn. Using a broadcast spreader *(page 85)*, distribute the seed over the entire lawn *(left)*. Check on the grass-seed bag, or with your Cooperative Extension Service for the recommended distribution rate; an established lawn usually requires double the amount of seed that is sown for a new lawn. Keep the lawn well-watered *(page 85)* for the first two weeks, until the seeds have rooted, then return to a normal watering schedule.

GROUND COVER

Ground cover is commonly welcomed as the busy gardener's alternative to the challenge of keeping a lawn in putting-green perfection. Because some varieties can flourish where grass will not—beneath shade trees or on a steep slope—the homeowner may mistake its versatility (illustrated by the examples below) for carefree maintenance. In fact, like most plants, a ground cover requires attention and care. Before planting a ground cover, study the light and soil conditions in the area you wish to cover and ask a reputable garden nursery to recommend a species that will readily adapt. Ground cover encompasses a wide variety of plants, many of which

naturally spread so quickly that they would be considered weeds if they turned up uninvited. They range from low-growing perennials *(Vinca)* and shrubs *(Juniperus)*, to familiar herbs such as thyme *(Thymus)*, to the ever-popular ivies *(Hedera)*. They may be deciduous like cranberry cotoneaster *(Cotoneaster apiculatus)* or evergreen like bearberry *(Arctostaphylos uva-ursi)*, broad-leafed like Bethlehem sage *(Pulmonaria saccharata)* or needle-leafed like Scotch heather *(Calluna vulgaris)*.

For the first couple of years after planting most new ground cover, your primary chores are to weed, water, fertilize and

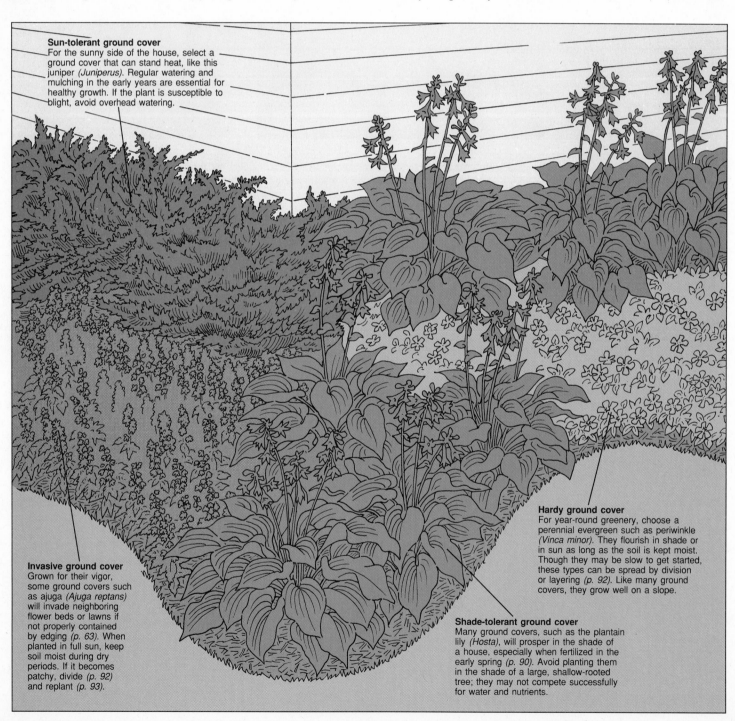

Sun-tolerant ground cover
For the sunny side of the house, select a ground cover that can stand heat, like this juniper *(Juniperus)*. Regular watering and mulching in the early years are essential for healthy growth. If the plant is susceptible to blight, avoid overhead watering.

Invasive ground cover
Grown for their vigor, some ground covers such as ajuga *(Ajuga reptans)* will invade neighboring flower beds or lawns if not properly contained by edging *(p. 63)*. When planted in full sun, keep soil moist during dry periods. If it becomes patchy, divide *(p. 92)* and replant *(p. 93)*.

Hardy ground cover
For year-round greenery, choose a perennial evergreen such as periwinkle *(Vinca minor)*. They flourish in shade or in sun as long as the soil is kept moist. Though they may be slow to get started, these types can be spread by division or layering *(p. 92)*. Like many ground covers, they grow well on a slope.

Shade-tolerant ground cover
Many ground covers, such as the plantain lily *(Hosta)*, will prosper in the shade of a house, especially when fertilized in the early spring *(p. 90)*. Avoid planting them in the shade of a large, shallow-rooted tree; they may not compete successfully for water and nutrients.

mulch much as you would a perennial flower bed *(page 52)*. When the ground cover becomes established and has grown dense enough to shade the ground and choke out weeds, you can begin to relax your vigil. Even then, continue to cast an attentive eye over the plants periodically. When patchy areas appear, replenish the threadbare carpet with existing ground cover by dividing or layering *(page 92)*. These propagation techniques save on buying more plants while ensuring a perfect match of type, species and color. Take into account the plant's growth habits, such as how fast it spreads, whether it thrives in sun or shade or whether spring pruning is required.

Many types of ground cover gain new strength from judicious pruning when spring comes; some can even be mowed *(page 73)*. Other, more vigorous species need no encouragement at all; the challenge with them is to control their spread.

To arrest problems, consult the Troubleshooting Guide below. In general, the most common symptoms are listed first in the chart. When you are referred to the Pests and Diseases chapter *(page 112)*, be sure to read the information on pesticidal control carefully. Further guidelines on the choice and use of pesticides are presented in Tools and Techniques *(page 129)*.

TROUBLESHOOTING GUIDE

continued ►

SYMPTOM	POSSIBLE CAUSE	PROCEDURE
Stunted growth, yellowed leaves; plants die, leaving bare patches of compacted soil	Excessive foot traffic	Install stepping stones; cultivate bare patches *(p. 19)* □○ and replant *(p. 93)* ▪○ with taller ground cover to discourage traffic; or replace with grass *(small area, p. 80)* ▪○; *(large area, p. 82)* ▪◑
	Heavy water flow from gutter or downspout	Correct or redirect water flow; cultivate bare patches *(p. 19)* ▪○ and extend ground cover over bare patch by layering or division *(p. 92)* ▪○
Leaves too small, pale green or yellow; plant growth slow; leaves drop or bare patches emerge	Soil pH wrong for plant; nitrogen deficiency	See Pests and Diseases *(p. 119)*. Test soil pH *(p. 23)* ▪○ and adjust *(p. 24)* ▪○; test soil nitrogen content *(p. 25)* ▪○, consult fertilizer chart *(p. 26)* and fertilize *(p. 90)* □○. Extend ground cover over bare patch by layering or division *(p. 92)* ▪○
Spindly growth, leaves dark green and sparse, leaves drop	Insufficient light	Prune tree or shrub to admit light *(p. 94)* ▪◑, or replant area with shade-tolerant ground cover *(p. 93)* ▪○
Bare spots develop in established ground cover	Dog or cat using ground cover	Spread commercial animal repellant; fence in ground cover
	Soil contaminated	Consult the cooperative extension service
Older (bottom) leaves turn yellow, growth slow, roots shallow and rotting	Soil too moist due to poor drainage, too much rain or overwatering	Dig up and dispose of rotted plants *(p. 133)* □○. Evaluate soil moisture *(p. 18)* □○ and allow it to dry out; evaluate drainage *(p. 27)* ▪○ and install a drainage system *(p. 30)* ▪● if necessary, or change soil structure *(p. 28)* ▪● and replant with new ground cover *(p. 93)* ▪○
	Soil too clayey (high clay content)	Evaluate soil texture *(p. 20)* ▪○; amend soil *(p. 21)* □○ and replant with new ground cover *(p. 93)* ▪○
Leaves pale green or yellow, edges turn brown and dry; plants wilt, bare spots emerge	Heat scorch or drought stress due to insufficient water	Water ground cover *(p. 90)* □○; install a drip irrigation system *(p. 36)* ▪◑
	Soil too sandy	Evaluate soil texture *(p. 20)* ▪○; amend soil *(p. 21)* □○ and replant with new ground cover *(p. 93)* ▪○
Blackened stems, distorted leaves, buds don't open	Winter kill (plants killed by cold or frost)	Prune damaged stems before new growth appears *(p. 91)* ▪○; mulch soil before next winter frost *(p. 134)* ▪○
Leaves brown and burnt-looking; stunted growth	Salty soil due to excessive fertilizing, road salt or sea salt	See Pests and Diseases *(p. 119)*. Leach soil *(p. 19)* □◑; amend soil *(p. 21)* □○
New leaves pale green or yellow; veins stand out	Alkaline soil; iron deficiency	See Pests and Diseases *(p. 119)*
Plant doesn't flower	Too much nitrogen fertilizer used	Test nitrogen level *(p. 25)* ▪○; leach soil of nitrogen *(p. 19)* ▪○ and amend soil *(p. 21)* ▪○
	Flower buds removed by pruning	Prune correctly in proper season *(p. 91)* ▪○
Sparse, straggly growth, low flower production	Neglect	Rejuvenate ground cover by pruning *(p. 91)* ▪○ or, if appropriate species, by mowing on highest setting of lawn mower *(p. 73)* □○
Ground cover invading lawn or garden	Naturally invasive species overgrown	Prune back stems and runners, and control growth by cutting through roots *(p. 91)* ▪○; install lawn edging *(p. 63)* ▪○

DEGREE OF DIFFICULTY: □ Easy ▪ Moderate ■ Complex
ESTIMATED TIME: ○ Less than 1 hour ◑ 1 to 3 hours ● Over 3 hours

TROUBLESHOOTING GUIDE (continued)

SYMPTOM	POSSIBLE CAUSE	PROCEDURE
Weeds invading ground cover	Young ground cover not yet established	Remove weeds (p. 52) □○; mulch (p. 21) □○
Leaves chewed along edges, stems chewed at ground level	Cutworms	See Pests and Diseases (p. 113)
Holes in leaves, leaves may be sheared off; silvery trails around plants	Snails or slugs	See Pests and Diseases (p. 113)
Leaves streaked and flecked, tiny insects on underside of leaves; when leaves disturbed, insects flutter	Whiteflies, aphids	See Pests and Diseases (p. 118)
Drying, dropping leaves with yellow spots	Spider mites	See Pests and Diseases (p. 118). Water and fertilize properly (p. 90) □○
Leaves spotted and discolored or powdery	Bacterial or fungal leaf spot disease, or powdery mildew	See Pests and Diseases (p. 120)
Brown or yellow spots on underside of leaves	Rust disease	See Pests and Diseases (p. 121)
White bumps on new growth; leaves discolored, dropping	Scale insects	See Pests and Diseases (p. 126)

DEGREE OF DIFFICULTY: □ Easy ◩ Moderate ■ Complex
ESTIMATED TIME: ○ Less than 1 hour ◔ 1 to 3 hours ● Over 3 hours

MAINTAINING HEALTHY GROUND COVER

Fertilizing. Consult a local garden nursery or a plant-specific gardening guide to learn your ground cover's fertilizing needs. Do not fertilize most established ground covers until soil tests for pH *(page 23)* or fertility *(page 25)* confirm the need for it. Choose a correctly balanced fertilizer *(page 26)*. Water the ground cover *(right)* the night before to moisten the soil. To fertilize small areas of sparse ground cover, lift the leaves or runners away from the soil. Wearing gloves, sprinkle the fertilizer in a thin layer around the base of each plant *(above)* and work it into the soil *(page 19)*. To fertilize a large, dense area, spray a liquid fertilizer over the ground cover using a hose-end sprayer *(page 139)*. Immediately wash the leaves with a brisk jet of water to prevent fertilizer burn.

Watering. To replenish dehydrated ground cover, place a lawn sprinkler on the border of the bed *(above)*, and adjust the spray so that it covers the entire area evenly. Leave it on until puddles start to form on the ground; this may take over an hour. Make sure that the watering moistens the soil to the full depth of the roots, usually 4 to 8 inches. Wait until the soil dries out before watering again. Assess soil moisture *(page 18)* to a depth of 2 inches; if it feels dry, water. Gently water newly-planted ground cover once or twice a day for about two weeks or until wilting stops, using a hose with a spray nozzle. If the ground cover was originally rooted in 2 1/2- to 4-inch pots, the root ball is established and the ground cover can be watered as shown above. A drip watering system *(page 36)* is also effective.

PRUNING GROUND COVER

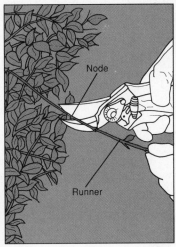

Pruning dead and diseased growth. Disease, insects, extremes of temperature, road salt and fertilizer are among the most common causes of discoloration and death in ground cover. Removal of damaged parts is necessary not only to halt the spread of disease, but also to rid the plant of weakened areas that might invite further infection. Wearing gloves, use pruning shears to cut straight through the healthy part of the stem, just above a leaf node beyond the damaged part *(above)*. If the plant was diseased, disinfect the shears with household bleach or rubbing alcohol after use, and dispose of all diseased growth carefully *(page 133)*.

Rejuvenating ground cover. Prune once a year, in early spring. A low-growing lawn substitute of the type that can be walked on can usually be mowed *(page 73)*; consult a gardening guide or your extension service to be sure. Most ground covers require hand pruning: Use pruning shears to cut through the stem or runner just above a node. To promote bushy growth of herbaceous ground cover such as Japanese spurge *(Pachysandra terminalis)*, cut back the stems about halfway *(above, left)*. To trim ground covers that send out runners, such as periwinkle *(Vinca minor)*, lift the runner and pull it taut, then cut it no closer than the third or fourth node from the parent plant *(above, right)*.

CONTROLLING THE SPREAD OF GROUND COVER

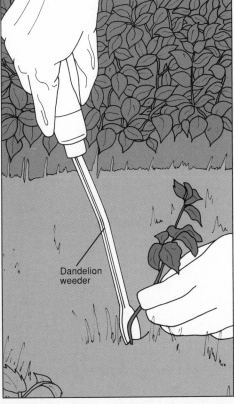

Restraining invading ground cover. Rampant ground cover with an underground-spreading root system, such as goutweed *(Aegopodium)*, can be temporarily contained by pruning with a sharp spade. Slice straight down into the soil at the edge of the ground cover to the full depth of the roots, usually about 6 to 8 inches *(far left)*. Repeat along the entire border. Control rapid-growing ground cover with surface runners, such as periwinkle *(Vinca minor)*, by pruning as shown above, right.

When ground cover begins to pop up in a lawn or flower bed, weed it out immediately before it grows beyond control. Use a dandelion weeder to remove deeply rooted plants *(near left)*; hold the base of the ground cover with one hand as you push the blade down into the soil alongside the root. Then lever the plant up with the weeder. You may be able to pull up shallow-rooted ground cover by hand. Otherwise, use a weeding fork *(page 52)*. Stop ground cover from encroaching on neighboring beds and lawns by installing lawn edging *(page 63)*.

PROPAGATING GROUND COVER BY LAYERING

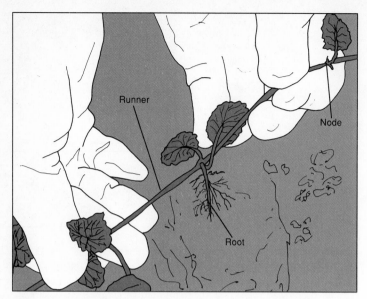

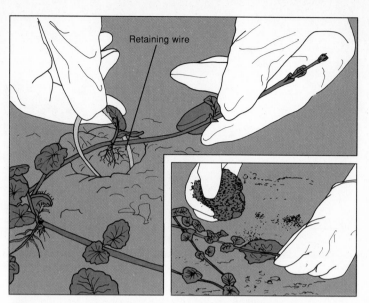

1 **Choosing a runner.** Plants such as creeping jenny *(Lysimachia nummularia, above)* and English ivy *(Hedera helix)* spread by sending out overground runners that root from nodes. Runners can be trained to cover a bare spot in a technique known as layering. Choose a runner close to the bare spot you want to cover and pull it up gently. A rooted runner *(above)* will resist a little. If the runner is unrooted, use a fingernail to wound it slightly near a node. The nodes of some ground covers, such as cotoneaster or scrambling forsythia, benefit from a dusting with root stimulator; consult a nursery.

2 **Burying the runner.** Prepare a small, dish-shaped hole 2 to 4 inches deep, using a garden trowel. Direct the runner over it so that its roots or the rooting node lie in the hole. If the runner springs up, pin it down with a 4-inch length of wire bent in a U shape; place it close to the node or root and press it into the soil *(above)*. Cover the runner with topsoil *(inset)*. Generally, to cover an area about 3 feet by 3 feet, you must repeat this procedure with three to five runners. Water the area thoroughly with a sprinkler or watering can, then mulch *(page 21)*.

PROPAGATING GROUND COVER BY DIVIDING

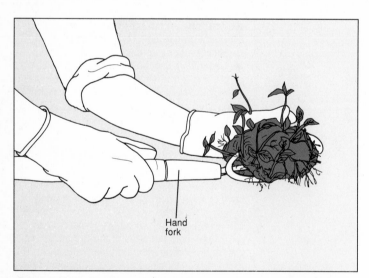

1 **Freeing a clump of plants for division.** Most established ground covers, especially those that grow in large clumps, can be divided and then replanted to fill bare spots or to start new areas of ground cover. Early spring, before growth begins, is the best time to divide. Water the ground cover thoroughly a couple of days ahead. Prepare the soil *(page 93, step 1)*, before digging up the clumps. Choose a clump of six to eight stems within a dense growth of ground cover. With a garden spade, cut a circle around the clump about 3 to 6 inches outside the roots. Then use a hand fork to lever it up *(above)*. Retain the soil around the root system.

2 **Dividing and trimming the plant.** Carefully pull apart the clump *(above, left)*. If the soil is densely packed around the roots, gently tap the roots against the ground to loosen the soil, then separate the stems by hand or with a hand fork. Use pruning shears to cut off dead stems or wilted leaves *(above, right)* and discolored or soggy roots. Repeat this procedure to divide other clumps. Replant one or two stems in each original hole *(step 2, page 93)* and prepare holes in the bare area for planting the remaining stems *(step 1, page 93)*.

PLANTING GROUND COVER

1 **Planting new ground cover.** Before planting a large area, either by division *(page 90)* or from nursery flats, test the soil pH *(page 23)* and fertility *(page 25)*, and evaluate the texture of the soil *(page 20)*. Before planting, adjust the soil as required: Use a garden fork or spade to break up the soil *(page 19)* and work in the appropriate amendments *(page 21)* to a depth of 6 inches. When planting ground cover from nursery flats, lift the rooting medium and plants from the flat, then carefully separate the stems as you would when dividing *(page 92)*. Prepare a small pocket in the soil about 4 to 6 inches deep using a garden trowel, and lower the plant into the hole with the other hand *(left)*.

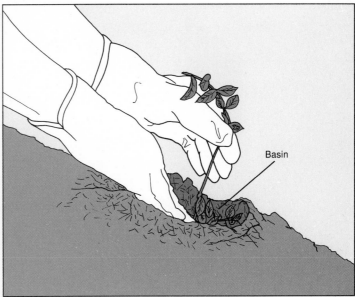

Basin

2 **Planting on flat and sloped surfaces.** Spread out the root system in the hole. With the back of the garden trowel, push the soil up against the crown of the plant (the juncture between root and stem) so that it settles level with the ground. Carefully tamp the soil flat around the crown of the plant with your hands *(above, left)*. If you are planting on a slope, mold a shallow basin around the lower side of the hole with your hand to prevent water runoff. Firm the soil around the crown of the plant *(above, right)*. Repeat this planting procedure, spacing the plants of a vigorous ground cover 1 foot apart, or of a slow-growing type 4 to 6 inches apart. Water thoroughly *(page 91)* and spray a pre-emergent herbicide on the soil to reduce weed growth *(page 79)*. To retain moisture and discourage weeds, lay 2 to 3 inches of mulch such as ground bark or pine needles around the newly-planted ground cover *(page 21)*.

TREES AND SHRUBS

Trees and shrubs, when injured or exposed to environmental stress, are slow to respond. Several seasons may elapse before they react with symptoms of ill health. For this reason their well-being is often ignored, their size and seeming invulnerability lulling the home gardener into a false sense of complacency. As with all plants, however, trees and shrubs need regular care and attention to reduce the need for repair. Water, mulch *(page 97)* and protect trees and shrubs from harsh weather *(page 104)* to help them resist pests and disease. When specific problems do arise, match their symptoms to those on the Troubleshooting Guide on page 95 and repair the plant as directed. If you suspect the presence of insects or disease, consult the Pests and Diseases chapter *(page 112)* for the recommended treatment.

The drawing below illustrates the role of trees and shrubs in defining a typical American home's lawn and garden. Whether chosen for shade or beauty, a tree lends a sense of permanence and grace to a residential landscape. Shrubs can soften the sharp corners of a house, or create a feeling of privacy when planted close together as a hedge. Before planting a tree or shrub, consult a reputable arborist, garden center or nursery to help you choose one that is suited to the soil and climate. Amending the soil to improve soil texture and structure is impossible because of the depth and spread of a tree's root system once it's established.

When a particular spot in the garden proves to be unsuitable for the tree or shrub growing there, consider removing the plant *(page 106)* and replanting it in a more appropriate site

Shade trees
Are frequently too large to be pruned by the average homeowner; call a tree specialist for removal of large branches above your head. The bark of hardwood trees such as the sugar maple *(left)* or red oak is particularly susceptible to sunscald and should be wrapped *(page 105)* when planted.

Flowering shrubs
When growing acid-loving schrubs such as azaleas *(above)* and rhododendrons, keep the soil acidic by mulching with pine needles or peat moss *(page 97)*.

Small deciduous tree
For an urban yard, consider a short, resilient deciduous tree such as a crab apple *(above)* that will fit under overhead powerlines. Avoid using herbicide-treated fertilizers on lawns surrounding trees or shrubs.

Evergreens
May be coniferous such as pine *(above, left)* or spruce *(above, right)*, or broad-leafed, such as holly. Water deeply before the winter since evergreens continue to lose water through their leaves even when their roots may no longer replenish the supply.

Hedges
May be evergreen or deciduous. When planted close together, shrubs or small trees form a single hege or screen. Make sure to prune *(page 103)* the top narrower than the base so that light reaches the lower branches.

(page 110). If the tree is over 8 feet tall, contact a landscaping firm to have it moved by professionals. Beware of transplanting a tree or shrub that is already weak; the shock of moving may kill it. It may be better to get rid of the plant altogether and plant a new one. In either case, carefully follow the procedures outlined in this chapter to keep root damage to a minimum. Deciduous trees and shrubs are best transplanted when dormant, usually in the fall after their leaves have dropped. Transplant evergreen trees and shrubs in the spring before their growing season has started.

The pruning of trees and shrubs should not be undertaken lightly. An improperly placed cut can seriously wound a plant, so follow the techniques described in this chapter and avoid cutting into the swelling at the base of the branch known as the branch collar *(page 99).* While dead, diseased or damaged branches should be removed immediately, you can perform most other pruning jobs, in the early spring, to give the plant time to heal before winter. One exception to this is the flowering shrubs that bloom in the spring; in this case, prune after they blossom. Since the approach to pruning deciduous shrubs is similar to that of climbing plants, refer to page 66 for more information.

A range of useful pruning tools is included in the chapter on Tools & Techniques *(page 130).* When pruning, make sure the cutting blades are sharp, keep an eye out for falling branches and work with your feet firmly planted on the ground. Avoid tackling major pruning jobs, particularly those that require a ladder, without first consulting a tree specialist.

TROUBLESHOOTING GUIDE continued ▶

SYMPTOM	POSSIBLE CAUSE	PROCEDURE
Tree or shrub in general decline; growth is slow, branches are weak and brittle. Leaves are dull, turn yellow, brown or grey-green prematurely, and drop. Conifer candles are small and pale, needles drop. Plant may ooze more sap than usual.	Overwatering or poor drainage	Check soil moisture *(p. 18)* ☐○ and water less frequently. Check soil drainage *(p. 27)* ◨○, install a drainage system *(p. 30)* ■●; if roots are rotten, plant new tree and shrub *(p. 110)* ◨◐
	Bark injured by lawn mower, car or animals	Clean wound *(p. 100)* ◨○ and water well; to protect tree from rodents, wrap trunk *(p. 105)* ◨○
	Soil pH wrong for plant; soil nutrient deficiency	Test soil pH *(p. 23)* ◨○▲ and adjust *(p. 24)* ◨○, test soil fertility *(p. 25)* ◨○▲ and fertilize *(p. 97)* ◨○
	Soil compacted by excess foot or machine traffic	Aerate *(page 86)* ◨◐▲ to a depth of at least 6 inches
	Roots are cut or soil grade around tree is raised or lowered by construction crew	Consult a tree specialist
	Young tree or shrub planted at wrong level	Remove the young tree or shrub *(p. 106)* ◨◐ and replant at correct level *(p. 110)* ◨◐
	Air pollution	Water thoroughly and consult tree specialist. If damage is serious, plant a hardier species *(p. 110)* ◨◐
	Road salt	Leach soil *(p. 19)* ☐○ and erect protective barrier or wrap trunk *(p. 105)* ◨○
	Lawn or flowers competing for soil nutrients and water	If surrounded by lawn, remove an area of sod at least 2 1/2 feet wide from around plant *(p. 78)* ◨○. If growing in flower bed, weed *(p. 51)* ☐○. In both cases, fertilize and mulch *(p. 97)* ◨○
	Surrounding lawn treated with herbicide or herbicide-treated fertilizer	Consult a tree specialist
	Wet root ball (especily on balled and burlapped trees planted in clayey soil)	Remove tree *(p. 106)* ◨◐ and let root ball dry out. Replant *(p. 110)* ◨◐ in well-drained, loamy soil
	Dry root ball (especially on balled and burlapped trees planted in sandy soil)	Water thoroughly and mulch *(p. 97)* ◨○
Tree swaying in the wind	Tree too slender to withstand force of wind	Brace with guy wires *(p. 104)* ◨◐
Leaves are dry and scorched	Lack of water	Water thoroughly and mulch *(p. 97)* ◨○
	If bark cracked and/or cankers growing on bark: Plant injured by sunscald	Trim damaged bark *(p. 100)* ◨○, protect trunk *(p. 105)* ◨○, water thoroughly and mulch *(p. 97)* ◨○
Leaves wilt; buds, flowers, needles wither and drop off. Bark may be cracked, branches broken	Winter damage (frost, wind or snow)	Trim damaged bark *(p. 100)* ◨○, prune damaged branches *(deciduous tree, p. 98, or shrub, p. 103; coniferous tree or shrub, p. 101)* ◨○. Wrap small trees and shrubs *(p. 104)* ◨○, or wrap unprotected bark *(p. 105)* ◨○. Water evergreens thoroughly in the fall

DEGREE OF DIFFICULTY: ☐ Easy ◨ Moderate ■ Complex
ESTIMATED TIME: ○ Less than 1 hour ◐ 1 to 3 hours ● Over 3 hours

▲ Special tool required

TROUBLESHOOTING GUIDE (continued)

SYMPTOM	POSSIBLE CAUSE	PROCEDURE
Leaves of recently trans-planted tree or bush wilt; buds, flowers or needles drop	Roots damaged during transplanting	Water thoroughly and mulch (p. 97) ◨○
Abundant foliage, few flowers	Excessive fertilizing	Stop fertilizing, water thoroughly
Spindly growth, few flowers	Sun-loving species grown in the shade	Remove tree (p. 106) ◨◕ and transplant to a sunnier location (p. 110) ◨◕
Branches straggly, few flowers, overgrown and unkempt appearance	Neglect	Evaluate plant's pruning needs and prune if necessary; (deciduous tree, p. 98, or shrub, p. 103; coniferous tree or shrub, p. 101) ◨◕
Branch rubbing against window or hanging over path	Tree planted too close to house, pruning has been neglected	Prune (deciduous tree, p. 98; coniferous tree, p. 101) ◨◕
Tip of spruce tree broken	Strong winds	Prune leader (p. 102) ◨○
	Spruce budworm	Prune leader (p. 102) ◨○ and see Pests and Diseases (p. 127)
Sewage system backing up	Roots are interfering with drainage system	Consult a tree specialist about pruning roots
Lower part of hedge is changing color, leaves or needles turn brown and drop	Lack of sunlight reaching lower portion of hedge due to neglect or incorrect pruning	Prune hedge narrower at the top (p. 103) ◨◕
Gap in hedge, interior branches bare	Dieback due to lack of sunlight and air reaching interior branches	Prune hedge (p. 103) ◨◕ to encourage growth to fill the gap
Leaves and flowers of rhododendrons, azaleas and camellias are growing slowly and yellowing. Flower buds may drop	Soil too alkaline	Test soil pH (p. 23) ◨○▲, lower pH (p. 24) ◨○ if necessary until pH level is 5.5. Mulch with acidic mulch such as peat moss or pine needles (p. 97) ◨○
Flowering shrubs such as hydrangeas are losing their flower color, top growth is dying	Soil too acidic	Test soil pH (p. 23) ◨○▲, raise pH (p. 24) ◨○ and avoid using acidic mulches such as peat moss or pine needles
Leaves covered with white powdery deposits	Powdery mildew	See Pests and Diseases (p. 121)
Leaves blotched, streaked with brown trails	Leaf miners	See Pests and Diseases (p. 121)
Leaves eaten by caterpillars, insect-woven bag may be hanging from branches	Gypsy moth, cankerworm, tent caterpillar, bag worm	See Pests and Diseases (p. 127). Prune branches of affected plant (deciduous tree, p. 98, or shrub, p. 103; coniferous tree or shrub, p. 101) ◨◕
Leaves chewed by large beetles	Japanese beetle	See Pests and Diseases (p. 116)
Leaves streaked and flecked; colonies of tiny insects on tender growth; leaves may look sooty	Wooly aphids and mealybugs	See Pests and Diseases (p. 126)
Evergreen buds are destroyed, needles are chewed. Small silken cases may be visible	Spruce budworm	See Pests and Diseases (p. 127). If a spruce leader is destroyed, train a new leader (p. 102) ◨○
American elm leaves droop and curl, turn bright yellow and drop	Dutch elm disease	See Pests and Diseases (p. 128)
Leaves, branches and trunk crusted with bumps, plant may look sooty	Scale insects	See Pests and Diseases (p. 126)
Bark cracked, growths on branches and trunk, dieback of foliage	Cankers, crown gall or fireblight	See Pests and Diseases (p. 128). Prune branches of affected plant (deciduous tree, p. 98, or shrub, p. 103; coniferous tree or shrub, p. 101) ◨○
Branches or trunks riddled with holes, dieback of foliage	Borer insects	See Pests and Diseases (p. 128). Prune branches of affected plant (deciduous tree, p. 98, or shrub, p. 103; coniferous tree or shrub, p. 101) ◨○

DEGREE OF DIFFICULTY: ☐ Easy ◨ Moderate ■ Complex
ESTIMATED TIME: ○ Less than 1 hour ◕ 1 to 3 hours ● Over 3 hours   ▲ Special tool required

MULCHING A TREE OR SHRUB

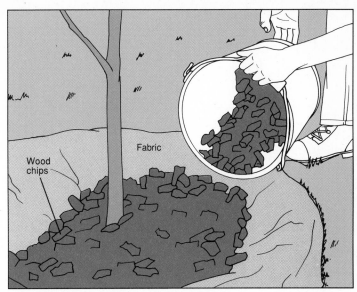

Laying an organic mulch. Place an organic mulch over the soil to keep in moisture and discourage weeds. For most trees and shrubs, use organic mulches such as partially decomposed wood, bark chips or composted materials *(page 21)* that will add nutrients to the soil. For flowering shrubs such as rhododendrons, azaleas and camelias, which grow well in acidic soil, choose pine needles or leaves. Using a spade, spread a 2- to 3-inch layer of mulch over the soil *(above)* and tamp it down lightly, leaving a band of bare soil around the base of the trunk to prevent rot.

Laying a fabric mulch. Landscaping fabric is non-degradable and will last several years before it needs to be replaced. Cut at least two pieces, large enough to fit around the base of the plant and, if it has a watering basin *(page 111)*, the edges of the basin as well. Butt the pieces together closely and cover them with a thin layer of wood chips *(above)* or crushed rock to weigh down the mulch and block sunlight. In windy areas, secure the edges of the fabric with small stakes. If the tree is surrounded by a lawn, cut and lift a one-inch band of sod with a square spade, and tuck the ends of the fabric under the sod.

FERTILIZING A TREE

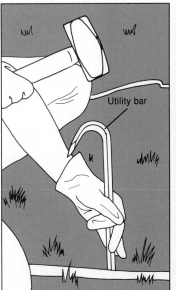

1 **Marking the drip line.** Consult your local Cooperative Extension Service for your particular tree's needs and choose a granular, slow-release fertilizer. Lay a soaker hose around the drip-line of the tree—the line directly beneath the tips of the widest branches—as a guide for making holes. Push small sticks at two-foot intervals along the hose *(above)*. Trees growing in a well-fertilized lawn may not need fertilizing. **Caution:** Do not apply herbicide-treated fertilizers.

2 **Applying the fertilizer.** Use a mallet to drive a utility bar *(above, left)* 8 inches into the soil at the points marked, making holes about 1 inch in diameter. To determine the quantity of fertilizer to add to each hole, divide the recommended amount by the number of holes. Pour the fertilizer granules into the holes, using a funnel *(above, right)* to avoid spilling them on the lawn. Remove the markers and turn on the soaker hose for 2 to 4 hours, allowing the water to soak down to the full root zone of the tree.

PRUNING A DECIDUOUS TREE

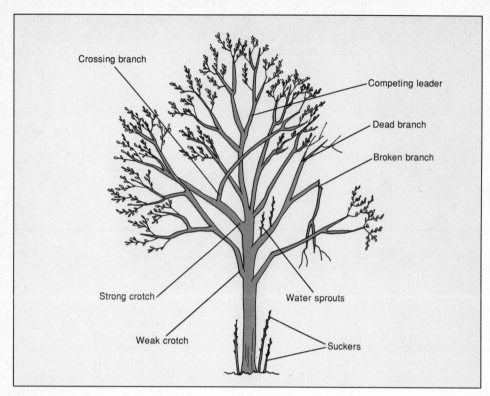

Evaluating the pruning needs of a deciduous tree. Before pruning a deciduous tree, consider the natural characteristics of the species in order to conserve them. Examine the shape of your tree, and look for the specific problems illustrated at left. Remove dead, damaged and diseased branches immediately, wiping tool blades with rubbing alcohol after each cut to prevent spreading disease, and dispose of the branches safely *(page 133)*. Prune crossing branches that rub against others and interfere with proper growth. For trees planted within the last year, remove side branches with weak crotches, or V-shaped angles. In a young tree, remove any leader that competes with the main trunk; it will weaken the tree as it matures. Prune water sprouts and suckers—those spindly, young shoots growing from branches or from the ground at the base of the trunk. Thin an established tree lightly to enhance its form and reduce branch crowding. Take care to space extensive pruning over a three-year period to minimize the stress on the tree. For best results, prune in early spring before leaves appear.

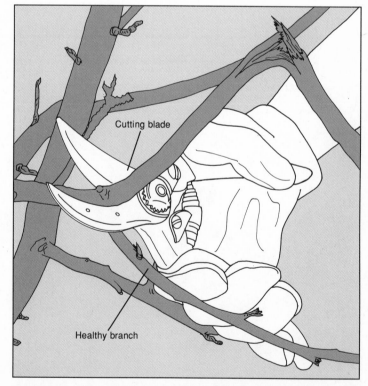

Removing suckers and sprouts. Remove a sucker by gripping it firmly at ground level and pulling it out, as shown. If necessary, dig a few inches into the ground with a garden trowel in order to grasp it closer to the root from which it has sprouted. Cutting a sucker at ground level will leave a stub that will send up new suckers. (If you cannot tear out the sucker, cut it close to the root with a sharp knife). Cut water sprouts close to the main branch with a pruning knife *(inset)* or other sharp knife.

Removing a very small branch. Use pruning shears to cut a branch up to 3/4 inch in diameter. Prune back to the nearest healthy branch, slanting the cut in the growing direction of the branch which will remain *(above)*. If you are cutting back to the trunk, position the cutting blade against the trunk, and make a clean cut. Take care not to twist the shears, or the bark will tear and wound the tree. If pruning diseased branches, wipe off the blades with rubbing alcohol after each cut and dispose of the branches safely *(page 133)*.

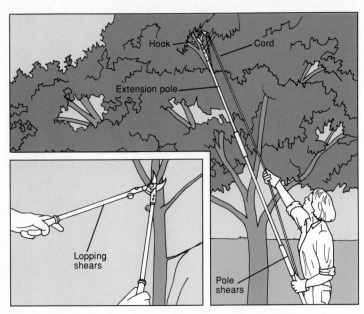

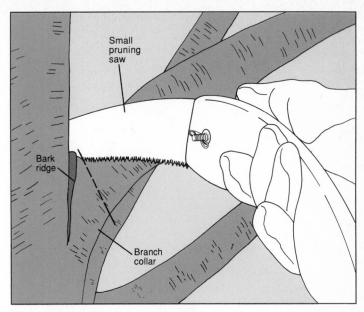

Removing a small branch. Cut branches 3/4 to 1 1/2 inches in diameter with pole shears or lopping shears. Use pole shears for pruning high up and attach extensions if necessary. Taking care to stand away from the branch, place the hook over the branch *(above)*, positioning the blade against the trunk or nearest healthy limb. Pull the pole cord to cut the branch. For pruning lower down, use lopping shears. Position the open jaws of the shears as far around the branch as possible. Cut with a firm, clean stroke to avoid tearing the bark.

Removing a medium-size branch. Use a small, curved pruning saw to remove branches 1 to 2 inches in diameter. Taking care to stand away from falling limbs, place the blade beside the branch's bark ridge. Then cut down through the branch, angling the saw away from the collar as shown. If the ridge and collar are not clearly visible, look for a raised swelling at the base of the branch where it joins the main trunk. If the bark is accidentally torn, trim the wound with a sharp knife *(page 100)*.

REMOVING A LARGE BRANCH

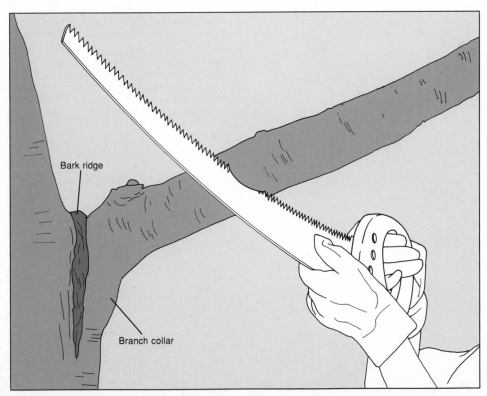

1 Making the first cut. When removing a branch 2 to 4 inches in diameter, make three cuts to ensure that the branch does not break away at the collar and tear the bark of the trunk as it falls. (Call a professional to remove a branch larger than 4 inches in diameter.) Before making the first cut, clear the area under the branch you intend to remove. Trim off all smaller branches to make the large branch more manageable. Position a pruning saw underneath the branch about 10 inches from the trunk. Grasp the saw firmly *(left)* and cut upward into the branch until the blade begins to pinch, about one-third of the way into the branch.

REMOVING A LARGE BRANCH (continued)

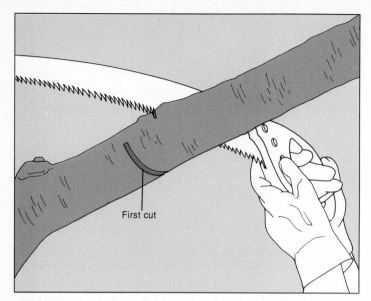

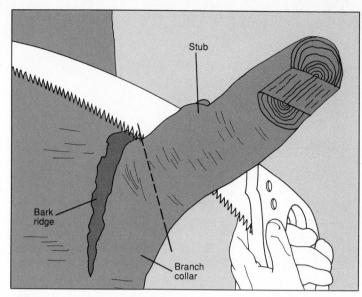

Stub

Bark ridge

Branch collar

2 **Removing the branch.** Make a second cut, positioning the saw on the upper side of the branch, about one inch farther from the trunk than the undercut. Standing out of the way of the falling branch, saw down toward the first cut. As you saw, the branch will kick back, splintering upward before it falls. To remove the remaining stub, go to step 3. If the branch was diseased, wipe the saw blade with rubbing alcohol and dispose of the branch safely *(page 133)*.

First cut

3 **Trimming the stub.** Position the saw outside the branch's bark ridge as shown and cut at an outward angle, following the branch collar. Saw cleanly and smoothly, removing all branch wood but taking care not to cut into the collar. If the edges of the pruning wound are smooth, leave them. Do not coat the wound with paint or wound dressings. Despite their widespread use, these products do not stop decay or stall rot. If the edges of the wound are jagged, trim them with a pruning knife *(below)*.

CLEANING A TREE WOUND

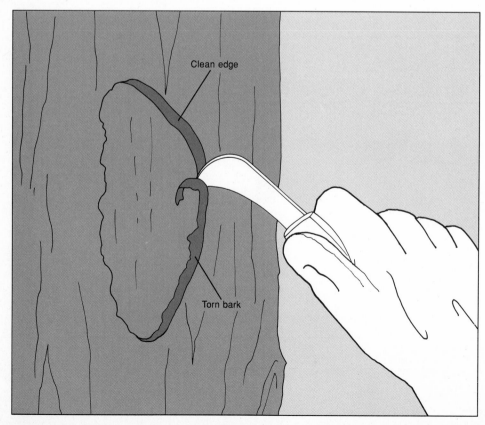

Clean edge

Torn bark

Trimming a wound. To prevent further damage and reduce scarring, clean tree wounds caused by fallen limbs, torn bark or other stresses. Wearing heavy gardening gloves, use a small, sharp pruning knife to trim torn or jagged bark edges *(left)* so that no pieces of dead or dying tissue are left on the tree to host infection. Take care not to cut into living bark. If the bark has split, shape the wound into a smooth oval to promote the forming of a hard callus which will protect the wound. If unprotected bark on a young tree has been split by frost or sunscald, consider wrapping the trunk *(page 105)*. Most tree specialists now recommend not to paint the wound.

PRUNING A CONIFEROUS EVERGREEN

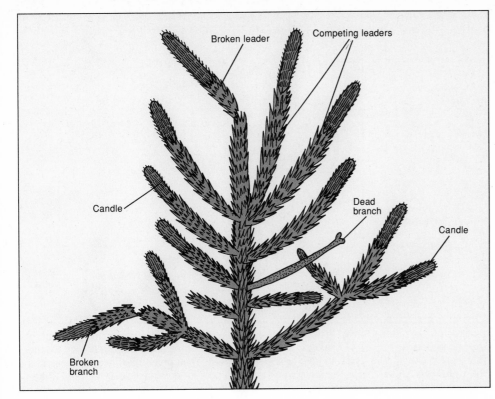

Evaluating a coniferous evergreen tree or shrub. Use the well-defined natural shape of an evergreen as a guide when pruning. First, remove damaged, diseased or dead branches and wipe tool blades with rubbing alcohol to avoid spreading disease. When possible, avoid cutting back to dead wood because new buds are seldom generated on old wood. Prune a broken leader, choosing another to dominate, and remove competing leaders. Consider carefully before cutting off the sweeping branches of an evergreen. Once removed, these branches will not be replaced.

Coniferous evergreens grow by sending out candles, finger-like projections which will later produce needles. Prune pines in early summer before the candles have hardened. Spruces, which are more tolerant, can be trimmed later into the summer. Prune new growth to dwarf or shape the tree, removing no more than one third of the new wood each year. Don't expect to keep evergreens small through severe pruning; they are hard to hold back. Instead, plant a species that will be smaller at maturity.

Pruning a pine, spruce or fir to redirect growth. Wait until the third growing season and prune in the late spring or early summer, before new growth is complete. Prune back new growth to promote a thick and bushy tree. Wearing gloves to protect your hands from sharp needles, use pruning shears to cut straight through the candle. Trim all the candles equally, including the leader, by about one third the length of the new growth *(above)*. Fir and spruce send out lateral buds from branches, and will become too dense if pruned every year.

Pruning a juniper or yew. Wearing gloves to protect your hands from the foliage, trim the new terminal growth of junipers with pruning shears. This will control their size and shape and help combat winter breakage, as well as prevent bare centers resulting from overgrowth. Prune early in the season to allow new growth to cover the wounds. When pruning a mature juniper, cut back to an overlapping branch that will conceal the cut *(above)*. This will maintain the natural, feathery appearance of a spreading juniper. To guard against snow breakage, shear narrow, upright trees lightly, like a hedge.

TRAINING A NEW LEADER

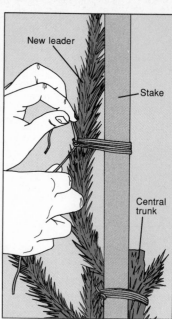

1 **Pruning the broken leader.** Remove the leader of an evergreen tree if it has been broken off by wind or damaged by insects or disease. Wearing gloves, use pruning shears (or lopping shears if it is more than 3/4 inch in diameter) to cut through the leader just below the point of breakage *(above)*. If the leader is diseased, wipe the blade after each cut with rubbing alcohol. When necessary, use a step ladder, taking care to position the feet firmly on the ground and supporting your body against the top steps.

2 **Cutting competing leaders and staking a new central leader.** Choose one lateral branch, close to the broken leader, to train as the new leader. Then prune back any branches that may compete with the new leader for dominance *(above, left)*. Cut a wooden stake about 18 inches long. Tie the lower end of the stake to the central trunk with medium-strength string, making sure the string does not constrict the trunk. Pull a neighboring lateral branch toward the stake and fasten it firmly, but not too tightly, with string. Fasten the new leader to the stake again 3 inches farther up *(above, right)*. Remove the stake and string after one or two seasons.

PRUNING DECIDUOUS SHRUBS

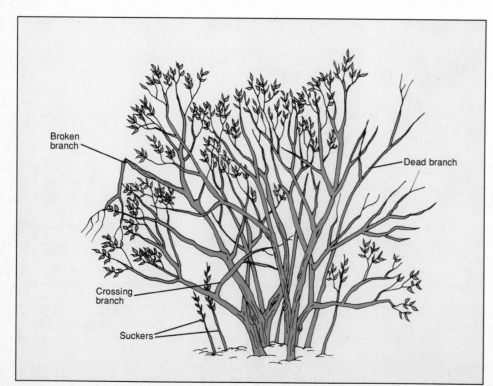

Evaluating a deciduous shrub. Before pruning, consider the natural characteristics of the species before pruning in order to conserve them. First remove dead, damaged or diseased branches. If the shrub is diseased, clean tool blades with rubbing alcohol and dispose of branches safely *(page 133)*. Next, prune crossing branches and straggly growth. Cut back to a bud or branch pointing in the direction you wish the new growth to follow. Thin dense growth to allow sunlight to reach the center of the shrub and promote larger, showier blossoms and foliage. To rejuvenate an old shrub, cut back one third of the old stems to the ground each year over a three-year period. Leave several suckers—the thin shoots growing vertically from the ground—to regenerate the shrub and produce foliage. To encourage dense growth at the tips of branches, head them back, trimming them to a new flower or leaf bud.

Prune summer- and fall-flowering shrubs in early spring, when the branching structure is visible. Prune spring-flowering shrubs after blooming.

PRUNING DECIDUOUS SHRUBS (continued)

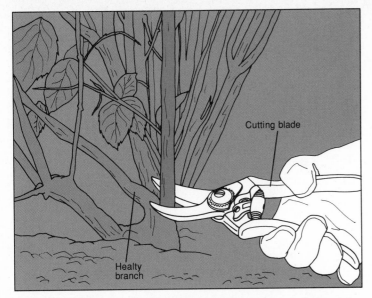

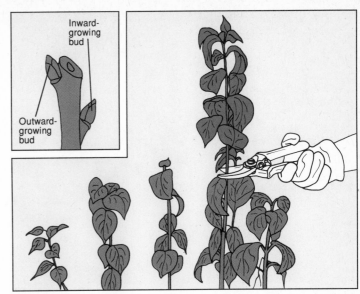

Thinning a shrub. To thin a shrub, cut branches back to their point of origin and stems back to the ground. Use pruning or lopping shears, and angle the cut in the growing direction of the nearest healthy branch *(above)*. Cut through in one clean stroke, taking care not to twist the shears. Remove all dead, damaged or diseased branches in this way. If thinning is required to open up the center of a dense, overgrown shrub, begin with the least healthy branches and stems, and do not remove more than one third of the healthy ones.

Heading back to a bud. Cut back top growth on a thin and straggly shrub to promote denser growth. Using pruning shears *(above)*, prune back to a leaf bud, sloping the cut in the direction of the bud growth *(inset)*. Choose the leaf bud carefully: Cutting to an outward-growing bud will promote an airy, light shape; inward-growing buds will promote a full and vigorous center.

TRIMMING A HEDGE

Shaping a hedge. Place stakes and string as a guide for cutting a straight and even hedge. With a hedge trimmer, shear the hedge straight across the top at this height. Then trim the sides of the hedge, sloping them slightly to shape the base wider than the top. Now round off the top and edges of the hedge *(shown)* to give it a natural form, and to allow sunlight to reach all branches. Shake the hedge to dislodge the clippings, and rake them away. For thick and woody branches that catch and tear with a power-operated trimmer, use hedge shears.

Filling in a gap. Rejuvenate a deciduous hedge which is straggly or sparse at the base by heading it back in the spring before growth starts *(top, right)*. To encourage the growth of foliage to fill in a gap in the hedge, use pruning or lopping shears to cut back inside branches to inward-growing buds *(shown),*. For an evergreen hedge, cut back new growth only *(page 101)*, since cutting back to deadwood will not produce new growth. Evergreens must never be severely headed back.

BRACING A TREE AGAINST THE WIND

Collar

Hose collars

Wire

Wooden stake

Bracing a tree for stability. A staked tree brought home from a nursery, or tree over 8 feet tall that has been moved into a very windy area may be temporarily braced with guy wires. Using a mallet, drive three wooden stakes into the ground equidistant from the tree and about one foot outside the planting area. Buy a roll of guy wire and at least 3 feet of rubber hose. Locate a strong crotch *(page 98)* one third to one half way up the tree. Measure the distance between the crotch and one of the stakes and add about 1 1/2 feet. Cut three pieces of guy wire to this length. Also cut three pieces of rubber hose, each twice the circumference of the tree trunk, to protect it from the cutting edge of the wire. Thread each wire through a length of hose and wrap it around the trunk, supporting it in the crotch *(inset)*. Pull each length of wire down to a wooden stake *(left)* winding the ends several times around the stake to secure it. Make sure the wires are taut. Trim the wire ends and mark the stakes to make them clearly visible. Remove the wires and hose collars after one growing season.

PROTECTING SHRUBS

String

Plastic netting

Wrapping shrubs for winter protection. To protect deciduous shrubs from winter damage, tie them up with medium-weight string. Using a ball of string, make a large loop at the base of the shrub. Tighten and knot the string but do not cut it. Walk around the shrub with the ball in your hands, winding the string higher on the shrub with each loop. Continue until the shrub is pulled in all the way up to the top *(far left)*. Make sure the string is not cutting into any branches, then tie a knot and cut the string. Protect narrow evergreen shrubs the same way, or use a tube of plastic netting, available from nursery centers. Place the collar of netting over the shrub and push it gently down to the base. Then open the netting, pulling it up over the shrub like a stocking *(near left)*. Remove the string or netting early in the spring, after the danger of snow and ice damage has passed.

INSTALLING A PROTECTIVE BARRIER

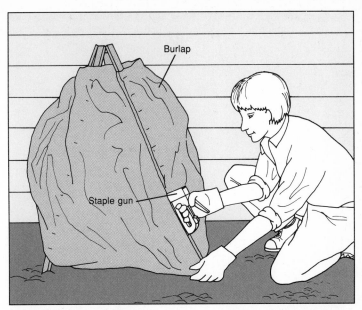

1 **Placing the stakes.** At the first warning of frost, install a temporary barrier to protect shrubs that may suffer winterkill from harsh winds and snow. Use a mallet to drive four wooden stakes into the ground *(above)*, equal distances apart and just at the limit of the branches. Push the stakes together at the top, to form a teepee-shaped structure over the shrub. If your area receives a lot of snow, also tie them together with string or twine.

2 **Attaching the burlap.** Cut several pieces of burlap to stretch over the wooden frame. Drape the pieces over the stakes to see if they will fill in the frame; cut more if necessary. In order to provide a snug fit, trim the pieces with scissors to make them narrower at the top. Then fold under the edges of the burlap and fasten them to the stakes with a staple gun. Burlap allows the air to circulate, while shielding the shrub. Use a plastic foam sheet, available at garden-supply stores, for shrubs that require insulated protection.

PROTECTING THE TRUNK

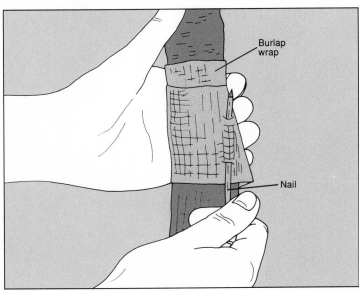

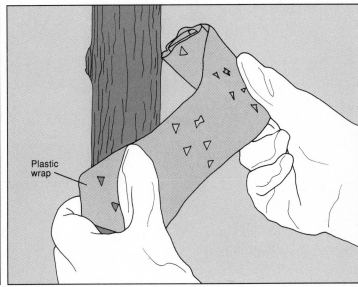

Wrapping the trunk. Wrap the trunk of a young tree if there is danger of sunscald or frost in your area. Cut strips of burlap 2 to 4 inches wide. Starting at the bottom of the trunk, wrap the burlap around the trunk up to the first branch, overlapping the wrap one inch each turn. To secure the wrap, or to fasten two short strips together, push a galvanized nail through the burlap *(above, left)*, taking care not to puncture the tree. Remove the burlap when there is sufficient foliage to protect the trunk, usually within two years. To discourage rodents from nibbling the trunk in the winter, use perforated plastic wrap *(above, right)*, protecting the tree up to one foot higher than the expected snow level. Remove it in late spring.

REMOVING A TREE FOR TRANSPLANTING

1 Outlining the root ball. Move only a very young tree; older trees, especially those taller than 8 feet, are extremely heavy. The night before you plan to move the tree, water it thoroughly to the full depth of its root zone—about 2 feet. The next morning, outline the circumference of the root ball by scratching a circle in the ground corresponding to the spread of the tree's branches, but no further than 12 inches from the trunk. Then, using a square spade upside-down, push away a 4-inch band of soil outside this line *(above)* to a depth of about 4 inches.

2 Severing the roots. Use a square spade with a sharp edge to cut through the roots at this level. Position the spade along the edge of the root ball at a 20- to 30-degree angle away from the trunk, so that the root ball will taper slightly. Place your heel on the spade and push it firmly to cut the roots cleanly in one strong stroke *(above)*. Continue severing the roots around the root ball.

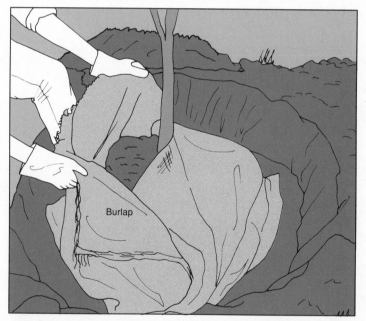

3 Detaching the root ball. Deepen the trench around the root ball to a depth of about 1 1/2 feet, severing the side roots as you go. Scoop out soil all the way around the tree, keeping one foot on the root ball to prevent the soil from crumbling away *(above)*. Stop whenever you hit a side root, and cut it cleanly as described in step 2. Be careful not to cut into the root ball itself with the side of the spade, and do not cut the main support root (tap root) that runs straight down into the ground.

4 Wrapping the ball with burlap. If the tree or shrub is very small, and the roots are holding the soil together, cut horizontally through the base roots and lift it out for planting *(page 110)* or for heeling-in *(page 109)*. For a root ball about 18 inches in diameter, such as the one shown above, wrap it in burlap to keep the soil from crumbling away. Place two pieces of burlap over the ball while it is still anchored by its tap root *(above)*. Be sure to leave enough burlap at the bottom of the trench to wrap beneath the root ball.

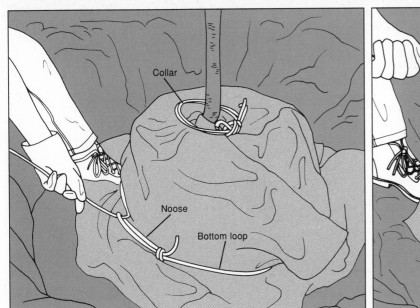

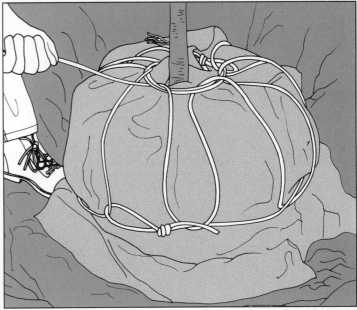

5 **Securing the root ball in burlap.** Loop a 36-inch length of strong twine twice around the base of the trunk and knot it securely to make a collar about 6 inches in diameter. Loop a second piece of twine 30 feet long around the bottom of the root ball. Make a small noose at one end of the twine, and pull the other end through *(above, left)*. Keeping the the bottom loop secure with one foot, pass the twine up and under the collar, then back down and under the loop. Continue weaving the root ball in this manner, tightening the twine as you go, until it is encircled *(above, right)*.

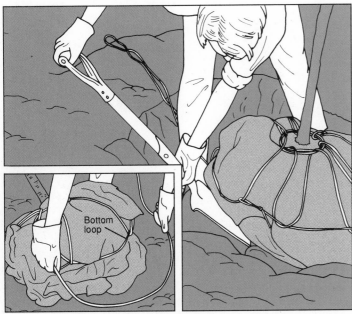

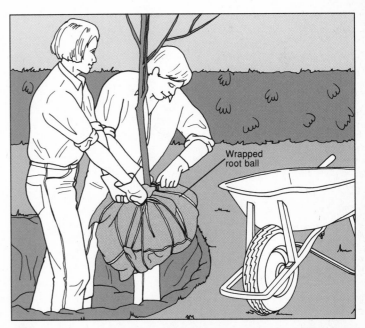

6 **Severing the tap root and securing the root ball.** Place the sharpened spade at the bottom of the root ball and thrust it horizontally to sever the tap root and other large roots *(above)*. Lever one side of the root ball up and tuck burlap underneath it. Do the same on the other side, overlapping the burlap as much as possible. Then take the end of the twine and pass it under the root ball, bringing it up to the bottom loop on the opposite side *(inset)*. Weave it back and forth twice, knot it securely and cut off the remaining twine.

7 **Lifting the root ball.** Even a small tree with a burlapped root ball is very heavy—do not attempt to lift it without a helper. With knees bent and back straight, hold on to the wrapped ball and lift the tree out of the hole. Place it in a wheelbarrow or on a heavy sheet of burlap or canvas that can be pulled to the new planting site. Plant the tree immediately *(page 110)* or set it in a shady spot for up to a week, keeping the burlap moist. If you cannot plant the tree in less than a week, keep it alive by heeling it in *(page 109)*.

PREPARING A CONTAINER-GROWN PLANT

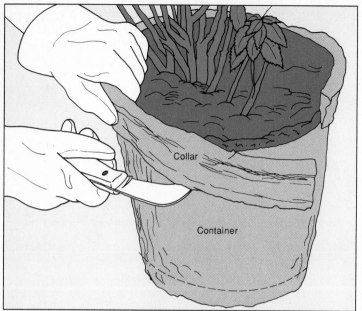

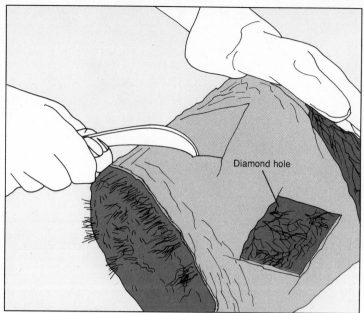

1 **Removing the container.** If possible, take the tree or shrub out of its container before transplanting to allow the roots to establish themselves in the new planting site. Rap the container gently, or squeeze and release the sides two or three times. Then hold the tree firmly at the base of its trunk and pull it up. If the tree lifts out of its container, go to step 2. For plastic or metal containers that do not slide off easily, cut the container from top to bottom in three or four

places with a pair of tin snips. Then pull the strips away and lift out the root mass without knocking off the soil. For peat containers, use a sharp knife to cut away the top collar *(above, left)*, and a 1/2-inch strip from the bottom. For a solid root ball, remove the rest of the container. If the soil crumbles away from the roots, leave the remaining band of peat to support the root mass, cutting diamond shapes in the side *(above, right)* to allow the roots to spread out once planted.

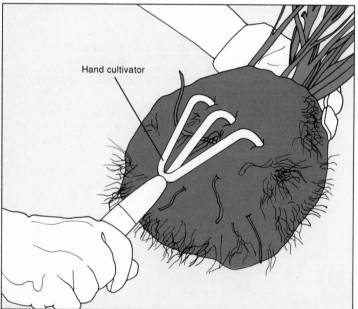

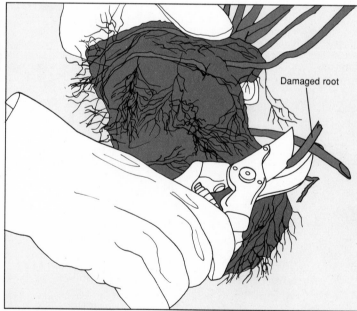

2 **Preparing the roots.** Look for root ends and tug gently to uncoil them so that they will not strangle each other or grow in circles. If the roots are compacted, use a hand cultivator *(above, left)* to gently scratch the edges of the root ball and loosen the roots. Then work the roots free with your hands. If the roots cannot be worked free, butterfly them *(page 109)*. Use pruning shears to trim damaged roots *(above, right)*. For a tree, also prune any large roots that encircle and constrict the other roots. They will eventually girdle the mature tree, cutting off its nutrient supply. The tree is now ready for planting *(page 110)*.

BUTTERFLYING A COMPACTED ROOT BALL

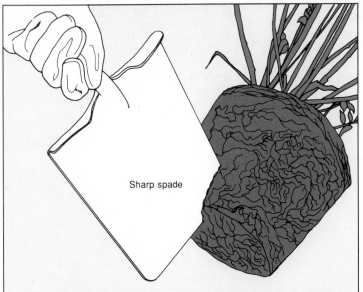

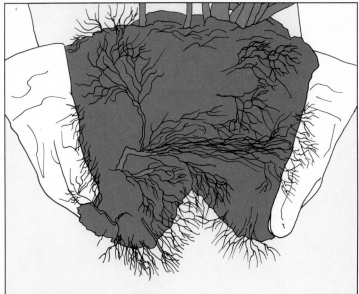

1 **Splitting a compacted root ball.** To prepare a container-grown tree or shrub with severely compacted roots for planting *(page 110)*, consider butterflying, or splitting the root ball as a last resort. This technique may also be necessary to discourage circular root growth when planting in heavy, clay soil. Use a sharp spade to cut into the bottom third of the root ball *(above, left)*. Then pull the two sides of the root mass apart to spread the roots *(above, right)*. When planting, make a small mound at the bottom of the hole and spread the edges of the rootball over it, in the shape of a butterfly.

HEELING-IN A TREE

Trench

Heeling-in a tree. Protect a tree or shrub that cannot be planted immediately by providing a temporary planting site. If you are planting it the next day, store it in a shady area and protect the roots with moistened burlap. Otherwise, choose a shaded area of the garden that is protected from wind, and dig a shallow trench 1/3 to 1/2 the depth of the root mass. Sandy soil is ideal for heeling-in. Lean the tree against one side of the trench, and cover the roots completely with soil *(left)*. If there is not enough soil, add an organic mulch *(page 21)*. For balled and burlapped trees, place a thin layer of soil over the entire root ball and tamp it with your hands. Water the root ball lightly every two or three days to keep it from drying out. Avoid overwatering or immersing the tree in water—the roots will rot if they get too wet.

PLANTING A TREE

1 **Preparing the planting site.** Plant on an overcast day in the fall or dormant season, when there is less risk of transplant shock. If the tree is balled and burlapped, keep the burlap moist to protect the roots from drying out. Choose a well-drained site, making sure that soil conditions and shade level are compatible with the tree. Use a sharp spade to mark a circle twice the diameter of the root ball. If the site is on a lawn, remove the sod *(page 79)*. Then dig a hole deep enough to generously accommodate the root ball—in this case, about 18 inches deep. Toss the soil onto a sheet of burlap, plastic or canvas, which will later serve as a firm surface for mixing in fertilizer. Use a garden fork *(left)* to break down clumps of soil and aerate the sides of the hole. Then push back the loosened soil from the sides and tamp the bottom lightly. If you are planting a container-grown tree, prepare the roots now *(page 109)*.

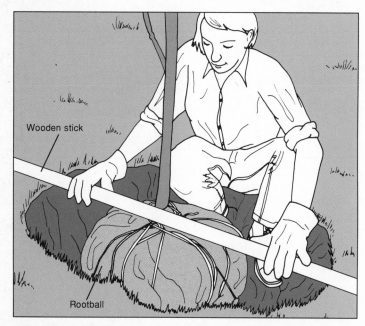

2 **Positioning the tree.** Measure the depth of the root ball with a yardstick, or by marking a piece of wood. Then add or remove soil until the planting hole is the same depth. For a bare-rooted or butterflied tree *(page 109)*, add soil to build a small mound in the center of the hole. With a helper, set the root ball in the hole and position the tree, spreading the roots over the mound. Lay the yardstick across the hole and check that the root ball is even with the ground or at the tree's original soil level, as indicated by a dark band at the base of the trunk. If the tree is too high or too low, lift it out and remove or add soil as necessary.

3 **Staking the tree.** Support the tree in its new site by staking it. For a bare-rooted tree, one stake is usually sufficient. For a balled and burlapped tree, use two stakes, each about 6 feet high. Position one of the stakes beside the root ball, taking care not to disturb bare roots. Using a mallet, drive the stake into the soil at the bottom of the hole to a depth of 6 inches, angling it slightly outward. Place the second stake on the other side of the root ball in the same way *(above)*.

4 **Backfilling the hole.** If the root ball is wrapped in a plastic sheet and nylon cord, remove them. Otherwise, leave the root ball fastened until step 5. Mix a slow-release granular fertilizer with a high phosphorus formula, such as 5-15-5, into the pile of soil from the hole. Using the spade, fill the planting hole halfway with the soil, gently tamping each layer to remove air pockets. Shake a bare-rooted tree from time to time to make sure the soil is settling, and work the soil between the roots with your hands. Water the soil in the hole thoroughly *(above)*.

5 **Completing soil placement.** Cut the twine of a balled and burlapped tree and open the burlap, spreading the ends over the soil in the hole. Continue to add soil *(step 4)* until the hole is filled, making sure to completely cover the burlap *(above)*. If left exposed to the air, burlap will encourage moisture to evaporate from the soil.

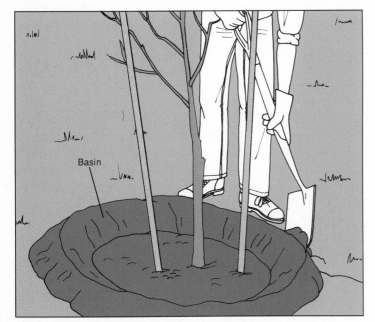

6 **Forming a basin.** Pile extra soil around the edge of the planting hole *(above)*, forming a small basin to hold water. Firm the soil with your hands and fill the basin with water. Allow it to drain and fill it again to thoroughly soak the root ball. Water frequently the next few weeks if the weather is warm and dry. Mulching *(page 97)* will help to keep moisture in and discourage weed growth.

7 **Securing the tree.** Cut two strips of a soft fabric such as burlap or nylon, or use pieces of hose and wire *(page 104)*, long enough to reach around the trunk and the stakes. Pull one of the angled stakes upright, parallel to the tree trunk. Then loop a strip of fabric around the tree trunk two-thirds of the way up the tree and tie it into a figure-8 around the stake. Repeat the procedure with the other stake *(above)*, making sure the ties do not cut into the tree bark. Remove the stakes after one season. Prune all broken and damaged branches *(page 98)*.

PESTS AND DISEASES

Any garden can become host to troublesome fungi, insects and bacteria. Many pests and diseases are always present in particular climates and soils, and wounded plants, or plants stressed by weather or by poor nutrition, may easily fall victim.

Tiny sucking insects such as aphids rapidly colonize, draining sap from leaves and killing plants. Chewing insects such as beetles and caterpillars eat holes in leaves and stems, defoliating plants. Disease organisms can enter from the soil, or through wounds made by tools or insects, stunting and wilting plants. Bacteria and fungi are spread by wind and splashing water, infecting leaves with spots and mold.

Pests and diseases should be spotted early and treated promptly. The key to early detection is vigilance; when you're in the garden, take time to look closely at your plants.

Keep an eye on the general condition of your plants. Are they growing steadily and vigorously, or do they look weak and unhealthy? Slow, distorted or stunted growth may signal disease or a lack of adequate light, water or nutrients. Are the plants a vibrant green? Dull color or brown or yellow foliage may indicate a nutrient or soil problem, disease, or even the presence of insects that kill plant tissue as they feed. Are plants losing leaves or dropping buds? If so, they may be diseased, or cut off by insects.

Regularly check the specific parts of plants where pest problems often first appear. Check leaf undersides; many insects feed there. Check stem bases at soil level for mold or discoloration caused by soil-borne diseases. Examine flowers and fruits for deformities, spots and holes. Check bark on tree trunks and branches for discoloration and holes.

Diagnosing problems correctly can be difficult, since their symptoms often look alike. For instance, plants that are yellowing and wilting may be suffering from wilt disease, or their roots might be eaten by maggots *(pages 114-115)*. And holes in leaves may be caused by a wide variety of insects *(pages 116-117)*. In addition, the symptoms of a disease may change as it progresses through various stages. For example, stripe smut *(page 125)* will first show up on a lawn as a pale area that grows more slowly than the surrounding grass. Later, this area will turn brown and die.

This chapter is designed as an aid to diagnosis. The section headings list symptoms of common plant problems, for example "Spots on Leaves" *(page 120)* or "Dieback of Tree and Shrub Foliage" *(page 128)*. Each section presents photographs of the insects, diseases or nutrient deficiencies that may be producing the symptom. For example, "Leaves Brown and Burnt Looking" *(page 119)* may be the result of potassium deficiency, salt toxicity or pesticide damage.

If you are having trouble with a specific type of plant, first refer to its chapter in this book for general information. The Troubleshooting Guide there will list several of the pests or diseases that affect the plant, and will direct you to the relevant pages in this chapter for details. Compare the photographs with the damage you see in your garden, and read the captions. The information they contain will help you decide which of the possible problems is affecting your plants.

Each caption begins with the problem's **Range**—the geographic area in which it is commonly found. Many pests survive only in specific regions. The caption then gives a **Description** of the problem—how the damage progressively develops, along with associated signs and symptoms. It then lists the **Affected Plants**—some problems are typically found only among certain types of plants. Each caption concludes with a **Control** strategy—the sequence of actions that should be taken to remedy the problem. These actions may include cultural control methods, such as adjusting the watering or amending the soil; and chemical control methods, such as spraying pesticides.

Cultural methods of pest and disease control are the most environmentally sound, and should always be tried first. Though pesticides can be a useful gardening tool, they are poisons that should be used with an eye to controlling pests, not eradicating them. Many pesticides are broad-spectrum, attacking not only the pest, but beneficial organisms as well. Also, insects in some areas have become resistant to certain pesticides. There is still much debate about the long-term environmental effects of pesticides, but if you watch your garden carefully, you may never need to resort to them.

Many insects and diseases can be successfully treated with chemicals only at certain stages of their life cycles. Consult the Cooperative Extension Service about the correct timing and frequency of spraying or dusting. Read the pesticide label closely to make sure your plant is listed. Most pesticides should not be used on food crops, although some pesticides may be used up to an indicated time before harvest. Before proceeding with a pesticide program, read about pesticides in the Tools & Techniques chapter *(page 129)*, and consult the Insecticides and Fungicides chart *(page 137)*.

The best treatment for pests and diseases is prevention. Clear the garden of debris, and weed regularly to eliminate host sites for troublesome organisms. Keep plants well spaced to allow ventilation and to reduce moisture buildup, which speeds the spread of disease. Diseases can migrate from plant to plant on clothing and tools, especially when plants are wet; avoid overhead watering, and don't work in a wet garden. Healthy, strong plants withstand insect and disease problems that would overcome weak, stressed plants. Ensure that your soil structure and pH *(page 16)* are good so that your plants can get the nutrients and moisture they need.

Occasionally, certain plants in a well-maintained garden will suffer recurring trouble with a specific disease or insect pest. Consult the Cooperative Extension Service or your local nursery for advice about hybrid varieties of the plant that are resistant to this particular invader.

Many insect pests are naturally controlled by so-called "beneficial" insects that prey upon them. Ladybugs, for instance, eat aphids. Some beneficials can be ordered by mail from garden supply companies to combat particular insect pests. Their effectiveness, however, depends on many climatic and garden conditions. Ask your Cooperative Extension Service or nursery about using beneficials in your area.

SEEDLINGS DYING

Damping off

Range: Continental U.S.

Description: Seedlings suddenly topple and die. Stem bases just above soil line are pinched and shriveled. Soil may be quite wet.

Affected plants: All seedlings, including grasses, when less than 2 inches tall.

Control: Dig up and destroy dead seedlings. Reseed *(pages 39, 80, 85)* with fungicide-treated seed, cover seed rows with a soilless mix, and thin seedlings when crowded. Check soil moisture *(page 18)* and reduce wetness as required.

Cutworms

Range: Continental U.S.

Description: Stems of young plants are severed at or just below soil level. Dark worms that curl up tightly when disturbed can be found in the soil beneath the surface at night. Cutworms also sever grass blades at soil surface, leaving dead patches. Climbing cutworms will eat above-ground leaves, buds and fruit.

Affected plants: All types.

Control: Scratch away soil and handpick *(page 137)* at night with flashlight. Install collars *(page 136)* around undamaged plants. Apply wood ash or sand to soil around plants. Spray plants and soil *(page 139)* with carbaryl, chlorpyrifos, pyrethrins or diazinon.

Slugs and snails

Range: Continental U.S.

Description: Seedlings are eaten. Low-growing plants have large ragged holes in leaves and stems near the ground. Trails of slime cover leaves and soil near plants. Dark, wet-looking, soft-bodied slugs *(above)* and hard-shelled snails feed on plants at night, and are found hidden in dark, damp garden locations by day.

Affected plants: Many types.

Control: Handpick *(page 137)* at dusk. Set traps or bait *(page 136)*. Dust soil around plants with wood ash, sand or diatomaceous earth. Broadcast metaldehyde bait *(page 136)*, water it lightly, and cover it with bricks or boards to keep birds and animals from eating it.

STUNTED PLANTS WITH DISTORTED, DISCOLORED LEAVES

Mosaic virus

Range: Continental U.S.

Description: Leaves have a yellow and green mottled or mosaic pattern, and may become curled and deformed. Plants may be stunted. Cucumber family fruits may be colored with a green and yellow mosaic pattern and covered with warts. Cabbage family vegetables may be stunted, with poorly developed heads.

Affected plants: All types.

Control: Dig up and destroy badly affected plants *(page 133)*. Control aphids *(page 118)*, leafhoppers *(page 118)* and cucumber beetles *(page 116)*, which may spread the disease. In the future, choose resistant varieties if available.

Aster yellows

Range: Continental U.S.

Description: Flowering plants have spindly stems, pale-veined leaves *(above, left)* and either do not flower or have distorted, green flowers *(above, right)*. Carrots have stunted yellow inner leaves, reddish-tipped outer leaves, and stunted, hairy taproots. Lettuce has stunted, curled, yellow inner leaves that do not form a head. Leafhoppers *(page 118)* may be found.

Affected plants: Flowers, carrots, lettuce, celery.

Control: Remove infected plants *(page 133)*. Weed thoroughly *(pages 35, 51)*, especially thistles, plantains and dandelions. Control six-spotted leafhoppers *(page 118)*, which spread the disease.

Curly top virus

Range: Western half of U.S.

Description: Leaves pucker along the veins, curl up or down at the margins *(above)*, and become either rough and brittle or tough and leathery. Plants become stunted, yellow and may die. Leafhoppers *(page 118)* may be found on plants or nearby weeds.

Affected plants: Beans, beets, cucumber family and tomatoes.

Control: Dig up and destroy infected plants *(page 133)*. Control beet leafhoppers *(page 118)*, which spread the disease. In the future, install a protective tunnel *(page 43)* over young plants in spring to keep leafhoppers from landing.

PLANTS YELLOWING AND WILTING, BOTTOM TO TOP

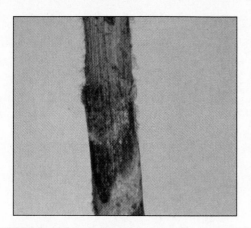

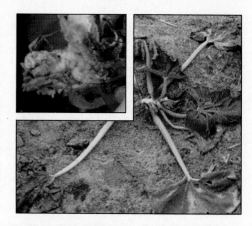

Stem rots

Range: Continental U.S.

Description: Leaves yellow, wilt and die. Stems weaken and collapse. Stems are soft and discolored, and may be slimy or mushy, or covered with mold *(above)*, fungal strands or pellets.

Affected plants: Many types, especially flowering plants.

Control: Cut out dying growth or remove badly diseased plants *(page 133)*. Check soil moisture *(page 18)* and drainage *(page 27)*. Consult the Cooperative Extension Service for information on drenching soil with fungicide when planting.

Crown rots

Range: Continental U.S., especially north central and northeast.

Description: Leaves progressively yellow and wilt, then stalks collapse and die. Stems just above the soil line or crowns just beneath the soil may become sunken and discolored. Weather may be very warm or cool and soil may be clayey and wet.

Affected plants: All types.

Control: Consult the Cooperative Extension Service for a specific diagnosis and for information about drenching soil with fungicide. Dig up and destroy badly infected plants *(page 133)*. Evaluate soil drainage *(page 27)* and improve as required.

Borer insects

Range: Continental U.S., except far west.

Description: All or part of a vine suddenly wilts. Below the wilted area are small bore holes exuding sawdust-like material. When vines are slit open, fat, white, brown-headed caterpillars, like the squash vine borer *(above)* are burrowed inside.

Affected plants: Many types, especially squash vine borer on cucumber family.

Control: Slit wilted vines, handpick and destroy borers *(page 137)*, and bury slitted part of vine in moistened soil to encourage rerooting. Ask the Cooperative Extension Service about proper times to spray egg-laying adult moths in your area. Spray or dust *(page 139)* with carbaryl. Plant resistant varieties.

Fusarium and verticillium wilts

Range: Southern U.S. for fusarium wilt and northern U.S. for verticillium wilt.

Description: Older, lower leaves yellow, curl and wilt, often only on one side of the plant *(above)*. With verticillium, plant growth will then slow and leaves drop. With fusarium, the whole plant will then wilt and die. When stems are cut across, brown staining is visible beneath the outer edge *(inset)*.

Affected plants: Many types.

Control: Dig up and destroy infected plants *(page 133)*. In the future, plant resistant varieties. Do not plant affected crops in the same soil for 3 years. Ask the Cooperative Extension Service about fumigating the soil if severe.

Bacterial wilt

Range: Continental U.S.

Description: At first, leaves wilt during daytime but recover at night. Later, leaves do not recover at all, and affected vines yellow and die. There may be cucumber beetles *(page 116)* on plants. When bases of cucumber vines are cut open, they are filled with sticky white sap.

Affected plants: Cucumber family, especially cucumbers and cantaloupes.

Control: Control cucumber beetles *(page 116)*, which spread the disease.

Nematodes (Eelworms)

Range: Continental U.S., especially south.

Description: Leaves begin to yellow and wilt. Leaves, flowers and stems become deformed and stunted. Plants may eventually die. When plants are unearthed, roots may be covered with small round nodules. Taproots, such as carrots, may develop many small side roots.

Affected plants: Many types, especially beans, tomatoes, celery, spinach, cucumbers, berries.

Control: If you suspect nematodes, consult the Cooperative Extension Service about testing and fumigating your soil. Dig up and destroy badly affected plants *(page 133)*. In the future, rotate crops and plant resistant varieties. Amend soil with manure to encourage nematode predators.

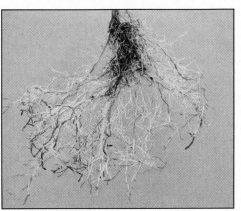

Root rots

Range: Continental U.S.

Description: Older leaves begin to wilt and yellow, and plants grow slowly or become stunted. In hot, dry weather, entire plant may wilt. When unearthed, roots may be soft, black and rotting *(above, left)* or brown and streaked *(above, right)*. Soil may be quite wet.

Affected plants: All types.

Control: Consult the Cooperative Extension Service for help in diagnosing a specific rot problem and for information about drenching soil with fungicide, if recommended. Dig up and destroy badly diseased plants *(page 133)*. Evaluate soil moisture *(page 18)* and soil drainage *(page 27)*; avoid overwatering.

Root maggots

Range: Central, western and northern U.S.

Description: Lower leaves wilt. Gradually, plants lose vigor, turn blue-gray and become stunted. Weather may be cool and wet. There may be tiny eggs on the soil at stem bases. When plants are unearthed, legless white maggots are found on roots or bulbs.

Affected plants: Many types, especially cabbage family, onions and carrots.

Control: Dust soil around plants with diatomaceous earth or wood ash to prevent egg-laying by flies. Clear plant debris thoroughly in fall to eliminate overwintering sites. In the future consult the Cooperative Extension Service for information about drenching the soil with diazinon before seeding or transplanting.

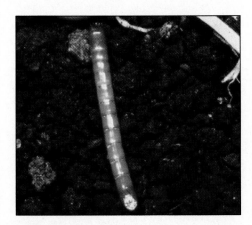

Wireworms

Range: Continental U.S.

Description: Plants are stunted and grow slowly. Plants may be growing on land that was recently in sod. When unearthed, segmented, hard-shelled, six-legged yellow to orange worms are feeding on roots and burrowed into tubers.

Affected plants: Many types, especially corn, potatoes, beets, carrots, turnips and grass.

Control: Cultivate soil thoroughly *(page 19)* in fall to expose larvae. Plant alfalfa or clover as a cover crop. Evaluate soil drainage *(page 27)* and improve as required. Ask the Cooperative Extension Service for information about drenching the soil with diazinon before planting.

Bulb rots

Range: Continental U.S.

Description: Bulbs either do not grow or bulb plants begin yellowing and wilting, starting with the lower leaves. New foliage is sparse and stunted. When unearthed, bulbs have only a few dark and rotting roots *(above, left)* or are rotted and without roots *(above, right)*. Rotted bulbs may be dark and spongy or dry and withered, and covered with discolored spots, lesions or mold.

Affected plants: Flowering bulbs and corms such as tulips, lilies, daffodils, gladiolus, freesias and crocuses, as well as onions.

Control: Ask the Cooperative Extension Service for help in diagnosing a specific rot problem and determining its treatment. Dig up and destroy diseased plants *(page 133)*. Evaluate soil moisture *(page 18)* and soil drainage *(page 27)* and reduce soil wetness as required. At the end of the season, dig up bulbs carefully to avoid wounds. Store bulbs in a cool, dry, airy place. Discard bulbs that rot in storage. Plant bulbs in a new location next season.

HOLES IN LEAVES, BUDS, FLOWERS AND FRUIT (INSECTS VISIBLE)

Japanese beetles

Range: Continental U.S., especially east.

Description: Flowers are frayed and eaten. Leaves are rapidly being eaten away between veins, leaving lacy skeletons. Dark, metallic, coppery-winged beetles are crawling on plants. Grubs feed on grass roots in lawns *(page 123)*.

Affected plants: Many types.

Control: Handpick *(page 137)*. Install scent traps *(page 136)* away from infested plants to lure beetles. Spray grubs *(page 139)* with *Bacillus popillae* (milky spore disease), or with carbaryl, diazinon or methoxychlor, at 10-day intervals. Cultivate soil *(page 19)* frequently to destroy grubs. Dust lawns *(page 140)* with *Bacillus popillae* to control grubs.

Colorado potato beetles

Range: Continental U.S., except California, Nevada and southern Florida

Description: Black and yellow striped adults *(above)*, and humpbacked red larvae *(inset)* eat large holes in leaves and stems. Plants may be rapidly defoliated. There may be clusters of yellow eggs on leaf undersides.

Affected plants: Potatoes, eggplants, peppers and tomatoes.

Control: Handpick *(page 137)*. Crush egg clusters. Spread diatomaceous earth on soil around plants to kill grubs. Spray *(page 139)* or dust *(page 140)* with rotenone, carbaryl, diazinon, dimethoate or malathion. In the future, mulch *(page 21)* in spring to stop adults overwintering in soil from climbing onto plants. Rotate crops.

Cucumber beetles

Range: Continental U.S., especially east.

Description: Leaves and flowers are eaten by yellow-orange, beetles *(above, left)* or black-spotted beetles *(above, right)*. Grubs feed on corn roots. Adults spread bacterial wilt disease *(page 114)* and mosaic virus *(page 113)*.

Affected plants: Many types, especially cucumber family.

Control: Handpick *(page 137)*. Weed thoroughly *(page 35)* to eliminate egg-laying sites. Dust *(page 140)* with wood ash, diatomaceous earth, rotenone or pyrethrins. Clear garden debris thoroughly in fall. In the future, rotate crops. Cultivate soil *(page 19)* before planting and mulch heavily to reduce overwintering beetles.

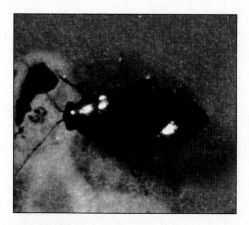

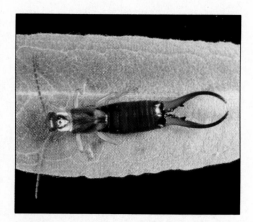

Flea beetles

Range: Continental U.S.

Description: Leaves are riddled with tiny holes. Leaves of young plants may be rapidly eaten. Growth of older plants may be slowed. When leaves are touched, tiny, dark, metallic beetles jump rapidly, like fleas. Flea beetles can spread early blight *(page 121)*.

Affected plants: Many types of vegetables.

Control: Dust immediately *(page 140)* with diatomaceous earth, rotenone, pyretherins, carbaryl, diazinon or methoxychlor, and repeat as necessary. Cultivate the soil *(page 19)* to destroy eggs and larvae. Install protective tunnel using fine mesh *(page 43)*. Clear garden debris thoroughly in fall.

Mexican bean beetles

Range: Continental U.S., except northwest.

Description: Leaves are skeletonized. Orange to coppery-yellow ladybug-like adults, with 16 black spots, and humpbacked, spiny yellow grubs *(above)* can be found on leaf undersides. There may be clusters of yellow eggs on leaf undersides.

Affected plants: Many types, especially beans.

Control: Handpick *(page 137)*. Crush egg clusters found on leaf undersides. Spray *(page 139)* with rotenone, pyrethrins, carbaryl, dimethoate, malathion or methoxychlor. Clear garden debris thoroughly in fall to eliminate overwintering sites.

Earwigs

Range: Continental U.S.

Description: Seedlings are chewed. Flowers are frayed. Ragged holes are eaten in leaves. Reddish-brown insects with pincer-like appendages crawl on plants at night. By day they are found in dark, damp hiding places.

Affected plants: Many types, including lawns.

Control: Trap *(page 136)* and destroy insects. Spray or dust plants *(page 139)* with diazinon or carbaryl, or broadcast carbaryl bait and cover it with boards to keep birds and animals away. In the future, cultivate soil thoroughly before planting *(page 19)* to destroy eggs in soil. Ask the Cooperative Extension Service about drenching the soil if the problem is extensive.

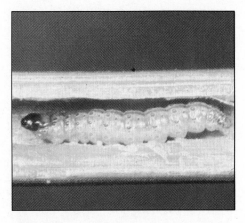

Tomato hornworms

Range: Continental U.S.

Description: Many leaves are eaten, with only their midribs left untouched. Holes are eaten in unripened or green vegetables. There may be black droppings on plants. Large, fat, green caterpillars with white diagonal bars on their sides and a small horn protruding from their hind ends are crawling on plants. There may be greenish-yellow eggs on leaf undersides.

Affected plants: Tomatoes, peppers and eggplants.

Control: Handpick *(page 137)* and destroy. If infestation is severe, spray or dust *(page 140)* with diatomaceous earth, *Bacillus thuringiensis*, carbaryl, pyrethrins or rotenone when worms are small. Cultivate soil in fall to destroy pupae *(page 19)*.

Cabbage worms

Range: Continental U.S.

Description: Pale green, white-striped cabbage loopers *(above, left)* or velvety green, yellow-striped imported cabbage worms *(above, right)* eat large ragged holes in leaves and flowers, and tunnel into vegetables. There may be masses of green-brown excrement on plants.

Affected plants: Cabbage family and some flowers.

Control: Handpick *(page 137)*. Spray *(page 139)* or dust *(page 140)* with diatomaceous earth, *Bacillus thuringiensis*, rotenone or carbaryl, especially when worms are young, and repeat as needed. In fall, clear garden debris thoroughly and cultivate soil to destroy pupae.

European corn borers

Range: Continental U.S., except south, southwest and far west.

Description: Pinholes in corn leaves and clusters of white eggs that look like fish scales may be found on undersides. Tan or pink worms with brown dots may be found on plants. Small holes may be bored into stalks and the bases of ears and stalks may be broken.

Affected plants: Corn; also peppers, tomatoes and potatoes.

Control: When leaf holes and eggs are seen, spray leaf whorls and ear bases, not tassels, weekly *(page 139)* with carbaryl or rotenone. When bore holes are found, slit stalks below holes with small knife and handpick insects *(page 137)*. Clear all plant debris in the fall. Plant early with resistant varieties.

Corn earworms (tomato fruitworms)

Range: Continental U.S.

Description: Leaves and flower buds may be chewed. Corn silks are eaten. Holes are bored into corn husks and other vegetables. Striped green, yellow, pink or brown caterpillars may be found.

Affected plants: Corn, peppers, tomatoes, potatoes, beans, peas, and some flowers.

Control: Dust worms on foliage *(page 140)* with *Bacillus thuringiensis* or carbaryl. Suffocate worms in corn ears with mineral oil applied to the tips once silk has wilted. Destroy other infested vegetables. In the fall, clear all plant debris and cultivate soil deeply *(page 19)* to prevent overwintering.

Stinkbugs

Range: Continental U.S., especially south.

Description: New shoots are wilted. Leaves are deformed and brown. Fruits and vegetables may be distorted. Shield-shaped insects that emit an odor when crushed, like the harlequin bug *(above)*, are on plants. There may be bright-colored, striped eggs on leaf undersides.

Affected plants: Many types.

Control: Handpick *(page 137)* in early morning when insects move slowly. Crush eggs. Weed thoroughly *(pages 35, 51)* to eliminate egg-laying and overwintering sites. Spray or dust *(page 139)* with carbaryl, methoxychlor or rotenone. Clear all garden debris in fall. Rotate crops in spring.

Sawflies

Range: Continental U.S.

Description: Holes are eaten in leaves, leaving only larger leaf veins. Older conifer needles are eaten. Branches may be rapidly defoliated. New shoots may be black and deformed. Small, soft, glistening, slug-like larvae or caterpillars with many legs—the larvae of certain wasps—are clustered on foliage.

Affected plants: Many trees, shrubs and flowers, especially roses and raspberries.

Control: Spray *(page 139)* or dust roses and other flowers, trees and shrubs with diatomaceous earth, carbaryl or acephate; on fruit trees, use methoxychlor.

117

LEAVES, BUDS AND FLOWERS STREAKED, PUCKERED AND CURLED (TINY INSECTS)

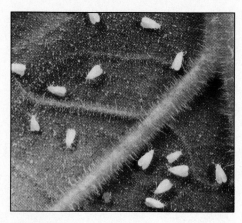

Aphids

Range: Continental U.S.

Description: Young shoots are curled. Leaves are curled and stunted and may be covered with sticky honeydew or a sooty black fungus. Tiny, pale, soft-bodied, pear-shaped insects are clustered on the tips of new shoots and the undersides of young, upper leaves. Aphids transmit mosaic virus *(page 113)*.

Affected plants: Many types.

Control: Hose off plants *(page 137)*. Spray *(page 139)* plants with insecticidal soap, carbaryl, methoxychlor, diazinon or malathion, thoroughly covering leaf undersides where insects feed. Mulch *(page 21)* with aluminum foil to reflect light, since aphids prefer darkness.

Whiteflies

Range: Continental U.S., especially southern and coastal areas.

Description: Leaves are mottled or yellowing, and may be withered and dying. They may be covered with sticky honeydew or a sooty black fungus. Leaf undersides are covered with tiny white flies, which flutter in clouds when leaves are disturbed.

Affected plants: Many types, especially tomatoes, cucumbers and lettuce.

Control: Spray *(page 139)* with insecticidal soap and set out yellow sticky traps. Shake plants periodically to disturb the flies and make them stick. In future, check nursery plants carefully for signs of infestation before buying. Control is difficult and must be repeated.

Leafhoppers

Range: Continental U.S.

Description: Leaves are lightly stippled white, yellow or pale green, and may be coated with sticky honeydew and burnt looking. Eventually leaves may curl. Small pale-green insects fly away from under leaves when plants are touched. Six-spotted leafhoppers *(above)* transmit aster yellows *(page 113)*, and beet leafhoppers transmit curly top virus *(page 113)*.

Affected plants: Many types.

Control: Weed thoroughly *(pages 35, 51)*, especially thistles, plantains and dandelions, to eliminate egg-laying sites. Ask the Cooperative Extension Service about optimal spraying times. Spray *(page 139)* with pyrethrins, rotenone, malathion, diazinon or carbaryl. Dust *(page 140)* with diatomaceous earth as a repellant.

Spider mites

Range: Continental U.S.

Description: Leaves become stippled, then dull bronze or yellow, dry and dirty looking. There may be fine webbing over leaves, shoots and buds. Weather may be hot and dry. When a sheet of paper is held beneath leaves and plant is tapped sharply, tiny reddish specks fall onto the paper.

Affected plants: All types.

Control: Hose off plants *(page 137)*, directing water to leaf undersides. If infestation is severe, spray vegetables and fruits weekly *(page 139)* with insecticidal soap, diazinon or malathion, and flowers and shrubs with dicofol, making sure to spray leaf undersides thoroughly.

Thrips

Range: Continental U.S.

Description: Blossoms wither. Flower petals are streaked and brown at the edges. Leaves are flecked and silvery, and may become bleached and withered *(above, left)*. Minute sliver-like insects, brownish-orange to black, found inside flowers *(above, right)*, and on leaves.

Affected plants: Many flowers, cabbage and onions.

Control: Pick off infested buds and blooms *(page 133)*. Hose off *(page 137)*. Mulch *(page 21)* with aluminum foil to reflect light, since thrips prefer darkness. Dust *(page 140)* with diatomaceous earth or spray *(page 139)* flowers with acephate, carbaryl, malathion or methoxychlor, and vegetables with diazinon or malathion.

Lacebugs

Range: Continental U.S.

Description: Upper leaf surfaces are speckled silvery gray and bleached looking. Foliage may curl, turn brown and drop. Leaf undersides are covered with hard, shiny black drops of excrement. Tiny, clear-winged insects with scalloped, lacey-looking bodies are found on the undersides of leaves.

Affected plants: Many ornamental trees and shrubs.

Control: Spray *(page 139)* with malathion, carbaryl, acephate or dicofol when damage is first seen, making sure to cover leaf undersides thoroughly.

LEAVES DISCOLORED (NUTRIENT DEFICIENCY)

Low phosphorus level

High phosphorus level

Nitrogen deficiency

Range: Continental U.S.

Description: Older, lower plant leaves become pale, then yellow, and may eventually drop. Newer, upper leaves are small. Overall growth is slow, and flower and fruit production is poor.

Affected plants: All types.

Control: Fertilize plants with nitrogen *(page 26)*. Test soil pH *(page 23)* and adjust if it is higher than 7.8 or lower than 5.5. Check soil drainage *(page 27)* and improve drainage *(page 30)* if soil is too wet; lack of oxygen prevents plants from utilizing nitrogen. Evaluate soil texture *(page 20)* and amend if soil is too sandy, allowing nitrogen to leach.

Phosphorus deficiency

Range: Continental U.S., especially south and southeast.

Description: Growth is slow or may stop, leaves remain small, and few flowers or fruits are produced. Leaves become dark and dull, and stems and leaf veins or margins may be tinged purple-red.

Affected plants: All types.

Control: If plants are seriously affected, fertilize immediately *(page 27)* with a high-phosphorus fertilizer. Check soil pH *(page 23)* and raise pH *(page 24)* if lower than 5.5. In the future, fertilize when planting with a starter solution high in phosphorus, and side-dress plants regularly *(page 27)* with a fertilizer containing at least 5% phosphorus.

Iron deficiency

Range: Continental U.S., especially western regions and Florida.

Description: Upper leaves become pale green or yellow between well-defined darker green veins. Lower leaves remain green. Rainfall in your area may be low. Lime may have recently been added to the soil or plants may be growing near a brick or concrete wall that leaches lime.

Affected plants: Many types, especially acid-loving azaleas, rhododendrons, camellias and raspberries and fruit trees.

Control: Check soil pH *(page 23)* and lower to 7.0 *(page 24)* if very alkaline. In one month, test soil fertility *(page 25)* and feed with a fertilizer containing chelated iron if required.

LEAVES BROWN AND BURNT-LOOKING

Potassium deficiency

Range: West coast and eastern half of U.S., especially south and southeast.

Description: Older leaves are mottled pale green or yellow, and have burnt-looking, spotted, curled and dying edges. Plants grow slowly and produce few flowers and fruits.

Affected plants: All types.

Control: Fertilize regularly *(page 27)* with a fertilizer containing at least 5% potassium. Evaluate soil texture *(page 20)* and amend if soil is too sandy, allowing potassium to leach away.

Salt toxicity

Range: Continental U.S., especially western half.

Description: Edges of leaves and areas between leaf veins turn brown, wither and die. Leaves may drop. Plants grow slowly or do not grow. Soil may be covered with a white or dark crusty material. Rainfall in your area may be low.

Affected plants: All types.

Control: Avoid amending soil with high-salt organic materials such as manure. Check soil drainage *(page 27)*. Leach soil *(page 19)*. If soil drains poorly, improve drainage *(page 30)*. In dry regions, mulch *(page 38)* to reduce evaporation and resulting salt accumulation.

Pesticide damage

Range: Continental U.S.

Description: Leaves suddenly develop irregular, burnt, brown blotches. Young leaves and blossoms may be distorted, brown and dying. Pesticides may have been sprayed nearby within the past 24 hours.

Affected plants: All types.

Control: Pick off and destroy *(page 133)* damaged parts. Keep plants well watered and control other pests and diseases to avoid additional stress. In the future, do not spray pesticides when it is windy or the temperature is higher than 90°F. Carefully follow directions on pesticide labels for proper application. Do not eat produce from these plants.

SPOTS ON LEAVES

Bacterial leaf spots

Range: Continental U.S.

Description: Plants infected by bacterial leaf spot diseases such as angular leaf spot *(above)* often have tiny angular spots on leaves and on other plant parts. Under humid conditions these spots are often rotting or oozing.

Affected plants: All types.

Control: Pick off and destroy *(page 133)* infected leaves and remove severely affected plants. Keep garden clear of debris. Avoid overhead watering. Ask the Cooperative Extension Service for a specific diagnosis and treatment. In general, spray *(page 139)* with basic copper sulfate or streptomycin at recommended times and intervals.

Fungal leaf spots

Range: Continental U.S.

Description: Plants infected by fungal leaf spot diseases such as septoria leaf spot *(above, left)* or cercospora leaf spot *(above, right)* often have small circular spots with distinct margins, usually only on the leaves. Spots may be covered with fungal growth. Spots may enlarge to form blotches, and leaves yellow and die, but often do not drop.

Affected plants: All types.

Control: Pick off and destroy *(page 133)* infected leaves. Keep garden clear of all debris and fallen leaves. Weed thoroughly *(pages 35, 51)*. Avoid overhead watering, which can spread fungi. Ask the Cooperative Extension Service for help in identifying a specific disease and its treatment. In general, spray biweekly *(page 139)* with benomyl, captan, chlorothalonil, maneb or zineb as long as weather is wet and spotting continues to prevent new leaf spots from developing. If plants do not respond to these fungicides, spots may be caused by a bacterial leaf spot disease *(left)*.

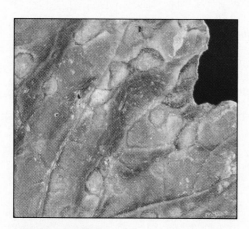

Anthracnose

Range: Eastern half of U.S.

Description: In warm, rainy weather, bean leaf undersides develop dark, elongated spots and darkened veins. Cucumber family leaves develop yellow, water-soaked spots that dry, brown and fall out; on watermelon leaves, spots blacken. Fruits and vegetables also affected.

Affected plants: Beans, tomatoes, cucumbers.

Control: Avoid working with wet plants. Mulch *(page 41)* or support *(pages 44-47)* plants away from soil. Spray *(page 139)* with chlorothalonil weekly while wet weather persists. Clean up plant debris thoroughly at the end of the season. Next year, rotate crops.

Black spot

Range: Continental U.S.

Description: Leaves develop black spots, often circled with yellow, that enlarge to form blotches, then fall. Plants may flower poorly.

Affected plants: Roses.

Control: Prune off *(page 59)* badly infected canes and dig up and destroy *(page 133)* badly diseased plants. Avoid overhead watering. Spray weekly *(page 139)* with benomyl, captan, folpet or triforine during wet weather, and biweekly during dry weather, covering leaf undersides thoroughly. Spray *(page 139)* pruned plants during dormant season with lime sulphur or chlorothalonil. In the future, plant tolerant varieties.

Alternaria leaf spot

Range: Continental U.S.

Description: In hot, wet weather, cabbage family leaves develop brown spots with concentric rings that become covered with dark felt-like mold. Cucumber family leaves develop water-soaked spots with dark concentric rings, then dry and drop. Carnation leaves develop dark purple spots with pale centers. Geranium leaves develop brown spots with dark centers.

Affected plants: Many types.

Control: Spray weekly *(page 139)* in wet weather with chlorothalonil or capstan. Clear all garden debris in fall. In the future, rotate plants.

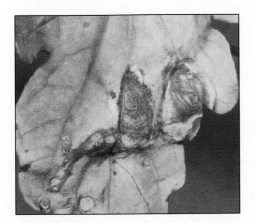

Early blight

Range: West coast and eastern half of U.S., especially north.

Description: Older leaves develop dark brown target-like spots with concentric rings, then yellow and die. Disease spreads gradually from older to younger leaves. Potatoes may be covered with brown, corky spots. Tomatoes develop black, sunken, leathery spots on their stem ends. Weather may be warm and humid.

Affected plants: Tomatoes and potatoes.

Control: Keep plants well fertilized *(page 27)* to produce vigorous new leaf growth. Furrow-water *(page 35)* or drip-irrigate *(page 36)* to avoid wetting foliage and spreading disease. Spray *(page 139)* with chlorothalonil, basic copper sulphate or maneb every 7 to 10 days if disease is severe.

Late blight

Range: West coast and eastern half of U.S.

Description: Lower leaves develop brownish-black blotches at the margins. Leaf undersides develop a white mold and infected leaves rapidly brown, wither and dry up. Tomatoes develop gray, water-soaked spots that become brown and corky. Potatoes develop brown spots that rot. Weather may be cool and wet.

Affected plants: Potatoes and tomatoes.

Control: Spray *(page 139)* with chlorothalonil every 7 to 10 days at first signs of disease. If potato foliage is badly infected in late summer, cut stems at ground level *(page 134)*, destroy vines and wait two weeks before harvesting to avoid infecting tubers. Clear plant debris thoroughly in fall.

Downy mildew

Range: Continental U.S.

Description: Upper leaf surfaces develop yellow patches that become brown and netted with dark markings. The undersides of these patches become covered with a downy white or purple mold in humid weather. Affected cucumbers and cantaloupes may be small and bitter, and cabbage heads covered with sunken black spots.

Affected plants: Many types, especially cabbage family and onions.

Control: Spray *(page 139)* with chlorothalonil. Spray onions with maneb. Furrow-water *(page 35)* or drip-irrigate *(page 36)* to avoid wetting foliage and spreading disease. In the future, plant resistant varieties, if available. Clear all debris in fall

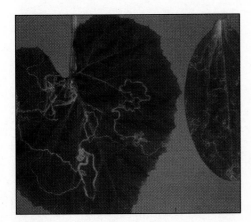

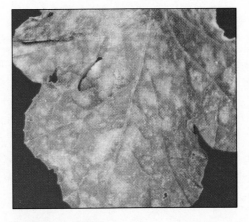

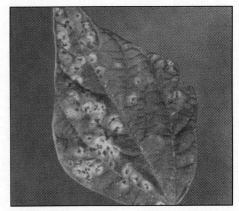

Rust

Range: Continental U.S.

Description: Leaf undersides and stems are covered with orange to red-brown, crusty spots or pustules. Affected leaves yellow, then brown and drop. Infected plants weak and stunted.

Affected plants: All types.

Control: Ask the Cooperative Extension Service for help identifying a specific rust fungus and its treatment. Pick and destroy infected leaves and prune off and destroy infected stems *(page 133)*. Avoid overhead watering. Spray *(page 139)* with sulfur, maneb, zineb or triforine. Clear all debris in fall. In the future, plant resistant varieties.

Powdery mildew

Range: Continental U.S.

Description: Upper surfaces of older leaves, as well as fruits and pods, are covered with powdery white growth, which may spread rapidly. Affected leaves may become yellow and dry. Plant growth may slow and yields may be small.

Affected plants: Many types, especially later in the growing season when they are mature.

Control: Avoid overhead watering. Spray weekly *(page 139)* with benomyl, captan, chlorothalonil, sulphur or folpet as long as infection persists. If many applications are required, alternate fungicides to avoid building up resistance. In the future, plant resistant varieties, if available. Rotate crops.

Leafminers

Range: Continental U.S.

Description: Pale, papery winding trails or blotches cover leaves. Beneath these trails are black specks of maggot excrement. Tiny maggots, the larvae of certain flies, tunnel through the inner layers of leaf tissue.

Affected plants: Many types, spinach, beets.

Control: Pick and destroy infested leaves *(page 133)*. Weed thoroughly *(pages 35, 51)*. If problem is severe, ask the Cooperative Extension Service when to spray adult flies during their egg-laying period, and spray *(page 139)* with diazinon, lindane or malathion. Cultivate soil in late fall and early spring to destroy pupae. Rotate crops.

SPOTTED, DISCOLORED OR ROTTING VEGETABLES

Sunscald
Range: Continental U.S.

Description: Young fruits develop light blistered areas that later become sunken and papery, and may begin to rot.

Affected plants: Tomatoes and peppers.

Control: Cage tomato vines *(page 45)* or prune staked tomatoes properly *(page 45)* to provide greater sun protection. Install a protective tunnel *(page 43)* to shade peppers. Avoid excessive pruning, which exposes developing fruit to excessive sun.

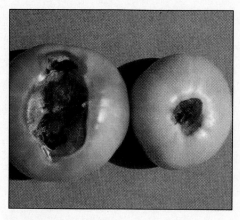

Blossom end rot
Range: Continental U.S.

Description: Due to calcium deficiency, vegetables develop water-soaked spots on their blossom ends. Spots enlarge, turn brown and leathery, and begin to rot. Soil may fluctuate between very wet and very dry, or be very high in salts, both of which inhibit calcium intake.

Affected plants: Tomatoes, peppers and cucumber family.

Control: Evaluate soil moisture *(page 18)* and adjust watering accordingly. Furrow-water *(page 35)* or drip-irrigate *(page 36)* to ensure uniform deep moisture. Mulch *(page 41)* to help conserve moisture if soil dries rapidly in hot weather.

Anthracnose
Range: Eastern U.S.

Description: Tomatoes develop sunken areas with a dark bull's-eye spot in the center *(above, left)*. Bean pods have round, black sunken spots *(above, right)*. Weather may be wet.

Affected plants: Many vegetables, especially tomatoes, beans and cucumber family.

Control: Avoid working with wet plants. Mulch *(page 41)* or support *(pages 44, 46)* plants to keep them out of contact with the soil. Spray *(page 139)* with chlorothalonil or capstan every 7 to 10 days while wet weather persists. Clean up plant debris thoroughly at the end of the season. Next year, plant susceptible crops in a new site.

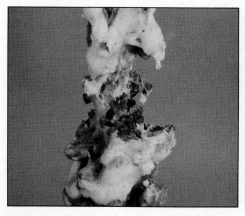

Molds
Range: Continental U.S.

Description: Leaves, stems and fruits develop water-soaked spots that enlarge, turn brown and become covered with mold in cool, humid weather. Two common molds are white mold *(above, left)*, which produces a fluffy, white fungus growth, and gray mold *(above, right)*, which produces a velvety, brown-gray fungus growth.

Affected plants: Many vegetables, especially beans and lettuce, for white mold, and many flowers and small fruits for gray mold.

Control: Prune off *(page 133)* infected plant parts. Dig up and destroy badly diseased plants *(page 133)*. Avoid overhead watering. Spray *(page 139)* plants infected with gray mold with captan, maneb, zineb or benomyl. Clear all debris from garden in fall. In the future, rotate plants affected by white mold, and do not overcrowd them when planting. As a preventive measure, spray *(page 139)* young plants susceptible to white mold with benomyl.

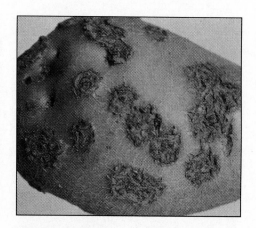

Common scab
Range: Continental U.S.

Description: Tubers become covered with brown, corky patches and pits. Rainfall may be low in your area, lime may have recently been added to the soil or plants may be growing near a brick or concrete wall that leaches lime.

Affected plants: Potatoes; also beets, turnips, carrots and parsnips.

Control: Avoid using fresh manure that may carry scab-causing bacteria. In the future, plant resistant varieties if available. Rotate affected crops for 3 years. Check soil pH *(page 23)* and adjust *(page 24)* if required.

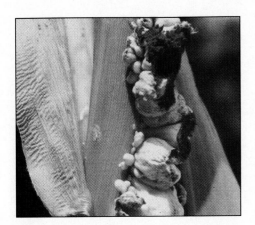

Corn smut

Range: Continental U.S., except northern midwest.

Description: Plants develop white, spongy galls that later turn gray-brown and become filled with powdery spores. Weather may be hot and dry.

Affected plants: Corn, especially when young.

Control: Prune off galls *(page 100)* as early as possible to avoid dispersing spores. Clean garden thoroughly at the end of the season. In the future, plant tolerant varieties.

Clubroot

Range: Continental U.S.

Description: At first, plants wilt during daytime but recover at night. Then older leaves begin to yellow and droop, plants become stunted and slowly die. When unearthed, roots are swollen and twisted.

Affected plants: Cabbage family.

Control: Dig up and destroy badly infected plants *(page 133)*. Do not plant cabbage family plants in same location for 7 years. In selecting a new site, test and adjust soil pH *(pages 23 and 24)* to keep it slightly alkaline.

Blackrot

Range: Continental U.S., especially east.

Description: Seedlings yellow and die. Older plants develop yellow, wilted V-shaped areas on the margins of their lower leaves, which spread inward and turn brown. Veins may be black. Cabbage heads may rot. Weather may be warm and humid.

Affected plants: Cabbage family.

Control: Dig up and destroy infected plants *(page 133)*. Furrow-water *(page 35)* or drip-irrigate *(page 36)* to avoid wetting plant tops and spreading disease. In the future, rotate cabbage family crops for 2 years.

LAWN THINNING, TURNING BROWN AND DYING IN PATCHES

Sod webworms

Range: Continental U.S., except southwest, midwest and northern midwest.

Description: The lawn develops dead patches in the driest, sunniest parts. Grass blades are chewed off at soil level. Tan moths may have been flying over the lawn at dusk. Birds may be feeding on the lawn in early morning. Black-spotted, tan or gray worms *(inset)* are nestled in web-lined tubes below soil surface.

Affected grasses: Many types; bentgrass.

Control: Mow and water the lawn, then spray *(page 139)* with *Bacillus thuringiensis*, carbaryl, diazinon or chlorpyrifos next day when grass is dry. Do not water for 48 hours after spraying.

Chinch bugs

Range: Continental U.S.

Description: The lawn develops large, irregular, yellowish, dead sunken patches, especially in hot, dry weather. When a bottomless can is pushed into the ground at the edge of a dead patch and filled with water, small black-and-white or brown-and-white insects *(inset)* float up.

Affected grasses: Many types, especially St. Augustine grass, bentgrass and bluegrass.

Control: Mow and water the lawn. Apply compost or lawn fertilizer, or spray *(page 139)* with carbaryl, chlorpyrifos or diazinon. Repeat several times during the season to control successive generations, especially in the south.

White grubs

Range: Continental U.S.

Description: The lawn develops irregular, yellow-brown dead patches, especially in areas lit at night. Birds may be feeding in these areas. Dead patches roll back easily, like carpet. Grass blades are severed. Fat, grayish-white, brown-headed, U-shaped worms are burrowed 1 to 3 inches into the soil beneath.

Affected grasses: All types. Also affects corn, strawberries, potatoes, onions.

Control: Roll up dead patches of grass, cultivate soil and handpick *(page 80)*. Consult the Cooperative Extension Service for optimal spraying times in your area. Spray *(page 139)* with carbaryl, diazinon or chlorpyrifos, then water deeply.

LAWN THINNING, TURNING BROWN AND DYING IN PATCHES (continued)

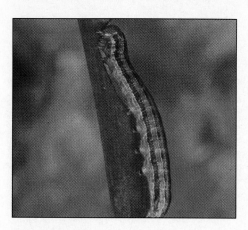

Armyworms

Range: Southwest, south, southeast and eastern U.S.

Description: The lawn develops bare patches, often beginning in spring after cold, rainy weather. Three-striped, tan to brown caterpillars can be found feeding on grass blades during the day.

Affected grasses: Many types; also vegetable crops.

Control: Mow and water the lawn, then spray *(page 139)* with *Bacillus thuringiensis*, carbaryl, chlorpyrifos or diazinon. Repeat throughout the season to control successive generations.

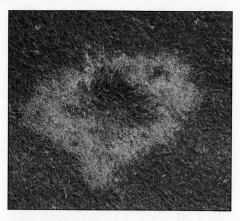

Fusarium blight

Range: Continental U.S., except midwest and north central.

Description: The lawn develops dead patches, or dead rings with green centers, in hot, dry weather. Grass blades look bleached and have brown or black bases. Lawn may not have been watered much, may have thick thatch, or may have been heavily fertilized with nitrogen.

Affected grasses: Bluegrass and bentgrass.

Control: Remove dead grass. Dethatch *(page 86)*. Reseed with resistant varieties. Do not fertilize. Next spring, before disease recurs, water thoroughly, spray *(page 139)* lawn with benomyl and water again. Repeat twice at two-week intervals to slow spread of disease.

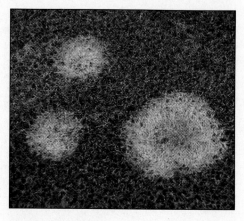

Pink snow mold

Range: Northern half of U.S.

Description: The lawn develops roughly circular, tan to yellowish dead patches when snow melts, or when weather is cool and wet in late fall or early spring. Dead patches may be pink around the edges and covered with greyish-white mold.

Affected grasses: Many types, especially bentgrass.

Control: Spray *(page 139)* the lawn in early spring, when disease first appears, with benomyl or chlorothalonil. In the future, keep lawn mowed throughout the fall to prevent long grass from matting beneath snow. Do not fertilize the lawn in fall. Spray again in late autumn, before snowfall.

Helminthosporium leaf spot

Range: Continental U.S., especially northwest, south, southeast and east coast.

Description: The lawn develops sparse brown areas in early summer. Grass blades are covered with small oval spots that have tan centers and purplish borders.

Affected grasses: Many types, especially Kentucky bluegrass.

Control: Spray *(page 139)* the lawn at least twice, at 10-day intervals, with chlorothalonil, maneb or mancozeb when spots first appear. Do not mow or water lawn within 24 hours of treatment. Dethatch *(page 86)* if required, and avoid over-fertilizing. If necessary, reseed *(page 85)* with resistant varieties.

Pythium blight

Range: South, southeast and east-coast U.S.

Description: The lawn develops dead patches in very hot weather. Grass first wilts and browns in small spots, which may then enlarge and spread quite rapidly. Grass blades in these areas mat together when they are walked on.

Affected grasses: Many types, especially ryegrass.

Control: Spray *(page 139)* with chloroneb at 10-day intervals and continue as long as disease persists. Avoid mowing or walking on infected areas and spreading fungus. If damage is severe, cultivate lawn and reseed *(page 85)* or resod *(page 83)*.

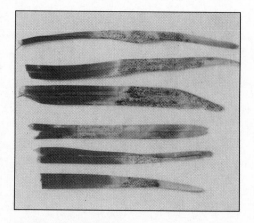

Septoria leaf blight

Range: Continental U.S., except far south and northern midwest.

Description: The lawn develops pale areas that have a gray cast, particularly in spring and fall when weather is cool and wet. Tips of grass blades are pale yellow or gray and may be covered with tiny black spots. Lawn may not have been fertilized for some time.

Affected grasses: Many types, especially Bermuda grass.

Control: Spray weekly *(page 139)* with chlorothalonil or maneb or iprodione as long as condition persists. Mow regularly to remove diseased tips. Keep lawn fertilized. If damage is extensive, reseed *(page 85)* with a tolerant mix.

Stripe smut

Range: Northeast and north central U.S.

Description: The lawn develops pale green or yellow areas in cool weather in the spring and fall. These areas grow more slowly than surrounding grass. Grass blades become streaked, first yellow, then gray or black, and begin to curl and shred. Lawn may be heavily watered.

Affected grasses: Many types, especially Kentucky bluegrass.

Control: Reduce watering. Spray *(page 139)* lawn with benomyl at least twice at two-week intervals when symptoms appear, and water thoroughly afterwards. Reseed *(page 80)* badly damaged areas with resistant varieties.

Rust

Range: South, southeast and northwest U.S., and east and west coasts.

Description: The lawn becomes sparse and pale. Grass blades are covered with orange or reddish powdery material that rubs off on the fingers. Weather may be warm and humid. Lawn may not have been fertilized much.

Affected grasses: Kentucky bluegrass and ryegrass.

Control: Fertilize to stimulate new growth. Mow regularly and remove infected clippings. If infection is severe, spray *(page 139)* the lawn with chlorothalonil, maneb or zineb every 14 days until infection disappears. If damage is extensive, cultivate lawn *(page 82)*, and reseed *(page 85)* with resistant varieties.

Brown patch

Range: Southeast U.S.

Description: The lawn develops roughly circular, expanding dead patches in warm, humid weather. Edges may have a dark, smoky color and centers may eventually recover, creating rings of dead grass. The lawn may be heavily shaded, have thick thatch, or have been heavily fertilized.

Affected grasses: All types.

Control: Spray *(page 139)* with benomyl or chlorothalonil every 10 days in warm, humid weather to slow disease. Do not mow or water lawn for 24 hours after treatment. Do not apply high-nitrogen fertilizer during hot weather. Dethatch *(page 86)* if required. Prune trees *(page 98)* or shrubs *(page 102)* to reduce shade.

Dollar spot

Range: Continental U.S., except southwest, midwest and northern midwest.

Description: The lawn develops many small, bleached dead spots in warm, wet weather. Spots merge to form large dead areas. Grass blades have bleached sections with reddish edges. Lawn may not have been fertilized much.

Affected grasses: Many types, especially bentgrass, Bermuda grass and bluegrass.

Control: Fertilize lawn *(page 75)*. Avoid walking on affected areas. Spray *(page 139)* twice at a 10-day interval with chlorothalonil or benomyl. Do not mow or water for 24 hours after treatment. Reseed *(page 80)* damaged areas with resistant varieties.

Red thread

Range: Pacific northwest and Atlantic northeast.

Description: The lawn develops small tan or yellow dead patches in mild, wet weather during the spring and fall. Pink or red fungal threads protrude from the tips of grass blades and are woven from one blade to another. Lawn may not have been fertilized much or soil may be acidic.

Affected grasses: Fine fescues, ryegrass, bluegrass and bentgrass.

Control: Fertilize *(page 75)*. If disease persists or worsens, spray *(page 139)* with chlorothalonil, mancozeb or benomyl at least 3 times at 10-day intervals. Check soil pH *(page 23)*. If below 5.5, adjust pH *(page 24)* until it is within the 6.0 to 7.0 range.

DISCOLORED DEPOSITS ON WOODY AND HERBACEOUS PLANTS

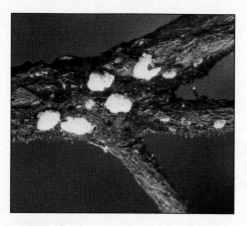

Wooly aphids

Range: Continental U.S.

Description: White, wooly tufts are deposited on leaves or needles, and trunks and branches, of trees and shrubs. Sometimes tufts affect roots. Beneath the tufts, dark, soft-bodied insects are clustered. Leaves may be curled and coated with sticky honeydew and a sooty, black mold. Conifer needles may be yellow. Trunks or branches may be covered with small galls.

Affected plants: Many woody plants, especially apple, hawthorn and mountain ash.

Control: Spray with insecticidal soap in the spring, or with petroleum oil in late winter or early spring. Spray *(page 139)* affected branches with malathion, diazinon or acephate when wool first appears. Consult the Cooperative Extension Service for information on drenching infested roots with disulfaton.

Mealybugs

Range: West coast, southwest, south and southeast U.S.

Description: Tiny, cottony tufts are deposited on leaf bases and stem bases, and in branch nodes. Beneath the tufts are clusters of soft, flat, white, oval insects. Leaves may be curled and covered with sticky honeydew or sooty mold. Severely infested branches may die.

Affected plants: Many woody plants, especially fruit and citrus trees.

Control: Hose off plants *(page 137)*. Spray *(page 139)* with insecticidal soap, malathion, diazinon or acephate. Repeat if plants become reinfested. In warm climates where insects can overwinter, spray *(page 139)* dormant citrus and fruit trees with petroleum oil.

Spittlebugs

Range: Continental U.S.

Description: Twigs and buds of trees and shrubs, or leaves, stems and flowers of herbaceous plants are covered with masses of white, frothy foam. Beneath the foam are small green or brown soft-bodied insects. Infested shoots may die. Conifer needles may yellow and drop. Heavily infested plants may be stunted.

Affected plants: Many types.

Control: Hose off plants *(page 137)*. Spray *(page 139)* trees, shrubs and flowers with insecticidal soap, malathion, acephate or resmethrin. Spray or dust *(page 139)* fruits and vegetables with insecticidal soap, diazinon, malathion, methoxychlor or carbaryl. Clear plant debris thoroughly in fall to eliminate overwintering eggs.

Scale insects

Range: Continental U.S.

Description: Foliage, twigs, branches and trunks of trees and shrubs are crusted with round or elongated bumps. They may be thick, white and cottony, like the cottony cushion scale *(above, left)* or small, waxy and dark-colored, like the lecanium scale *(above, right)*. Plants may be coated with sticky honeydew and sooty mold. Foliage of severely infested plants may be yellowing.

Affected plants: Many types of trees and shrubs.

Control: Hose off scale-infested plants to get rid of dust that keeps away natural scale parasites and predators. Ask the Cooperative Extension Service to help identify a specific scale pest and determine optimal times and frequencies for spraying scale larvae (crawlers). In general, spray *(page 139)* woody ornamentals with insecticidal soap, acephate or dicofol, and fruit trees with insecticidal soap, malathion or diazinon to control larvae when weather warms in spring. Spray dormant trees with petroleum oil to control overwintering adults and eggs.

Leaf galls

Range: Continental U.S.

Description: Leaves develop deformed growths. They may range in size from numerous small blisters *(above)* to large tumor-like swellings. There may be yellowing and dieback of foliage, but plant health is usually unaffected by these growths, which result from the feeding and egg-laying of a variety of tiny insects.

Affected plants: Many trees and shrubs.

Control: Remove affected foliage *(page 133)*. If galls are unsightly or weaken young trees, control the insect responsible. Ask the Cooperative Extension Service to help identify the specific pest and treatment. In general, spray *(page 139)* recommended pesticides during dormancy or in spring, as new growth begins.

HOLES IN TREE AND SHRUB FOLIAGE

Gypsy moths

Range: Atlantic northeast.

Description: Hairy, dark, red-and-blue-spotted caterpillars are eating foliage and may rapidly defoliate woody plants. There may be excrement beneath infested plants. Hairy masses of yellow eggs may be found on many outdoor objects.

Affected plants: Many trees and shrubs, especially oak.

Control: Destroy egg masses. For light infestation, band trees *(page 105)* with burlap in spring, and handpick *(page 137)* and destroy trapped larvae. Or apply sticky insect barrier *(page 138)*. For heavier infestations, spray *(page 139)* with *Bacillus thuringiensis*, carbaryl or acephate in spring or early summer when larvae are small. In the future, plant less susceptible tree and shrub species.

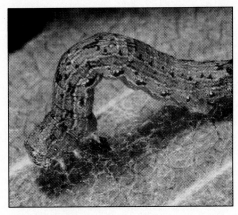

Cankerworms

Range: Continental U.S., except southwest, south and southeast.

Description: Green or brownish worms with legs only at their front and rear ends are feeding on unfolding leaves and buds in the spring. These worms move by pulling their back ends forward to form a loop. Leaves are completely eaten except for midribs and large veins. Heavily infested trees may appear scorched.

Affected plants: Many trees and shrubs.

Control: Paint trunks in late fall and early spring with a sticky barrier to trap egg-laying moths *(page 136)*. Spray *(page 139)* with *Bacillus thuringiensis*, carbaryl, diazinon or acephate in spring after leaves have fully expanded.

Spruce budworms

Range: Continental U.S., except southwest, south and southeast.

Description: Needles on the tips of conifer branches are being eaten by small, reddish-brown caterpillars with raised spots, in late spring and early summer. Branch ends may turn reddish brown in summer. There may be clusters of pale green eggs on needles in late summer.

Affected plants: Many coniferous trees, especially spruce and fir.

Control: Spray *(page 139)* with *Bacillus thuringiensis* or carbaryl in spring as buds begin to open. Timing is critical.

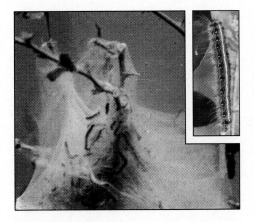

Tent caterpillars

Range: Continental U.S.

Description: There are tent-like silken nests in the branch forks of trees and shrubs *(above)*. Sparsely hairy, dark caterpillars, with a white back-stripe and blue, brown and yellow marks on the sides *(inset)* are found in nests, on branches and chewing on leaves. Brown, shiny, foam-like collars of eggs may girdle twigs.

Affected plants: Many types, especially apple, crabapple and flowering cherry.

Control: Remove and destroy egg masses in winter or early spring. Wipe tents off branches with a kerosene-soaked rag in spring. Spray *(page 139)* with insecticidal soap, *Bacillus thuringiensis*, malathion, carbaryl or diazinon when caterpillars are first seen.

Bagworms

Range: Southwest, south, southeast, east-coast and northeast U.S.

Description: Small, brown "bags" *(above)* hang from tree branches. Bags are made of dead foliage and twigs woven together with silk. Inside each bag is a dark caterpillar. Leaves are chewed and branches may be badly defoliated.

Affected plants: Many trees and shrubs, especially spruce and cedar.

Control: Handpick and destroy bags *(page 133)* in winter when they are filled with eggs. Spray *(page 139)* young caterpillars with *Bacillus thuringiensis*, carbaryl, diazinon or acephate in late spring and early summer when they hatch and emerge from bags to feed.

Leafroller caterpillars

Range: Continental U.S.

Description: Leaves are rolled tightly with webbing. Inside is a small, greenish-brown caterpillar. Nearby leaves may be skeletonized, and buds and fruit may be eaten.

Affected plants: Many woody plants, especially fruit trees and roses.

Control: Pinch leaves to kill insects, then pick and destroy *(page 133)* them. Ask the Cooperative Extension Service to help identify a specific leafroller and its treatment. In general, clear all garden debris in fall to eliminate some overwintering larvae and pupae. Spray next spring *(page 139)* with *Bacillus thuringiensis*, malathion, diazinon or carbaryl before caterpillars roll leaves.

DIEBACK OF TREE AND SHRUB FOLIAGE

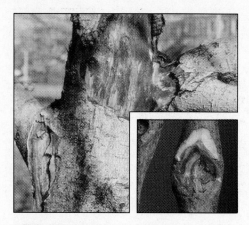

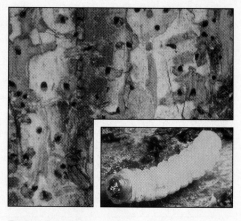

Cankers

Range: Continental U.S.

Description: Irregular, dark areas develop on trunks *(above)* or branches *(inset)* of woody plants where bark may have been injured by sun, frost, tools or insects. As these infected areas grow, they may ooze sap, become sunken, crack and peel. Where cankers girdle branches or cover large trunk areas, branches beyond them may progressively die back from their tips.

Affected plants: Many trees and shrubs.

Control: Prune off branches *(page 98)* at least 6 inches below cankers that girdle them. Cut out trunk cankers, removing all brown, stained inner bark and leaving smooth edges to promote quick callusing and healing. Sterilize tools *(page 133)* after each cut.

Fireblight

Range: Continental U.S.

Description: Blossoms and leaves suddenly wilt, as if scorched, and wither, particularly when weather is warm and wet in spring. The bark at the base of affected twigs or branches is cankered and may be covered with orange bacterial ooze.

Affected plants: Many trees and shrubs, especially apple, pear, crabapple, quince, mountain ash, cotoneaster and hawthorn.

Control: Prune off *(page 98)* twigs 6 inches below cankers, and branches 12 inches below. Sterilize tools after each cut. Next spring, before bud break *(page 133)*, spray *(page 139)* affected plants with copper or streptomycin. Repeat at 5-day intervals until blooming finishes. In the future, plant resistant varieties.

Borer insects

Range: Continental U.S.

Description: Branches are weak, with dying, discolored foliage. Branches or trunks may be covered with small holes *(above)* that exude sawdust or sap. Borers *(inset)*, the larvae of many different beetles and moths, have tunnelled into trees and are disrupting water and nutrient flow.

Affected plants: Many trees and shrubs.

Control: Ask the Cooperative Extension Service to help identify a specific borer and the required type and timing of treatment. In general, prune off *(page 98)* and destroy dead and dying branches. Spray *(page 139)* adult moths or beetles with lindane or carbaryl at egg-laying time. Wrap trunks of young trees *(page 105)* for 2 years to inhibit egg-laying on bark.

Dutch elm disease

Range: Continental U.S., except southwest.

Description: Leaves in the top of the tree wilt, yellow and drop, and small branches or entire limbs die. There may be small holes in the bark of infected branches that are made by the borer larvae of elm bark beetles, which spread the fungus.

Affected plants: Elm trees.

Control: Contact the Cooperative Extension Service or a professional arborist. Curing a tree is usually impossible, but treatment may prevent or delay the spread of the fungus. In general, prune off and destroy *(page 98)* all dead and dying wood that harbors disease-carrying insects. Sterilize tools *(page 133)* after each cut.

Crown gall

Range: Continental U.S.

Description: Brown, corky galls, or swellings, develop on plant crowns at soil level, and sometimes on stems and roots. Depending on the plant, they may be walnut- to football-size. Plants with many or large galls may be weak and have dying branches with yellowing leaves.

Affected plants: Many trees and shrubs, especially roses, fruit trees and fruit canes.

Control: There is no chemical control for the condition, which is caused by a soil bacterium. Prune off and destroy *(page 98)* diseased stems. Sterilize tools *(page 133)* after each cut. Contact a professional arborist to remove large galls. In the future, plant resistant varieties.

TOOLS & TECHNIQUES

This section introduces tools and techniques that are basic to maintaining your lawn and garden in good health. They include instructions on the use of a power tiller *(page 132)*, special seasonal preparations for winter and spring *(page 134)* and the mixing and application of pesticides *(pages 139-140)*. You can do most of the repairs described in this book with the tools shown below and on pages 130-131. Power tools can be rented from tool rental shops. Some garden supply stores will lend tools if you buy materials from them.

Buy the best tools you can afford, use the right tools for the job, and take the time to care for them properly. Wash caked-on mud and grime from tools. When dry, wipe metal surfaces with a rag moistened with a few drops of light oil. To remove rust, rub with fine steel wool or emery cloth. Store tools in a shed or storeroom. Pesticides should be labelled and locked up separately as described on page 141.

To prevent accidents in the garden, work in daylight. Use ear protectors when operating noisy power tools for a long period of time. Wear safety goggles if stones may be cast up by the action of a tool or when dusting fungicides or spraying pesticides overhead. Read the Emergency Guide *(page 8)* before you apply pesticides and keep the phone number of your physician handy.

Insects and fungi are present in every lawn and garden. Many are beneficial but some are pests, particularly when their numbers get out of control. Before applying any insecticide or fungicide listed in the chart on pages 137-138, consider whether the extent of damage warrants chemical treatment. If the damage is limited to a few leaves or buds, or one branch or plant, try controlling the problem by pinching, pruning or removing the entire plant *(page 133)*. Install the appropriate bait, lure, trap, barrier or repellant *(page 136)*, or remove the pest by hand or with water *(page 137)*. If these measures don't work or aren't applicable to your problem, spray or dust with extreme care

Before buying a pesticide, make sure it can be used safely on the plant in question; study the product label and consult with the supplier. Keep in mind that the use of some pesticides is not permitted in certain areas. If in doubt about its application or effects, call your local Cooperative Extension Service. The service answers questions on a range of subjects including pest controls, toxic waste disposal and the legal aspects of performing certain gardening tasks in your area. It also offers diagnostic services by mail and the local offices are well-versed in the special problems of gardening in your area, from soil conditions to weather.

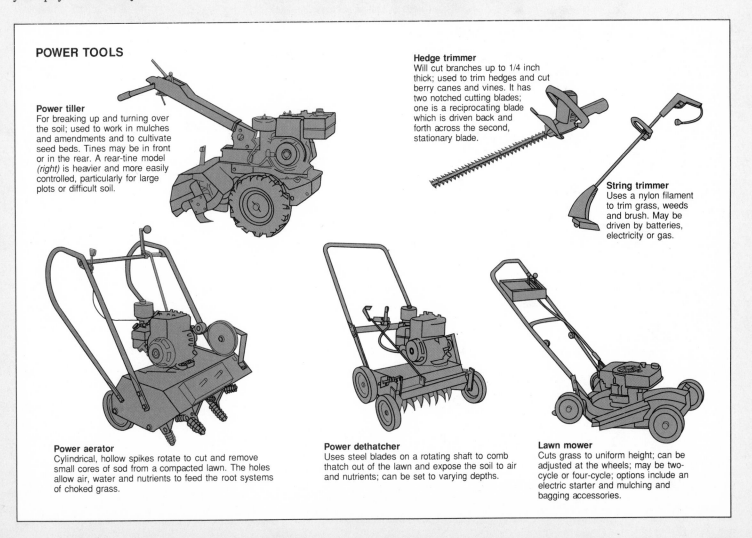

POWER TOOLS

Power tiller
For breaking up and turning over the soil; used to work in mulches and amendments and to cultivate seed beds. Tines may be in front or in the rear. A rear-tine model *(right)* is heavier and more easily controlled, particularly for large plots or difficult soil.

Hedge trimmer
Will cut branches up to 1/4 inch thick; used to trim hedges and cut berry canes and vines. It has two notched cutting blades; one is a reciprocating blade which is driven back and forth across the second, stationary blade.

String trimmer
Uses a nylon filament to trim grass, weeds and brush. May be driven by batteries, electricity or gas.

Power aerator
Cylindrical, hollow spikes rotate to cut and remove small cores of sod from a compacted lawn. The holes allow air, water and nutrients to feed the root systems of choked grass.

Power dethatcher
Uses steel blades on a rotating shaft to comb thatch out of the lawn and expose the soil to air and nutrients; can be set to varying depths.

Lawn mower
Cuts grass to uniform height; can be adjusted at the wheels; may be two-cycle or four-cycle; options include an electric starter and mulching and bagging accessories.

HAND TOOLS

Weeding hoe
Cuts weeds 1 to 2 inches below the surface when pulled through loose soil.

Hand fork
For loosening compacted soil in a small bed or digging up small plants by the roots.

Garden trowel
A multi-purpose general digger, especially useful for transplanting small plants.

Hand cultivator
Multi-purpose tool with three curved tines for breaking up the top 1 to 3 inches of garden soil for seed bed preparation, or aeration of small areas.

Dandelion weeder
Uses a notched blade to cut and pry up tap-rooted weeds several inches below the surface.

Gardening gloves
Protect hands from damage by friction or chemicals. Use leather (above) for general purposes, rubberized or vinyl gloves for protection against pesticides.

Weeding fork
Useful for removing weeds with spreading roots from loose soil or lawns.

Garden hoe
Multi-purpose tool with a flat, sharp blade for loosening compacted soil, weeding, and making irrigation furrows between rows of plants.

Scuffle hoe
Used to cut weeds 1 to 2 inches below the surface when pulled and pushed through well-tilled soil. Also used for shallow-surface cultivating.

Lawn rake
Has dull, flexible teeth. Use like a broom to sweep up clippings and leaves without harming the lawn.

Garden rake
For breaking up clods of soil, distributing mulch and soil amendments, and when turned over, for leveling soil.

Spade
A multi-purpose digger. Pointed blade is useful for digging into compacted soil; square blade for slicing through sod or edging around a bed. Use one with a long handle (below) for trenching or digging deep planting holes.

Garden fork
For turning the soil, digging and prying up plants for transplanting. Also useful for dividing perennials with dense, tangled root clumps.

Lawn edger
Sturdy, half-moon blade cuts through sod to trim edges of walks, driveways and garden beds.

Rotary edger
For cutting through grass encroaching on walks, driveways or garden beds.

Bulb planter
Cuts cylindrical holes in the soil for planting bulbs or plugs of grass.

Pruning knife
For small operations such as pruning sprouts or trimming damaged bark.

Hedge shears
For pruning or trimming hedges with branches up to 1/2 inch in diameter.

Lopping shears
For cutting branches 3/4 to 1 1/2 inches in diameter. The long handles provide leverage and are separated by rubber cushions that absorb the shock when the blades close.

Grass shears
Used to trim grass where the lawn mower blades can't reach, such as around trees and fences.

...uning shears
...arp, short-handled, multi-purpose ...tter used for pruning stems and ...nches up to 3/4 inch in diameter and ...harvesting fruit and vegetables.

Pruning saws
For cutting branches larger than 1 inch in diameter; the blades are curved to draw their teeth down into the wood when pulled across the branch. They can handle soft or hard wood.

...le shears
...ed to prune high branches 3/4 to ...1/2 inches in diameter; has a pul-...r-operated, hooked cutting blade. ...r longer reach, add the telescop-...g fiberglass extension.

Hose-end sprayer
Mounted on the end of a hose; it controls dilution ratio of water to liquid pesticide or fertilizer stored in the container.

Trigger nozzle
The trigger adjusts the volume of water and the nozzle adjusts the pattern of spray.

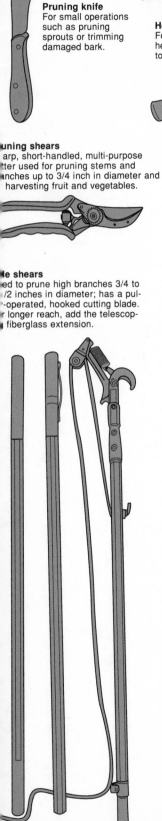

Pressure sprayer
Tank contains up to 3 gallons of pesticide. Use with shoulder strap and wand to reach large areas; nozzle adjusts to spray a mist or high pressure stream reaching up to 30 feet.

Watering wand with a fan-spray nozzle
Wand extends hose to water plants in hard-to-reach spots; use with a fan-spray nozzle for gentle watering of delicate plants and flowers.

Crank duster
The crank drives a fan that mixes dust and air and produces a cloud of pesticide. The nozzle rotates to direct the dust up or down.

Mist nozzle
May be attached to hose or wand to deliver a foglike spray on delicate plants.

Watering can
May be copper, brass, galvanized steel or plastic. Use with various threaded attachments for applying liquid in mist, or gentle or heavy spray.

Soaker hose
For deep, slow watering of plant roots. Water seeps through porous walls; is attached to a regular hose and is often left in position in the garden or around the base of trees.

Sprinkler
Oscillates back and forth to provide even water coverage over a rectangular area; can be adjusted to move through all or part of an arc.

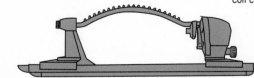

Garden hose
May be made of rubber, nylon, vinyl or plastic; use with different nozzles and heads. To maintain, coil carefully and avoid kinking.

OPERATING A POWER TILLER

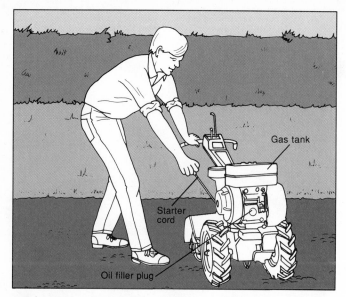

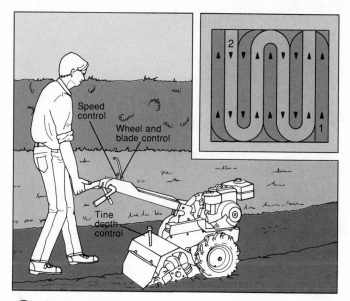

1 **Starting up.** Check soil moisture *(page 18)* and cultivate when the soil is cool and barely moist. Hard, dry soil can be softened for tilling by soaking and waiting two or three days. Before starting up a power tiller, read the manufacturer's operating manual. On a rear-tine, gas-powered tiller such as the one shown here, first check the gas tank and, if low, top it up. Unscrew the oil filler plug, check and fill it as well. Switch on the gas cock mounted on the line between the gas tank and the carburetor. Make sure the wheel and blade control is set to Neutral and attach the spark plug wire to the top of the spark plug as shown in step 3. Move the tiller into position at one corner of the bed. Set the tine depth control for shallow digging and move the speed control lever into its starting position. Standing clear of wheels and tines, pull the starting cord with a smooth, fast motion *(above)*.

2 **Cultivating with a rear-tine power tiller.** With one hand firmly grasping the tiller handlebar, move the wheel and blade control into Forward; the tines will immediately start to bite into the ground, so don't be suprised by the sudden thrust forward. Guide the tiller *(above)* along one side of the bed (1). When you reach the far end, make a broad turn and cultivate a second row parallel to the first. Continue this U-shaped pattern *(inset)* until you reach the other side of the bed. Then shift into Neutral and roll the tiller to the nearest untilled row (2). Shift back into Forward and, repeating the same pattern, turn over the remaining untilled soil in the bed. If you are amending *(page 21)*, spread the amendments over the ground in a 3- to 4-inch layer. Then set the tines to their lowest level and cultivate a second time at right angles to the first pass.

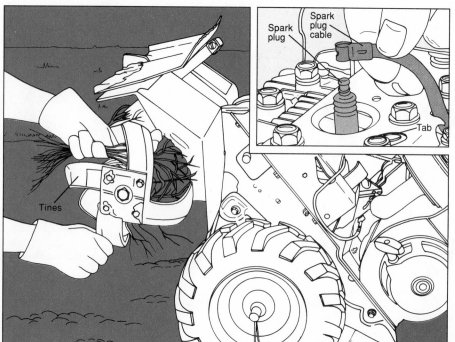

3 **Finishing up.** If the tiller jerks and gyrates during operation, slow down. When the job is finished or when the tines or axle load up with dirt and vegetation, stop the tiller by moving the wheel and blade control into Neutral and pulling the speed control back to Off. Always unplug the spark plug cable *(inset)* and hook it under the tab when the machine is not in use. To clean the tines, tip the tiller forward onto its front end. Pull free any vegetation from around the axle and remove clumps of dirt from the tines *(left)*.

Before storing the machine between uses, allow it to cool and work through the following list: Check the air filter and, if it looks dirty, clean or replace it as instructed in the manufacturer's manual; wipe off any dirt or oil from the engine and body; clean the tines; top up the oil reservoir and gas tank; and store the machine in a cool, dry place.

RECYCLING LEAVES

Plywood

Shredded leaves

Shredding leaves with a lawn mower. Leaves are best shredded with a high-powered lawn mower before being applied as a mulch or an amendment. Rake the leaves into small piles and let them dry. Make sure there are no rocks or branches hidden among the leaves. Check your lawn mower blade; sharpen it if necessary *(page 74)*. To catch the leaves once they're shredded, use a lawn mower with a portable bag attachment or lean a piece of plywood against a tree and pile the leaves close by. The plywood will stop the leaves from spewing over the entire lawn. Turn the mower on high speed, lean on the handlebar and raise its front end. Then lower the mower slowly onto the pile so that the blade will shred the leaves into tiny pieces *(left)*. You may need to raise and lower the mower several times before most of the leaves are shredded. Collect the leaves in bags and use them as a mulch or an amendment *(page 21)* or compost them *(page 22)*.

REMOVING AND DISPOSING OF DISEASED PLANTS

Diseased plant

1 Removing diseased plant material. Examine plants carefully to see how far the infection has spread and refer to Pests and Diseases *(page 112)*. Wear gloves to pinch off damaged or diseased buds, blooms or leaves. When climbing plants *(page 66)*, ground cover *(page 91)* or trees and shrubs *(page 98)* are diseased, prune them. If you suspect fungal, bacterial or viral disease to be the cause of the damage, disinfect the pruning shears in rubbing alcohol between cuts and after pruning is completed. When a plant is badly diseased, dig it up by the roots with a garden fork *(above)*, keeping as much of the surrounding earth as possible. When an entire tree is affected, consult a tree specialist before having it cut down; sometimes a tree will recover even after it has been defoliated for a couple of years.

2 Disposing of infected plants. Place diseased plant material in a plastic garbage bag at the site of removal. If brush or branches are too long or sharp for bagging, bundle them tightly *(above)*. Dispose of bags or bundles with the rest of your garbage.

SEASONAL MAINTENANCE OF YOUR LAWN AND GARDEN

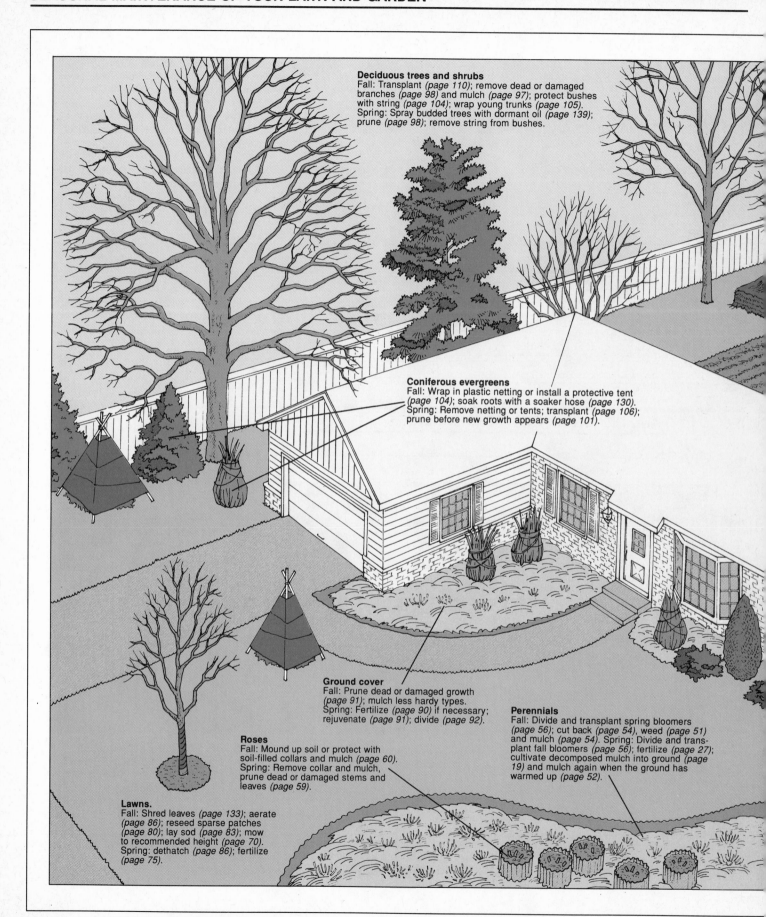

Deciduous trees and shrubs
Fall: Transplant *(page 110)*; remove dead or damaged branches *(page 98)* and mulch *(page 97)*; protect bushes with string *(page 104)*; wrap young trunks *(page 105)*.
Spring: Spray budded trees with dormant oil *(page 139)*; prune *(page 98)*; remove string from bushes.

Coniferous evergreens
Fall: Wrap in plastic netting or install a protective tent *(page 104)*; soak roots with a soaker hose *(page 130)*.
Spring: Remove netting or tents; transplant *(page 106)*; prune before new growth appears *(page 101)*.

Ground cover
Fall: Prune dead or damaged growth *(page 91)*; mulch less hardy types.
Spring: Fertilize *(page 90)* if necessary; rejuvenate *(page 91)*; divide *(page 92)*.

Perennials
Fall: Divide and transplant spring bloomers *(page 56)*; cut back *(page 54)*, weed *(page 51)* and mulch *(page 54)*. Spring: Divide and transplant fall bloomers *(page 56)*; fertilize *(page 27)*; cultivate decomposed mulch into ground *(page 19)* and mulch again when the ground has warmed up *(page 52)*.

Roses
Fall: Mound up soil or protect with soil-filled collars and mulch *(page 60)*.
Spring: Remove collar and mulch, prune dead or damaged stems and leaves *(page 59)*.

Lawns.
Fall: Shred leaves *(page 133)*; aerate *(page 86)*; reseed sparse patches *(page 80)*; lay sod *(page 83)*; mow to recommended height *(page 70)*.
Spring: dethatch *(page 86)*; fertilize *(page 75)*.

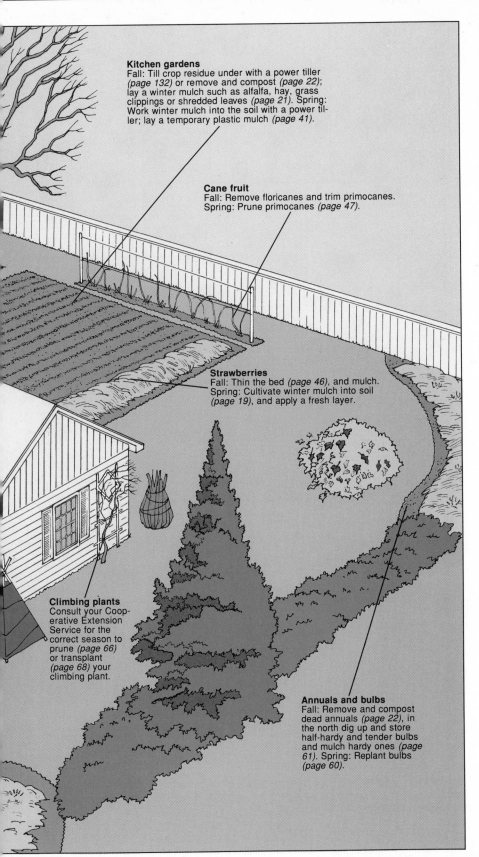

Kitchen gardens
Fall: Till crop residue under with a power tiller *(page 132)* or remove and compost *(page 22)*; lay a winter mulch such as alfalfa, hay, grass clippings or shredded leaves *(page 21)*. Spring: Work winter mulch into the soil with a power tiller; lay a temporary plastic mulch *(page 41)*.

Cane fruit
Fall: Remove floricanes and trim primocanes. Spring: Prune primocanes *(page 47)*.

Strawberries
Fall: Thin the bed *(page 46)*, and mulch. Spring: Cultivate winter mulch into soil *(page 19)*, and apply a fresh layer.

Climbing plants
Consult your Cooperative Extension Service for the correct season to prune *(page 66)* or transplant *(page 68)* your climbing plant.

Annuals and bulbs
Fall: Remove and compost dead annuals *(page 22)*, in the north dig up and store half-hardy and tender bulbs and mulch hardy ones *(page 61)*. Spring: Replant bulbs *(page 60)*.

Seasonal preparations. Before both the dormancy period and the growing season begin, test soil pH *(page 23)* and add pH adjusters *(page 24)* if necessary. Similarly, test soil fertility *(page 25)* and amend *(page 21)* with organic materials such as peat moss and manure, or fertilize *(page 26)*.

Each year, prepare your lawn and garden for the winter. In colder climates this will involve installing special protections against frost and wind *(left)*. Consult your local Cooperative Extension Service for recommendations for winter preparations in your area.

In the fall, clean up and compost crop residue, leaves and other garden debris *(page 22)*. When finished with hand tools for the year, clean, sharpen and repair them as necessary. Consult manufacturers' manuals for instructions regarding proper storage of your gas-powered tools. Make sure you disconnect the spark plug and drain the gas tank. Store stakes, ties, cages and fences. Dispose of pesticides beyond their expiry date *(page 141)*. Note the location of perennials and bulbs to help you plan your new flower garden in the spring. If you intend to rotate your crops the following year, keep track of where each type of vegetable was grown. Consult a vegetable gardening guide for information on sowing a cover crop of annuals such as rye, winter wheat and buckwheat in your vegetable bed.

In the spring, while the garden is still dormant, remove any debris that may have accumulated over the winter. Turn under the winter mulch by hand *(page 19)* or with a power tiller *(page 132)*. For many plants, this is the time to prune; read a reputable pruning guide for information on long-range pruning needs. Begin a compost heap *(page 22)* if you don't already have one. Consult seed mail-order catalogues and order your seeds now. Before shopping for supplies, check over your tools to see if any need replacement or servicing. After danger of heavy frost or snow is over, remove winter coverings.

CONTROLLING PESTS

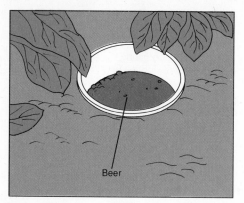

Organic slug and snail bait. In the evening, bury a container of stale beer mixed with a tablespoon of flour among slug-infested plants. Slugs, attracted by the yeast, crawl into the container and drown.

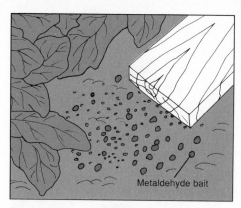

Chemical slug and snail bait. Sprinkle pesticide granules such as metaldehyde *(page 138)* around infested plants; avoid contact with edible plants. Water granules and cover with boards to protect children and pets.

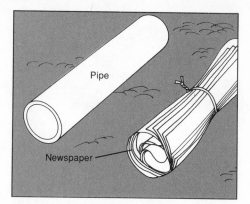

Slug, snail and earwig lures. For slugs, use a short length of pipe; for earwigs, use damp rolled newspaper. Place lure among infested plants in the evening. At dawn, the insects crawl into the pipe or newspaper to escape the light.

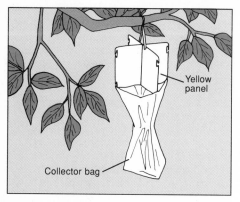

Japanese beetle trap. The panel is yellow and coated with a sex pheromone to attract beetles. Hang traps several feet off the ground on the windward side of the garden and at some distance from the garden to draw beetles away.

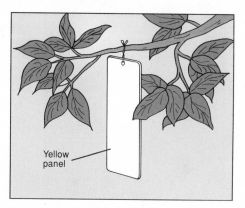

Aphid, whitefly and thrip trap. The panel is coated with a sticky substance. Place discreetly among infested foliage in order not to attract insects from farther away. Shake plants occasionally to dislodge insects.

Bird and insect barrier. Drape fine-mesh netting over plants and secure it to the ground. Remove when plants blossom to allow bees to pollinate.

Crawling insect barrier. Paint a band of sticky compound around the trunk of a tree about 2 1/2 feet high to stop invading insects.

Cutworm barrier. Collar seedlings with plastic foam cups. Remove the bottom of the container and cut the sides to 3 inches high.

Imitation predator repellant. Place inflatable owls or snakes in highly visible locations in the garden to frighten birds and small animal pests.

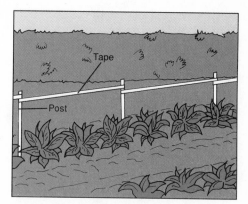

Bird repellant tape. Stretch the tape between posts set up among threatened plants. Some versions vibrate in the wind, emitting a noise that frightens birds and rabbits.

Protecting your garden. The baits, lures, traps, barriers and repellants pictured above represent a sampling of the many devices that can be set up to frustrate pests. Use them in combination with good cultural practices such as keeping your garden free of debris that attract and shelter pests. As soon as signs of a pest problem appear (if not before), make or buy the appropriate control. Start with a few and monitor them regularly to see whether they are having an effect on the pest population. Add a few more if needed. Clean out baits, lures and traps daily; throw dead pests into the garbage. If the pests are still alive, dispose of them more carefully *(page 137)*. In many cases, these measures will be sufficient; however, if the pests get out of control, you may have to consider a more drastic approach such as spraying with a chemical pesticide *(page 139)*. When gophers, raccoons, deer and other animals are a problem, the first defense is usually the building of a fence; consult your Cooperative Extension Service for suggestions regarding animal controls.

REMOVING INSECTS

Removing pests by hand. Handpick visible insects such as caterpillars and beetles off plants or from the ground. To kill them, drop them into a jar filled with soapy water and flush them down the drain. Look under and between leaves, along stems and at the base of your plants for insect evidence. Pinch off leaves with egg clusters hugging their undersurfaces. Use a flashlight and pick night-crawling pests such as cutworms and collect snails, slugs and earwigs lured into daytime hiding places *(page 136)*.

Removing pests with water. Knock small insects such as aphids, thrips, mites, whiteflies and many insect larvae from plants with a brisk jet of water. Use a hose with a trigger nozzle to spray foliage; carefully avoid hitting blossoms which may be easily damaged. Remove larger insects from the ground *(left)*. Don't repeat more often than every 3 or 4 days, as spraying will knock off beneficial insects as well and the water removes dust that inhibits scale parasites.

INSECTICIDES AND FUNGICIDES continued ▶

NAME	TYPE	REMARKS
INSECTICIDES		
Acephate	Spray; kills pest on contact and by ingestion of plant material.	May be used on most non-edible plants; absorbed by plant; highly toxic to bees, toxic to birds.
Bacillus popillae	Organic control; spray or dust; kills by infection with bacterial disease.	May be used on lawns and soil; apply in early morning or late afternoon; store in cool, dark place; non-toxic to fish or wildlife.
Bacillus thuringiensis	Organic control; spray, dust or granules; kills by infection with bacterial disease.	May be used on most plants; apply in early morning or late afternoon; store in cool, dark place; non-toxic to fish or wildlife.
Carbaryl	Spray or dust; kills pest on contact and by ingestion of plant material.	May be used on most plants; highly toxic to fish and bees.
Chlorpyrifos	Spray or granules; kills pest on contact.	May be used on lawns, avoid edible plants; toxic to fish, birds and other wildlife.
Diatomaceous earth	Organic control; spray or dust; kills by dessicating pest.	Use only agricultural diatomaceous earth; may be used on all plants; toxic to beneficial insects, non-toxic to fish and wildlife.
Diazinon	Spray, dust or granules; kills pest on contact and by ingestion of plant material.	May be used on most plants; effects persist up to 10 days; highly toxic to bees, toxic to fish, birds and other wildlife.
Dicofol	Spray; kills pest on contact and by ingestion of plant material.	May be used on non-edible plants only; highly toxic to bees, toxic to birds.
Dimethoate	Spray; kills pest on contact and on ingestion of plant material.	May be used on non-edible plants only; absorbed by plant; apply after eggs are laid in spring; highly toxic to bees, toxic to fish, birds and other wildlife.

INSECTICIDES AND FUNGICIDES (continued)

NAME	TYPE	REMARKS
Insecticidal soap	Organic control; spray; kills pest on contact.	May be used on most plants; apply to both sides of foliage; toxic to beneficial insects.
Lindane	Paint, spray or dust; solution and vapor kill pest on contact and by ingestion of plant material.	May be used on woody ornamentals; do not apply within 60 days of harvest; highly toxic to bees, toxic to fish, birds and other wildlife.
Malathion	Spray or dust; kills pest on contact and by ingestion of plant material.	May be used on most plants; is absorbed by plant; highly toxic to bees, toxic to fish.
Metaldehyde	Granules or liquid drops; kills pest by ingestion.	Molluscicide; apply to wet soil at base of plant, reapply every second week; keep children and pets away from treated area until granules are consumed; toxic to birds and other wildlife.
Methoxychlor	Spray or dust; kills on contact and by ingestion of plant material.	May be used on most plants; absorbed by plant; sometimes found in combination with malathion and captan; highly toxic to bees and fish.
Petroleum oil (dormant oil)	Organic control; spray kills pest by suffocation.	May be used on woody ornamentals including fruit trees and shrubs; may damage evergreens and certains species of maple, biron and beech.
Pyrethrins (pyrethrum)	Organic control; spray or dust; kills pest on contact.	May be used on most plants; toxic to bees and fish.
Rotenone	Organic control; spray or dust; kills pest on contact.	May be used on edible plants; highly toxic to fish.

FUNGICIDES

NAME	TYPE	REMARKS
Copper sulfate	Spray; kills fungus on contact.	May be used on most plants; also controls bacterial leaf spot; toxic to fish and wildlife.
Benomyl	Spray or granules; kills fungus on contact.	May be used on most plants although less readily absorbed by woody plants.
Lime sulfur	Organic control; spray; kills fungus on contact.	May be used on fruit, roses and trees; apply as prevention in fall, winter or spring before buds open; wash fruit before eating it; toxic to fish.
Captan	Spray or dust; kills fungus on contact.	May be used on most plants; toxic to fish.
Chlorothalonil	Spray; kills fungus on contact.	May be used on most plants; can be applied up to 3 days before harvest; toxic to fish.
Dinocap	Spray or dust; kills fungus on contact.	May be used on most plants; toxic to fish.
Folpet	Spray or dust; kills fungus on contact.	May be used on most plants; sometimes used in combination with other fungicides or insecticides; toxic to fish.
Iprodione	Spray; kills fungus on contact.	May be used on lawns, toxic to fish.
Maneb	Spray; kills fungus on contact.	May be used on most plants; sometimes used in combination with other fungicides or insecticides, toxic to fish.
Streptomycin	Spray; kills fungus on contact.	Antibiotic; may be used on most plants.
Sulfur	Organic control; spray or dust; kills fungus on contact.	May be used on most plants; do not apply to foliage when temperatures exceed 85° F; avoid using within four weeks of spraying dormant oil; keep away from sparks or flame.
Triforine	Spray; kills fungus on contact.	May be used on roses and flowers; apply at 7- to 10-day intervals in spring and fall; sometimes used in combination with various insecticides; toxic to fish.

Choosing an insecticide or fungicide. The list above contains some of the more common insecticides and fungicides available today. It also includes the molluscicide metaldehyde and the antibiotic streptomycin. Consult your Cooperative Extension Service before applying any chemical that is listed as toxic, or if the problem doesn't respond to treatment; some areas regulate the use of certain pesticides and certain insects are now resistant to their chemical controls. When possible, choose a product that is listed as organic. These are naturally occurring products and are usually less toxic to the environment than those synthesized in a laboratory.

When mixing *(page 139)*, spraying *(pages 139-140)* or dusting *(page 140)* any one of the above insecticides or fungicides, always check the product label and follow its instructions closely. Consult the safety tips on page 8, and be sure to wear goggles and a respirator when dusting with a fungicide or spraying at eye level or above. Also avoid spraying or dusting edible plants too near harvest; the label will tell you when the last application should be made. When a chemical is considered toxic to fish, don't let the spray contact water. If it is toxic to bees, avoid spraying while plants are in blossom. After spraying, keep children and pets away from the treated plants until the spray has dried.

MIXING A PESTICIDE

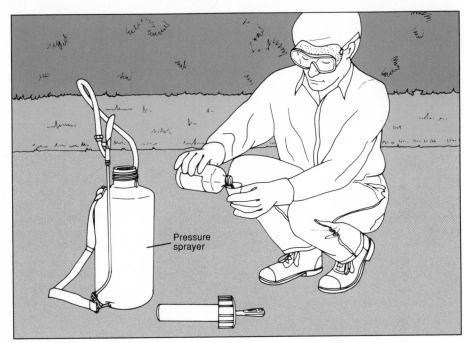

Mixing pesticides with water. Refer to the insecticide and fungicide chart *(page 137)* or the herbicide chart *(page 76)* for an appropriate pesticide. Many products come ready-to-use in their own applicators. If you buy one as a liquid concentrate or a wettable powder, dilute it according to the instructions on the product label. Never use an insecticide or a fungicide in an applicator that was used for herbicides. Use clean measuring spoons and containers kept for garden use only. Wear rubber gloves and long sleeves and do the mixing on the ground in a well-ventilated room or outdoors *(left)*. Mix less rather than more to avoid having any leftover mixture. To mix liquid concentrates, fill the canister with water first and then add the pesticide. Close the applicator tightly and shake it. If mixing wettable powders, combine them first with water in a bucket and then pour the solution into the canister. When spraying wettable powders, shake the canister frequently during application. After mixing, store pesticides safely *(page 141)*.

Pressure sprayer

SPRAYING LIQUID PESTICIDES

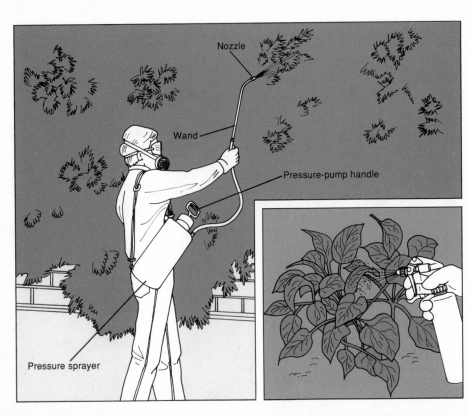

Nozzle

Wand

Pressure-pump handle

Pressure sprayer

Spot applications. Always follow all instructions on the pesticide label and spray on a calm day. For controlled spraying of pesticides, use a pressure sprayer. Mix the pesticide in the sprayer *(above)*. Pressurize the canister by vigorously pumping the pressure-pump handle. To spray above your head *(left)*, wear goggles and a respirator along with gloves and long sleeves. Aim the wand at the affected plants and squeeze the trigger. Spray as much of the undersides of leaves as possible. When the spray slows down, pump the handle again to increase the pressure. If applying dormant oil to a tree, adjust the nozzle to a narrow stream and coat branches and trunk with the oil.

For spot applications at close range, use a spray bottle with an adjustable nozzle *(inset)*, and label it. Wear rubber gloves and aim the nozzle adjusted to a fine mist spray at the affected plant. When you have finished applying the pesticide, dispose of or store remaining pesticide and clean your equipment carefully *(page 141)*.

APPLYING LIQUID PESTICIDE

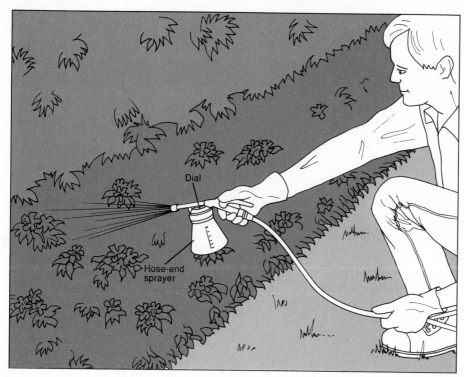

Dial

Hose-end
sprayer

Broadcast spraying. Use a hose-end sprayer *(left)* to cover a wide area, particularly below eye level. Hose-end sprayers are available premixed with pesticide; following manufacturer's instructions, attach them to the end of your hose. If mixing the pesticide concentrate yourself *(page 139)*, wear rubber gloves, boots and long sleeves. Use a hose-end sprayer such as the type shown here with ounces calibrated on the side and a dial that controls the amount of water that can pass through the sprayer. Pour the concentrate into the sprayer, noting the amount in ounces, then turn the dial to the appropriate setting. The product label will instruct you on the correct dilution ratio in ounces per gallon. Attach the sprayer to the hose and turn on the water. Aim the nozzle toward the area to be covered, squeeze the handle to release the water and move your arm from side to side to assure even coverage. When you have finished, clean your equipment and dispose of any leftover pesticide carefully *(page 141)*.

DUSTING PLANTS WITH INSECTICIDES AND FUNGICIDES

Plastic
bottle

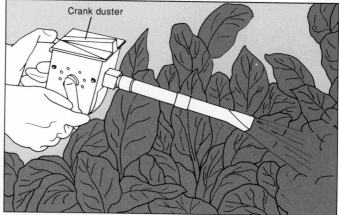

Crank duster

Dusting diseased or pest-infested plants. Never dust when it's windy and always follow the instructions on the product label. Wear rubber gloves, long sleeves, goggles and a respirator. Dust pesticides require no mixing and unused portions can be returned to their original containers. Dust the plants when wet from dew or rain, or dampen them with water from a plastic spray bottle. Many general and multi-purpose dust pesticides come in squeezable plastic bottles useful for spot applications. Shake the bottle with the cap closed, open it, then squeeze dust onto both the top and bottom surfaces of the leaves *(above, left)*. For larger areas fill a rotary crank duster with the appropriate pesticide and crank out a fine cloud *(above, right)* to cover the top and bottom surfaces of all affected foliage. Clean equipment and store the pesticide as described on page 141.

DISPOSING OF PESTICIDES

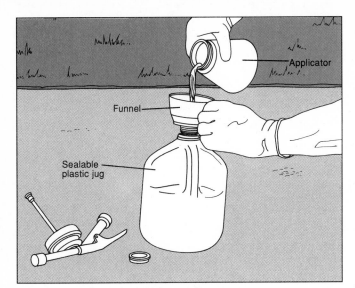

Applicator

Funnel

Sealable
plastic jug

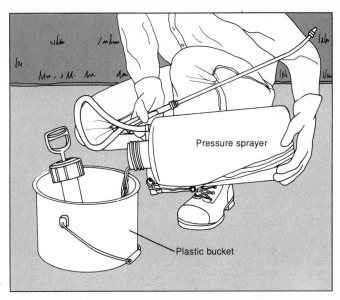

Pressure sprayer

Plastic bucket

1 Disposing of unused pesticides. Contact the toxic waste disposal facility nearest you by calling your local municipality or Cooperative Extension Service and follow their instructions regarding the safe disposal of leftover or expired pesticides. Pour leftover pesticide from the applicator *(above)* into a sealable plastic container with the aid of a funnel. If you spill any on the ground, dilute it thoroughly with water. Then label the jug and lock it away until delivered to the proper authorities. Pesticides which have reached the expiry date indicated on their labels should also be handed over to the appropriate authority.

2 Cleaning spraying or dusting equipment. Rinse a reusable applicator such as the pressure sprayer *(above)* with water over a plastic bucket. One rinse is sufficient for a crank duster. Spray applicators need to be washed more thoroughly. After rinsing, mix dishwashing soap and water in the applicator, screw the top back on and shake it. Then remove the top and pour the soapy water into a plastic bucket *(above)*. Undo nozzle and wand connections where possible and wash out any clogged material in the rinse water.

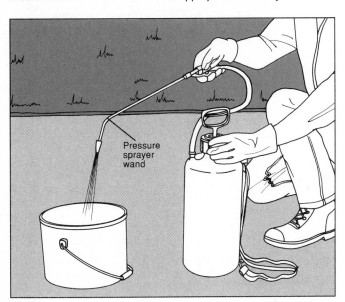

Pressure
sprayer
wand

3 Rinsing and drying the sprayer parts. Add more soap and water to the spray applicator and pump it through the sprayer wand and into the bucket *(above)*. Thoroughly rinse out the canister three times with fresh water and then spray more water through the sprayer until the water runs free of soap. Dispose of all rinse water by pouring it into a 2- to 3-foot hole dug in unused, well-drained soil, away from streams, septic fields or drainage systems.

4 Storing applicators and pesticides. Once applicators are dry, lubricate all moving parts, rubber and leather seals with oil. If the duster is metal, lubricate with graphite. Make sure all pesticides are clearly labelled. Store applicators with pesticides in a cool, dry cupboard or storeroom. Keep them locked up and out of reach of children and pets.

INDEX

Page references in *italics* indicate an illustration of the subject mentioned. Page references in **bold** indicate a Troubleshooting Guide for the subject mentioned.

ACKNOWLEDGMENTS

The editors wish to thank the following:

John Alexander, Arnold Arboretum, Jamaica Plain, Mass.; Dr. Michael Atkins and Fred DeFinis, Safer Inc., Wellesley, Mass.; Timothy O. Bakke, Popular Science Magazine, New York, N.Y.; Luci Barnas, University of Illinois, Rolling Meadows, Ill.; Trevor Cole, Dominion Arboretum, Ottawa, Ont.; Gerry Chevrier, Macdonald College, Montreal, Que.; William H. Gathercole, O.J. Co. Ltd., Sherrington, Que.; Tony A. Glover, Dr. C.C. Mitchell Jr. and Dr. Coleman Ward, Auburn University, Auburn, Ala.; Richard Grandy, Easy Gardener Inc., Waco, Tex.; Dr. Stuart B. Hill, McGill University, Montreal, Que.; Karl C. Kaukis, Jim Peterson and Dr. James R. Watson, The Toro Company, Minneapolis, Minn.; Bill Koury, Raindrip Inc., Chatsworth, Calif.; Dr. Glen P. Lumis and Marilyn Dykstra, University of Guelph, Guelph, Ont.; Luster Leaf Products Inc., Crystal Lake, Ill.; Dr. Jim Midcap and Dr. William I. Segars, University of Georgia, Athens, Ga.; John H. Nelson, Mona, Meyer & McGrath, Bloomington, Minn.; C. Peter Prakke, Smiths Falls, Ont.; Dr. Amalia Pucat and Christianne Ranger, Agriculture Canada, Ottawa, Ont.; Dr. George Puritch, Safer Ltd., Victoria, B.C.; Dr. Eliot Roberts, The Lawn Institute, Pleasant Hill, Tenn.; John Romero, Ortho Consumer Products, San Ramon, Calif.; Harry R. (Pat) Ryan, Bellingrath Gardens, Theodore, Ala.; Lowell True, University of Arizona, Maricopa County, Ariz.; Steve Vander-Mark, Cornell University, Canton, N.Y.; Bruce Van Duyne, Rutgers University, New Brunswick, N.J.; Carl Wilson, Colorado State University, Denver County, Colo.

The Staff of the Montreal Botanical Garden:

Pierre Brochu, Pascal Callea, Benoît Chartrand, Raymond Cochez, Robert Contant, Normand Fleury, Egon Fritz, Martin Gaudet, R. Girouard, Alain Joly, Rémi Laforest, Robert Malo, G. Nanni, Michel Otis, Normand Rosa, Armand Roy, Jean Wergifosse, Jacques Zapfrany.

Photo credits:

After each photographer's name are the pages on which his or her photographs appear.
The letter following the page number indicates the position of the photograph on the page, from left to right. A lower-case letter "i" refers to an insert photograph; "l" and "r" refer to double pictures.

James R. Baker: 113C, 118E(r), 119F, 126A, 126D, 127A, 127F; T. E. Bilderback: 119E; Canadian Forestry Service, Laurentian Forestry Centre: 128D, 128D (i); Ken Horst, Cornell University: 114A, 120E R.K. Jones: 113A, 113D, 113E (l), 115B, 115F, 119C, 122E, 123C, 128A (i), 128-B; Ray R. Kriner: 123E (i), 127-B; Montreal Botanical Garden: 122B, 126F, 127D, 128C; New York State Agricultural Experiment Station: 114E, 115C, 116D, 116F, 117D, 118C, 122D, 123D, 123D (i), 123E; New York Turfgrass Association Inc: 124B; D. G. Nielsen, Ohio State University: 127C; Nathan Peck, New York State Agricultural Experiment Station (Geneva): 119B (l), 119B (r), 119D; Richard W. Smiley: 124C, 124E, 124F, 125A, 125B, 125C, 125D (i) 125E, 125E (i); K.A. Sorensen: 114C, 114C (i); United States Department of Agriculture, Agricultural Research Service, Maryland: 116B, 117B (l), 118A; United States Department of Agriculture, Agricultural Research Service, Pacific West Area: 113F; United States Department of Agriculture, Photography Division, Washington, D.C.: 113B, 114D, 114D (i), 114F, 115D, 116A, 116B (i), 116C (l), 116C (r), 116E, 117B (r), 117C, 117E, 117F, 118B, 118F, 118F (i), 120A, 120B, 120C, 120D, 120F, 121A, 121C, 121D, 121E, 122C (l), 122C (r), 123A, 123F, 124A, 124D, 126B, 126C, 127D (i), 127E, 128C; University of Guelph, Pest Diagnostic & Advisory Clinic, Department of Environmental Biology: 113E (r), 115A, 115E, 117E, 118E (l), 119E, 121B, 122A, 125D, 126E, 128A, 128E; Thomas G. Zitter, Cornell University: 114B, 118D, 121F, 122F, 123B.

The following persons also assisted in the preparation of this book:
Marie-Claire Amiot, Claude Bordeleau, Arlene Case, Richard Fournier, Patrick J. Gordon, Julie Léger, Michael Mouland, Robert Paquet, Natalie Watanabe, Billy Wisse.

Typeset on Texet Live Image Publishing System.